Strengths-Based Approaches in Indigenous Education

This book brings together Indigenous thinkers and scholars with Western theories and practice frameworks to propose a theory for a strengths approach to knowledge production in Indigenous education.

The text traverses disciplines and fields that have advanced strengths-based approaches in providing practitioners, researchers, and policy makers a way of reframing problems to start from a place of strength and capital. Strengths approaches have gained traction in various contexts in Indigenous education; however, this book is the first of its kind to explore the field more broadly and consider its potential for a way forward in Indigenous education. Using existing scholarship to consider how Indigenous education has been positioned in the past and present, it puts forward compelling reasons why new approaches grounded in strengths-based approaches are necessary for reimagining the possibilities for Indigenous education.

Offering a theoretically robust framework, this is an essential resource for educators, researchers, and policy makers interested in transformative action in Indigenous education.

Marnee Shay is an Associate Professor and Deputy Head of School in the School of Education at the University of Queensland, Australia. She is an Aboriginal woman whose maternal family is from the Ngen'giwumirri language group. She researches in the fields of Indigenous education, policy studies, flexi schooling, and youth studies. She advocates for strengths-based approaches and the development of Indigenous-informed evidence in advancing Indigenous education.

Grace Sarra is a Professor at the School of Education in the Faculty of Creative Industries, Education and Social Justice at the Queensland University of Technology (QUT), Australia. She is of both Aboriginal and Torres Strait Islander heritage from the Bindal and Birriah clan groups of the Birrigubba nation and Torres Strait Islander heritage of Mauar, Stephen, and Murray Islands. Her research work utilises Indigenous knowledges and frameworks with theoretical frameworks to contest prevailing assumptions and stereotypes that contribute to the lack of success of Aboriginal and Torres Strait Islander young people in schools.

Strengths-Based Approaches in Indigenous Education

Research and Practice

Edited by Marnee Shay and Grace Sarra

Routledge
Taylor & Francis Group

LONDON AND NEW YORK

Designed cover image: Tara-Rose Butterworth-Gonebale

First published 2026
by Routledge
4 Park Square, Milton Park, Abingdon, Oxon OX14 4RN

and by Routledge
605 Third Avenue, New York, NY 10158

Routledge is an imprint of the Taylor & Francis Group, an informa business

British Library Cataloguing-in-Publication Data
A catalogue record for this book is available from the British Library

Library of Congress Cataloging-in-Publication Data
Names: Shay, Marnee editor | Sarra, Grace editor
Title: Strengths-based approaches in indigenous education : research and practice / edited by Marnee Shay and Grace Sarra.
Description: Abingdon, Oxon ; New York, NY : Routledge, 2026. | Includes bibliographical references and index. |
Identifiers: LCCN 2025022011 (print) | LCCN 2025022012 (ebook) | ISBN 9781032445632 hardback | ISBN 9781032445618 paperback | ISBN 9781003372783 ebook
Subjects: LCSH: Indigenous peoples--Education
Classification: LCC LC3715 .S77 2026 (print) | LCC LC3715 (ebook)
LC record available at https://lccn.loc.gov/2025022011
LC ebook record available at https://lccn.loc.gov/2025022012

ISBN: 9781032445632 (hbk)
ISBN: 9781032445618 (pbk)
ISBN: 9781003372783 (ebk)

DOI: 10.4324/9781003372783

Typeset in Sabon
by KnowledgeWorks Global Ltd.

Contents

List of Contributors

Fred Cobbo is a Wakka Wakka traditional owner. He holds a Bachelor of Applied Science (Indigenous Community Management and Development). He has extensive experience in community development, education, leadership, and cultural knowledges. He was a Chief Investigator on the Binung Ma Na Du: Cultural Stories and Living Histories on Wakka Wakka Country project.

Suraiya Abdul Hameed, of Malay Indigenous heritage from Singapore, is an interdisciplinary educational leadership expert at the University of Queensland. Her research spans leadership, global policy, equity, and inclusion. She leads international projects improving educational outcomes worldwide. Her leadership experience enhances student engagement and bridges theory with practice, earning her an ACEL Commendation award for leadership and research.

Margaret Kettle is an applied linguist who researches and teaches in second language education and Teaching English to Speakers of Other Languages (TESOL). Her research and teaching focus on the factors impacting language use in diverse social settings including the development and implementation of Indigenous languages in schools. Margaret has led and been a member of a number of research projects including three Australian Research Council (ARC) projects, three large Queensland Department of Education projects, and a number of university and philanthropic projects.

Jo Lampert is a white woman, originally from Canada. She has lived in Australia for over 25 years where she has continuously learned from her Indigenous colleagues and focusses on social justice and teacher education. Jo is a Professor of Teacher Education for Social Transformation in the Faculty of Education, Monash University.

Ian Mackie has had a long and distinguished career in schools as a teacher and Principal. In the 1990s, he was President of the Teachers' Union and went on to a 25-year long career as a very senior public servant. He is well known for his work on "job guarantees" and the use of "Nudge Theory" in education. His doctoral research covered models for improving education for First Nations students.

Gary MacLennan is a former teacher, academic and public servant. He has delivered papers at international conferences in Europe, Canada, China and Australia. His current interests are in theorising and advocating for a Reconciled Australia. Gary is a Critical Realist and is at present pursuing the relevance of the affective and ethical turns in current philosophy, especially in the field of Indigenous Education

Jodie Miller is an Associate Professor in mathematics education, in the School of Education at The University of Queensland. Her research focusses on improving the educational outcomes of students most at risk of marginalisation in school, particularly in the fields of Mathematics and Indigenous education.

Ren Perkins is a Quandamooka man with connections to the Wakka Wakka Nation. Ren's PhD research focussed on the experiences of Indigenous teachers who remained in the profession. His research interests include Indigenous education, Indigenous teachers, and Indigenist research standpoint. Ren is a Lecturer at Griffith University.

Toni Torepe is a senior lecturer in the Faculty of Education at the University of Canterbury. Her primary area of research is Māori educators' experiences in Western education institutions and has a particular focus on cultural taxation. More generally, she has an interest in Māori education and success, and research that makes positive contributions to Māori advancement.

About the Cover Designer

Tara-Rose Butterworth-Gonebale is a proud Wagiman Woman from the Western Suburbs of Naarm (Melbourne). She has been an exhibiting artist from as young as 8 years of age and has worked in Aboriginal community services for the last 10 years. Tara is currently working with mob in the correctional space as a Aboriginal Mental Health Worker.

1 Introduction to Strengths-Based Approaches in Indigenous Education

Research and Practice

Marnee Shay and Grace Sarra

Introduction

The premise of this book is to provide anyone working in education a strengths-based lens through which to embark on their work in Indigenous education, whatever that may be. We are two Indigenous women who have applied strengths approaches in various educational roles over decades, including in our work as researchers. Applying this approach has been challenging in a problem-based industry such as research. We are indeed still working on developing our ideas and practices using strengths-based approaches (SBA hereafter). Our purpose and aim in writing this book are to generate new and transformative conversations in the field and inspire researchers, practitioners, and policymakers working in the field to approach old and persisting problems with rigorous tools underpinned by SBA.

If you have lived in this country, you have absorbed deficit ideas about who Indigenous people are and what we are capable of. These deficit ideas are generated via the media, schools, policies, governments, legal systems, and social discourses. In education policy, these have been exacerbated by three words that have dominated policy approaches since 2012 – Close. The. Gap. The original intent of Close the Gap was a call to arms to end the generational disparity between Indigenous and non-Indigenous peoples in Australia. However, through the language and framing of the campaign, it has reproduced ideas in educational discourses that Indigenous people are a problem to fix and positioned us as the location of the problem.

This is not a book purporting to have the answers to how we can fix the pervasive and complex problems in Indigenous education. We do not propose that applying an SBA will be a panacea to the entrenched deficit discourses in Indigenous education and, indeed, about Indigenous peoples more broadly. We aim to provide anyone working in Indigenous education with an alternative to current frameworks such as Close the Gap. We have invested in developing our scholarship in SBA, as we have observed the notable differences that can be made in various educational settings when applied rigorously and effectively. Such approaches have enabled us to contribute new ways of approaching old problems, resulting in new findings and knowledge

DOI: 10.4324/9781003372783-1

that provide different Indigenous-centric understandings of various pervasive problems in education.

A Note about Language

We use Aboriginal, Torres Strait Islander, and Indigenous interchangeably throughout this book. We will also reference different mobs and languages, including Aboriginal English. We do so by understanding and respecting the great diversity among Aboriginal and Torres Strait Islander people. We also recognise that the term First Nations is preferred in other places in Australia. We pay our respects to the traditional owners, their ancestors, and Country.

Who We Are

Marnee Shay

I am an Aboriginal woman and my maternal family is from Wagiman Country in the Daly River Region from the Ngen'giwumirri language group; my family are Scully and Cummings. I also have Scottish and English ancestry through my paternal side of the family. I was born in Brisbane and raised by my Mum, my Aboriginal parent, so my Aboriginality has strongly influenced my cultural identity. I was raised on the north side of Brisbane in my early years. We then moved to Gubbi Gubbi Country (Sunshine Coast), where we were, and still are, connected to the local Aboriginal community. Although I didn't grow up on my Country, through being part of the community where I lived, I quickly learned the significance of knowledge in the community and how important it is to learn from and be connected to other Aboriginal and Torres Strait Islander peoples. When I was younger, I was part of an Indigenous youth group called "Walpara", where, as young people, we would organise different events and gatherings for mob to keep us strong and connected. During this time, being Indigenous was broadly not accepted to be positive – it was widely attributed to the racist stereotypes that we have all heard (and sadly continue to hear). There were no Indigenous media outlets to counter these stereotypes, very few Indigenous authors writing our stories, and even fewer Indigenous faces on television. Through my Mum, family, and community, I observed the contrast in the real experiences of our mob and how we are portrayed in just about every aspect of society.

My identity has played a significant role in my career path. I first attended university at 17 through an Indigenous entry programme. I studied through one of the few Indigenous colleges established in the 1990s that ran Indigenous Studies programmes. I completed an entire bachelor's degree in Indigenous Studies, where most of my lecturers were Indigenous. I am very fortunate to have had this unique experience of further learning about our experiences as Indigenous peoples in an academic setting. It set me on a path of wanting to learn more about these systems that had caused so much harm to our people and communities. The programme's interdisciplinarity grounded me in understanding that if I am going to work with our mobs in any way, no matter what profession or discipline, there is an interconnection for us with history, health, education, law, and culture. For example, history for us is not just about the past, it is about the present and the future equally. A further example is the relationship between education and health – the two are heavily interrelated. I undertook roles in higher education and the community sector when I decided that I wanted to go back and study while working. After doing a case management role with young people at risk of disengaging from schooling, I heard many times from young people the impact that teachers had on their learning experiences and overall engagement with school. I decided to re-train and become a secondary school teacher during my time in this role.

When I completed my studies, I commenced classroom teaching and taught mostly in a school setting called "flexi schools". They are schools for young people who have been pushed out of the mainstream system (formally or informally). I felt at this time it allowed me to use my previous experience working with young people (deemed) at risk. While challenging at times, teaching and leading in flexi schools taught me a great deal about myself and what it means to be an effective teacher. What fascinated me the most was that we had this cohort of young people who were "disengaged" from schooling and, in some cases, hadn't attended school in years. However, many of these young people attended school enthusiastically, even when they weren't well enough to be at school! It sparked my curiosity to understand our approach to teaching and learning in flexi schools and why it effectively re-engaged young people in schooling. After a short time teaching at TAFE (Technical and Further Education), I realised I was ready to study again. I enrolled in a Master of Education (Research) and commenced learning about what research is, and I developed my research project based on my work in flexi schools.

I enjoyed the process of research and bridging theory, practice, and research, especially focusing on flexi schooling and Indigenous education. After completing my master's degree, I commenced a full-time academic role and started my doctoral studies full-time, finishing that in three years. I loved (almost) every aspect of my PhD journey. I was deeply inspired by the potential knowledge production can have in informing systemic change. I have been working as a full-time academic for 10 years now. I have a large, externally funded research programme in flexi schooling, Indigenous education, and Indigenous education policy studies. A recurring theme throughout my research career has been using SBA. My colleague and co-author of this book, Grace, and I have had many yarns over the years about SBA and ways of applying it in our research and teaching practice. I have enjoyed continuing this thinking and these yarns in writing this book as we seek to strengthen SBA in theorising this philosophy in an attempt to provide practitioners, policymakers, and

researchers with a robust framework for seeking new answers to old problems in Indigenous education.

Grace Sarra

I am a professor in the School of Education in the Faculty of Creative Industries, Education and Social Justice at the Queensland University of Technology (QUT) in Brisbane, Australia. I am of both Aboriginal and Torres Strait
Islander heritage from the Bindal and Birriah clan groups of the Birrigubba
nation and Torres Strait Islander heritage of Mauar, Stephen, and Murray
Islands.

My work over the past 35 years has predominately been spent in education with a well-formed sense of social justice. My research work utilises
Indigenous knowledges and frameworks with theoretical frameworks to contest prevailing assumptions and stereotypes that contribute to the lack of
success of Aboriginal and Torres Strait Islander young people in schools. Furthermore, this work has provided opportunities to work with educators and
their communities primarily from Indigenous and low-socio-economic backgrounds from all levels of education in early childhood, primary, secondary,
and vocation education sectors to integrate cross-disciplinary approaches to
service delivery to improve educational outcomes for students.

I have been a chief investigator on several research projects which have
included an ARC Indigenous Discovery research project to work with incarcerated Indigenous and low socio-economic status youth and their teachers
to improve learning outcomes in mathematics and research funded project by
the CRC for the Lowitja Institute (National Institute for Aboriginal and Torres Strait Islander Health Research) on Cultural identity in schools. This project explored the importance of cultural identity to health and well-being of
Aboriginal and Torres Strait Islander young peoples being educated in diverse
school settings. It aimed to co-construct spaces where the physical/cultural/
social/emotional and spiritual well-being of Indigenous young peoples were
supported, and their voices were centred.

Currently, I am a chief investigator working with projects including the
$35 million QUT-led ARC Centre of Excellence for the Digital Child, which
is dedicated to creating positive digital childhoods for Australian children
aged from birth to eight years. In addition, an ARC Indigenous discovery
research grant aims to provide an evidence base and framework for the new
co-design approach being implemented across State and Commonwealth Indigenous policy domains. This project investigates co-design within the context of Indigenous education policy within Queensland to create a large data
set on how co-design is conceptualised and enacted.

My teaching and research work through knowledge mobilisation and exchange in higher education, schools, detention centres, and in communities
is influenced by the Stronger Smarter philosophy. The Stronger Smarter approach advocates SBA, indicating a "belief in the capacity" of children and

education colleagues to perform well regardless of the complexities of any social and cultural context. Similarly, this has transferred throughout my research work in schools with professionals and para-professionals and these approaches are just as effective across organisations that are open to change and are willing to engage in positive dialogue to foster a highly constructive environment.

Indigenous Education in Australia

Education on this continent now called Australia has been a fundamental aspect of how Aboriginal people sustained human life, Country, and animals here for millennia. Indigenous education is a relatively contemporary term that has only acknowledged Indigenous knowledge paradigms and ways of being, knowing, and doing in the past few decades. The term "Indigenous education" will hold different meanings depending on who uses it and for what purpose. The fundamental purpose of this book is to deeply engage with the philosophy and practice of SBA to improve educational outcomes for Aboriginal and Torres Strait Islander peoples. This aim is tied to the provision of schooling in Australia, which is predominantly provided by the State or private schooling sector.

We wrote this book in a political era of debates about voices and Indigenous sovereignty. On 14 October 2023, a historic referendum was held to allow the Australian people to change the Constitution to recognise Indigenous Australians in establishing a body called the Aboriginal and Torres Strait Islander Voice (Carson et al., 2024). The referendum was unsuccessful, with only 39.9% of the population voting in support of the Voice (Berry, 2024). The outcome of the referendum was devastating for many. It has also left our people in an ambiguous place; despite the analysis of voting showing many reasons purported the yes vote was so low (Carson et al., 2024), the result for Indigenous Australians is a lack of political direction for addressing the ongoing cycles of disadvantage. It also implicitly sent a message that our voices don't count or matter in matters about us. The ripple effects of the failed 2023 referendum demonstrate the importance of putting Indigenous voices back on the table. In Indigenous education, elevating Indigenous voices has been a long-standing aspiration. We propose that an SBA approach can advance some of these goals.

We acknowledge the ongoing impact of colonial educational institutions and how they can work against principles of Indigenous sovereignty. Rigney et al. (2024) remind us of the real consequences of poor schooling experiences: "Toxic learning environments imbued with formal epistemic violence blame Aboriginal students for their failure when their lived experiences, knowledge and cultural intelligences are positioned as antithetical to learning success" (p. 78). However, there are possibilities for improving Indigenous peoples' educational experiences and outcomes by interacting with these systems. We explore these ideas throughout the chapters of this book.

Indigenous education has increasingly included many aspects of educating Indigenous students. Still, recently, there has been recognition of the role Indigenous education can play in the experiences of all students in Australian schools. Indigenous education can include:

- Supporting Indigenous students in their academic outcomes
- Connections between schools and Indigenous communities
- Embedding Indigenous knowledges across the curriculum
- Culturally responsive pedagogies
- Employment of Indigenous staff across leadership, teaching and support roles
- Indigenous language revitalisation
- Learning Indigenous local histories and cultures
- The whole of school culture in addressing issues such as racism
- Cultural safety
- Celebrating Indigenous identities and cultures.

The above is a broad list of examples that may be included when discussing Indigenous education. We will provide many detailed examples throughout the book, identifying where schools and educational practitioners have been successful in these areas and how SBA played a role in the outcomes.

The past in Indigenous education is inherently connected to the present and future. As Phillips (2012) reminds us, the past is a shared history – including historical events that continue to impact today. There is a duality in how the same event can advantage one group while simultaneously disadvantaging another. Using SBA is not about erasing the past to focus on the positives (Pulla, 2017). Those who use SBA advocate truth-telling and deliberately seeking strengths and positives to be taken into account in a situation. In outlining the truth about colonisation in Australia, its violence and brutality make applying SBA seem like an overwhelmingly challenging task.

Massacres of Indigenous peoples have been documented up until the year 1930, only 95 years ago (Ryan et al., 2024). We know that the attempted erasure of us as a people continued through policies such as assimilation, whereby historical documents support a large-scale removal of Indigenous children of mixed heritage from their parents to remove them from their culture and Indigeneity (Payne, 2024). We know that Indigenous Australians continue to be the most incarcerated people on the planet (Anthony, 2017). We know that we continue to experience poorer health and education outcomes (Australian Government, 2024).

As a social determinant of health, education has played a damning role in contributing to poorer health and education outcomes (The Lancet Public Health, 2020). Poorer education is a precursor to the likelihood of interaction with the criminal justice system or incarceration (Australian Government, 2023). In the not-to-distant past, Indigenous people were termed uneducable, with many Indigenous children deemed unable to participate in academic study and destined for cheap labour roles such as cooking, cleaning, gardening, etc. (Price, 2012).

The antidote to these facts is that we are still here. We survived as a people, and some of us are thriving. We remember those who did not survive and champion change for our mob who are not thriving. While we never forget these histories, our people are steadfast in strategising to change the systems perpetuating these inequalities for future generations. Our people have a long history of advocacy in education. Holt (2021) documents the staunch voices of our Elders and people in education over decades, which resulted in significant policy advancement and improved outcomes.

We must not lose sight of the inequalities and injustices that persist. Still, we must recognise that some people in our communities experience wellness and happiness. We have an emerging middle class. The challenges we face are not our only story. The Indigenous business sector was found to have generated $16.1 billion in 2022 and was recognised for its innovations in Indigenous employment, creation of intergenerational wealth, trust building with the wider community, and accelerating self-determination (Evans et al., 2024). We have mob in leadership roles in most universities. Although elected to represent political parties and their interests, we have mob as elected members of parliament. We have Indigenous media outlets. Things have improved for some people in our communities. We know how much more there is to do. But if we do not stop to see how much has changed for the better and where there are strengths to build from, we perpetuate a story of helplessness and pathology.

SBA and Hope

Hope is a multifaceted and controversial topic when delving into the philosophy and science of it. There is no concrete definition (Graham, 2023) and, like many concepts in this book, there are many ways of understanding and studying it depending on the theoretical or discipline lens. We recognise this complexity and acknowledge that we cannot discuss every theory and perspective on hope. However, we need to foreground the book by addressing hope within the context of SBA. Historically and even contemporaneously, hope is portrayed as both negative and positive. Famous quotes from prominent thinkers such as Benjamin Franklin caution about the risks of relying on hope: "he that lives on hope will die fasting", and Plato calls hope a "foolish encounter" (Snyder, 2000, p. 4).

The fundamental premise of SBA is that things can change, including people and situations (McCashen, 2005). The presupposition, then, is that hope can play a role in facilitating such change. Saleebey (2013) explains:

> The central dynamic of the strengths perspective is precisely the rousing of hope, of tapping into the visions and dreams of the individual, family or community. Circumstances of bad luck, unfortunate decisions, the

harshness of a life lived on the hard edge of need and vulnerability, of course, may smother these. Nonetheless, it is this flicker of possibility that can ignite the fire of hope, and start the engine of positive change.

(p. 8)

Hope is not just an idea that may or may not render a positive impact. Scientists have increasingly been interested in the mindset of hope and how it impacts our bodies and minds (Beachboard, 2022). For example, Corn et al. (2020) analysed studies investigating hope as a direct or secondary factor of an outcome. While hope is determined by individual personalities and environmental contexts, they found potential "for hope to alter oncological outcomes with cancer and the opportunity for improvement in quality of life" (p. 452). Beachboard (2022) reports that many studies explore hope and causation and test their impact. They outline that in psychology studies, evidence supports that those with high hope levels show more resilience and better life satisfaction, irrespective of their family background or socioeconomic level.

For our people, hope has kept the fire burning to keep advocating for change in the aftermath of colonisation. If we resign hope, the prospect of change dims. There would be no point in continuing the legacy of change-making that so many Elders fought for. Eminent Elder, educator, and scholar Miriam-Rose Ungunmerr-Baumann speaks of hope from her cultural perspective as a Ngangikurungkurr woman from Daly River. She shares:

We are River people. We cannot hurry the river. We have to move with its current to understand its ways... we hope that the people of Australia will wait. Not so much waiting for us – to catch up – but waiting with us, as we find our place in this world.

(Ungunmerr-Baumann, 2022, paras 19–20)

Where Do We Want to Be?

Some tensions exist among many of our people when thinking about this question. Concerns have always been expressed that surviving or achieving in Western education means giving up your culture or assimilating to Western values. Are we seeking sovereignty and independence in pursuing better educational outcomes after the system has demonstrated its inability to support success for many Indigenous people? Or are we seeking widespread systemic change, which would result in the system catering to all Indigenous people (and, consequentially, all disenfranchised learners)? We are not advocating for one or other and see the answer as more nuanced than one singular approach.

Research demonstrates a positive relationship between localised and contextualised approaches and positive impacts for Indigenous, and indeed all, students (Harrison et al., 2023). We have written elsewhere about the value of listening to local knowledge holders and grounding oneself within the community to understand local histories, cultures, and politics (Shay et al., 2022). We also write about the importance of valuing local wisdom and knowledges in applying SBA in Chapter 7 of this book. Yet, educational policy continues to reinforce homogeneity in the approaches we take in Indigenous education. Community members we work with express continued frustrations about the lack of regard for Indigenous people from the community and the skills and expertise that are so often overlooked. Many ill-conceived assumptions and ideas about Indigenous communities can be debunked through authentic relationships with parents, families and local community members. Misconceptions can also be countered through elevating Indigenous knowledges and knowledge paradigms. For example, in his book, *Strength Basing, Empowering and Regenerating Indigenous Knowledge Education*, Dr John Davis outlines a place-based, strengths-based framework he developed called 'Riteways Flows'. Riteways Flows centres Indigenous knowledge systems and ways of being, knowing and doing alongside contemporary education practice, which approaches teaching and learning from building on the strengths of Indigenous children and young people in classrooms (Davis, 2024).

While there have been some positive gains in past decades in improving year 12 completion rates, university completions and enrolments in early childhood settings, there are still gains to be made in many areas in education. We know that improving outcomes for Indigenous students and providing all Australian students the opportunity to learn about Indigenous histories, cultures and peoples are overarching aspirations nationally. We also know that if we continue using the same methods and policy approaches as we have been, progress will be too slow, so our book is timely in bringing forward different approaches.

Book Overview

This book considers the role of process, philosophy, and approach in achieving these aspirations. Politicians, policymakers, educators and school leaders are often drawn to quantifiable solutions that are not required to be heavily resourced and are proven to solve a problem in a specific timeframe. Shifting how we think about and approach our work is a starting point, and even this shift takes time. SBA is about cultural shift and systemic change. In this book, we explore the theoretical origins of SBA in the broader literature (Chapter 2 – Shay and Sarra) and through a deep exploration of the thinking and work of SBA in Indigenous education champion Chris Sarra (Chapter 3 – Sarra, Shay, McLennan, and Mackie). Chapters 4 (Sarra and Shay) and 5 (Shay and Sarra) explore existing SBA frameworks, their application in research and practice, and case studies from our research over the past decade. Chapter 6 (Shay, Sarra, Lampert, and Miller) presents an evidence-based, Indigenous-informed framework for strengths-based codesign, providing conceptual clarity between approaches such as consultation and co-design. Chapter 7 (Shay, Cobbo, Sarra, and Kettle) explores the importance of local wisdom and knowledge in applying SBA in Indigenous education. This chapter also provides a case study from the communities of Murgon and Cherbourg. Chapter 8 (Hameed and Torepe) shifts to exploring SBA in a global context, Singapore and New Zealand, unpacking the emphasis on bilingual education, national cohesion, cultural identity, and culturally responsive pedagogies as a vehicle for achieving equity for Indigenous students. Chapter 9 (Perkins) shares the story of a new generation of Indigenous education researchers applying the strengths inherent in family, Country, culture, and community in research settings. Chapter 10 (Shay and Sarra) develops a theoretical lens for SBA in Indigenous education. Building on foundations from Indigenous theorists and other SBA theories, the theory provides a lens from which researchers and practitioners can apply SBA holistically in their work in Indigenous education.

References

Anthony, T. (2017). FactCheck: Are first Australians the most imprisoned people on earth? *The Conversation*. Retrieved from https://theconversation.com/factcheck-are-first-australians-the-most-imprisoned-people-on-earth-78528

Australian Government (2023). *Adults in prison*. Australian Institute of Health and Welfare. Retrieved from https://www.aihw.gov.au/reports/australias-welfare/adults-in-prison#:~:text=In%202022%2C%20prison%20entrants%20were,1.1%25%20had%20no%20formal%20schooling

Australian Government (2024). *Health and wellbeing of First Nations people*. Australian Institute of Health and Welfare. Retrieved from https://www.aihw.gov.au/reports/australias-health/indigenous-health-and-wellbeing

Beachboard, C. (2022). *The school of hope: The journey from trauma and anxiety to achievement, happiness, and resilience* (1st ed.). Corwin.

Berry, M. (2024). The voice referendum. *The Journal of Australian Political Economy*, (92), 240–248.

Carson, A., Evans, M., Strating, R., & Grömping, M. (2024). Voiceless: A multi-level analysis of the 2023 Voice to Parliament referendum outcome and its implications: An introduction. *Australian Journal of Political Science*, 59(3), 308–313.

Corn, B., Feldman, D., & Wexler, I. (2020). The science of hope. *The Lancet Oncology*, 21(9), e452–e459. https://doi.org/10.1016/S1470-2045(20)30210-2

Evans, M., Polidano, C., Dahmann, S. C., Kalera, Y., Ruiz, M., Moschion, J., & Blackman, M. (2024). *Indigenous business and corporation snapshot study 3.0*. The University of Melbourne. https://fbe.unimelb.edu.au/cibl/research

Graham, C. (2023). *The power of hope: How the science of well-being can save us from despair* (1st ed.). Princeton University Press.

Harrison, N., Tennent, C., Burgess, C., Vass, G., Guenther, J., Lowe, K., & Moodie, N. (2023). Knowing in being: An understanding of Indigenous knowledge in its relationship to reality through enacted curriculum. In N. Moodie, K. Lowe, R. Dixon, & K. Trimmer (Eds.), *Assessing the evidence in Indigenous education research: Implications for policy and practice* (pp. 125–139). Springer International Publishing.

Holt, L. (2021). *Talking strong: The National Aboriginal Education Committee and the development of Aboriginal Education policy*. Aboriginal Studies Press.

McCashen, W. (2005). *The strengths approach: A strengths-based resource for sharing power and creating change.* St Luke's Innovative Resources.

Payne, A. M. (2024). "Never again"?: Resonances of the past in contemporary Aboriginal and Torres Strait Islander child removal. *Cosmopolitan Civil Societies, 16*(3), 104–122. https://doi.org/10.5130/ccs.v16.i3.9294

Phillips, J. (2012). Indigenous knowledge perspectives: Making space in the Australian centre. In J. Phillps, & J. Lampert (Eds.). *Introductory Indigenous studies in education reflection and the importance of knowing* (2nd ed, pp. 9–25). Pearson.

Price, K. (2012). A brief history of Aboriginal and Torres Strait Islander education in Australia. In K. Price (Ed.), *Aboriginal and Torres Strait Islander education: An introduction for the teaching profession* (pp. 1–20). Cambridge University Press. https://doi.org/10.1017/9781108552905

Pulla, V. (2017). Strengths-based approach in social work: A distinct ethical advantage. *International Journal of Innovation, Creativity and Change, 3*(2), 97–114.

Rigney, L.-I., Mikulan, P., & Zembylas, M. (2024). Culturally responsive pedagogies: Australian Colonial Logic of the Centre and Aboriginal Refusal. In *Working with theories of refusal and decolonization in higher education* (1st ed., Vol. 1, pp. 77–92). Routledge. https://doi.org/10.4324/9781003367314-8

Ryan, L., Debenham, J., Pascoe, B., Smith, R., Owen, C., Richards, J., Craig, H., Gilbert, S., Anders, R., Usher, K., Price, D., Newley, J., & Brown, M. (2024). *Colonial frontier massacres in Australia, 1788-1930.* The University of Newcastle. Retrieved from https://c21ch.newcastle.edu.au/colonialmassacres/introduction.php

Saleebey, D. (2013). *The strengths perspective in social work practice* (6th ed.). Pearson.

Shay, M., Sarra, G., & Woods, A. (2022). Grounded ontologies: Indigenous methodologies in qualitative cross-cultural research. In P. Liamputtong (Ed.), *Handbook of qualitative cross-cultural research methods: A social science perspective* (pp. 26–39). Elgar Publishing. https://doi.org/10.4337/9781800376625.00011

Snyder, C. R. (2000). *Handbook of hope: Theory, measures and applications.* Academic.

The Lancet Public Health (2020). Education: A neglected social determinant of health. *The Lancet. Public Health, 5*(7), e361.

Ungunmerr-Baumann, M. R. (2022). *Dadirri – A reflection by Miriam-Rose Ungunmerr-Baumnann.* Emmaus Productions. Retrieved from https://www.dadirri.org.au/wp-content/uploads/2015/03/Dadirri-Inner-Deep-Listening-M-R-Ungunmerr-Bauman-Refl1.pdf

2 Theories and Strengths-Based Approaches

Marnee Shay and Grace Sarra

Introduction

It is important to foreground the coming chapters by understanding how the concept of epistemology impacts how we think we know and how we (re)produce dominant ways of knowing. Epistemology is the term commonly used to describe the theory of knowledge and how we come to know. It is a complex concept; contested, debated, and theorised across disciplines and paradigms for centuries and is as old as philosophy itself (Steup & Neta, 2002). In the social sciences, most epistemic foundations are produced through what is broadly recognised as positivist, naturalist, or constructivist paradigms (Silverman, 2013). Positivism is directly connected to scientific paradigms, underpinned by objectivity, and where studies are generally concerned with explanatory factors or causal relationships (Park et al., 2020). Naturalism is a model of qualitative research that focuses on the "factual characteristics of the object under study" and involves observations of phenomena in real-life settings (Silverman, 2013, p. 106). Constructivism is deeply concerned with the how in phenomena: how social realities are developed, enacted, and sustained (Holstein & Gubrium, 2013).

Most of the scholarship in the three examples above (and many more in what can only be described as an extensive body of literature) has drawn from Western thinking and cultural norms. Walter (2019) articulates that "as with social assumptions, dominant ways of knowing and the dominance of some knowers over others are embedded into our society. Social research is conducted against a background of these dominant ways of knowing" (p. 15). As how knowledge is produced impacts how Indigenous knowledges are valued or dismissed, it is vital to consider epistemology's role in this book's context.

Martin (2008) outlines "the separation and severance from our Stories and our knowledge occurring through weapons of colonialism such as schools, literature, multi-media technologies, universities and research" (p. 25). This powerful statement is a provocation for educational institutions and anyone working within them (including policymakers) to consider how dominant cultural norms impact their thinking about their

DOI: 10.4324/9781003372783-2

cultures and cultures outside of the prevailing norm. Anyone living and working on this continent must know that many epistemologies have existed here for at least 50,000 years (Sapfo Malaspinas et al., 2016). While they could be categorised in collective terms of Indigenous knowledge now, before colonialism attempted to erase Indigenous peoples, languages, and knowledge, there were at least 300 distinct languages with many hundreds more of language varieties of dialects (Simpson & Wigglesworth, 2019).

We must recognise that Aboriginal and Torres Strait Islander knowledge holders keep this knowledge alive every day. We have continued to advocate and insist on this knowledge as valuable and necessary to sustain humanity, Country, culture, and all living beings over the next 50,000 years. This recognition and advocacy have been occurring since colonisation. However, it is through the work of Indigenous scholars that Indigenous knowledge has recently been established as a knowledge paradigm through the corpus of literature in Western institutions (Shay et al., 2023).

So Why Talk about Epistemology in a Book about Strengths-Based Approaches?

Many epistemic theorists agree that the scientific knowledge paradigm continues to dominate how we conceive quality knowledge (Park et al., 2020; Saarela, 2019). Therefore, if we are limited by relating how we come to know about Indigenous people through scientific discourses, we are likely to assume that Indigenous people are meant to be the researched and not the researcher (Tuhiwai Smith, 2021). These limitations lead to an assumption that Indigenous knowledge can only be understood through Western theories. Some scientific paradigms reinforce racial hierarchies that position Indigenous people and knowledge as inferior and unable to determine what is right for our people and communities. Interrogating the role of knowledge production and how knowledge is theorised is necessary in education, as education departments, early childhood settings, schools, and universities are culpable in how knowledge is produced and (re)produced.

There has been extensive interrogation and theorisation of epistemologies for at least two centuries. However, Norris (2005) contends that what epistemology ought to be immediately concerned with is how individuals and society contend with "statements, truth-claims, opinions, moral and political viewpoints... [and] just what or whom to believe" (p. 1). The foundations of strengths-based approaches (SBA henceforth) require a shift from pathologising and emphasis on problems enculturated in every aspect of our lives (Saleeby, 2013). Therefore, deep thinking about how knowledge is theorised, produced, and perceived as valid is essential in theorising SBA approaches in Indigenous education.

Indigenous Theories

We need to preface this section by stating that this is not an extensive attribution to the corpus of Indigenous-based theories. We have focused here on Indigenous theories that we see as closely aligned with SBA and those that we have applied extensively throughout our work as Indigenous researchers. Indigenous people have theorised and observed, creating sophisticated knowledge that sustained people in harsh environments for thousands of years. While colonisation caused significant disruption, and many people were subject to brutal and violent dispossession of their lands, much of this ancient knowledge is used today (Moreton-Robinson, 2016). Like all cultures and knowledge paradigms, Indigenous knowledge is not static and continues to be modernised and grown. For example, scientific epistemologies and practices in the 1700s vastly differ from scientific discourses and practices in the 21st century. Consequently, as the environment, socio-cultural, and socio-political conditions change, so does how we think about knowledge and knowledge paradigms.

Any Indigenous theory within the academy has come from Indigenous knowledge and, therefore, Indigenous knowledge holders. We must acknowledge the systemic exclusion of Aboriginal and Torres Strait Islander peoples in higher education (and therefore knowledge production) for much of the 18th and 19th centuries (Rigney, 2001), meaning that most of the knowledge produced about us before our presence in the academy was very much through what is commonly termed as the "white gaze" (Paris, 2019, p. 218). Research has been inseparable from "European imperialism and colonialism", and this "collective memory of imperialism has been perpetuated through the ways in which knowledge about indigenous peoples was collected, classified and then represented in various ways back to the West" (Smith, 2012, p. 1). Indigenous scholars have developed theories against this backdrop and deeply embedded history of Western superiority, steeped in notions of science as the chief knowledge paradigm (Macdonald et al., 2023). Not all Indigenous knowledge has been theorised in knowledge production settings such as research. In developing a path forward for theorising SBA in Indigenous education, we share the three most significant theories of Indigenous knowledge that have shaped our research. But we acknowledge there are further theories (and theorists) in this space that are just as significant and have contributed in deeply significant ways (perhaps even to the development of the theories we will discuss).

Standpoint Theory

Indigenous standpoint theories' origins are from feminist epistemologies and theories founded on the recognition that there are subjectivities in how we come to know (Sabzalian, 2018). Feminist theories are focused on the notion of gender and how gender shapes not only how we come to know but how we perceive to know (Harding, 2004). It interrogates power structures and how gender reinforces ideas about who are more legitimate knowers. Standpoint theories have also included analysis of the role of race, class and sexuality and their intersections in knowledge production (Harding, 2004). Indigenous writers build on these ideas by critically analysing how Western epistemologies dismiss Indigenous knowledge paradigms and the Indigenous bodies that hold this knowledge within the academy (Moreton-Robinson, 2013).

Torres Strait Islander scholar Nakata (2007) argues that the Indigenous standpoint does not pre-exist based on one's Indigeneity but rather is a "distinct form of analysis, and is itself both a discursive construction and an intellectual device to persuade others and elevate what might not have been a focus of attention from others" (p. 214). Nakata further explains that Indigenous positionality is not about producing a particular truth based on lived experiences of being Indigenous, but rather is about unravelling deeper understandings of Indigenous knowledge production and how Indigenous people are implicated in these at the "cultural interface". Nakata (2007) defines the cultural interface as:

> Constituted by points of intersecting trajectories. It is a multi-layered and multi-dimensional space of dynamic relations constituted by the intersections of time, place, distances, different systems of thought, competing and contesting discourses within and between different knowledge systems, and different systems of social, economic and political organisation.
>
> (p. 199)

In simple terms, the cultural interface is about different cultures and cultural knowledges coming in contact with one another. Nakata's scholarship on the cultural interface has significantly shaped discourse about Indigenous standpoint in knowledge production. Moreton-Robinson (2013) questions Nakata's omission of the role of gender in his development of Indigenous standpoint theory. Moreton-Robinson (2013) contends, "Indigenous women's standpoint theory is where embodied knowledge provides the entry point for generating our problematics and research, conceptualised as situated, critical practice of activities, articulation and relationality" (p. 343). A commonality in this ground-breaking scholarship is the consensus that Indigenous standpoint theory is needed in the ongoing struggle to contest Western knowledge produced *about* us and without a theorising of our presence in the role of knowledge production, mistruths and biased understandings of Indigenous ways of being, knowing and doing will continue. Nakata (2007) concludes that it is unjust that one knowledge system (western/science) bases its judgment on what is valid or truthful in accordance with its own standards and understandings of truth validity (Nakata, 2007).

Indigenist Research

In response to being the most researched people in the world where much harm has resulted in knowledge produced about us, Narungga, Kaurna, and Ngarrindjeri scholar, Lester-Irrabinna Rigney, developed "Indigenist research" (Rigney, 1999). Rigney (2001) has deeply critiqued how scientific paradigms have dominated and "widely accepted as authoritative in constructing 'truthful' realities in modern Western societies" (p. 2). Rigney developed an Indigenist research paradigm to offer counter-narratives from the colonialist, hegemonic versions of who we are as Indigenous people and to provide Indigenous scholars with a place to debate ideas and knowledge from our perspectives as Indigenous researchers.

Indigenist research principles were developed as a form of "critical Indigenous scholarship" in response to Indigenous critiques of science and as a way of developing more Indigenous-based knowledge paradigms (Rigney, 2001, p. 7). Although framed as a critical approach, the impetus of its development is pushing back on the violence of Western epistemes and developing an approach that allows for Indigenous transformation, authority, rights, and rigour (Rigney, 2001). Indigenist research has three core principles: resistance as the emancipatory imperative, political integrity, and privileging Aboriginal and Torres Strait Islander voices (Rigney, 1999, 2001). These principles were developed with the aim of liberation from oppression and developing new knowledge that Rigney (1999) frames as "liberatory epistemologies" (p. 14). Indigenist research principles are now widely used by Indigenous Australian scholars and beyond and have deeply influenced our work as researchers. We always consider our role as researchers and the responsibility to ensure our research contributes to a liberatory agenda. The three Indigenist principles are inherently strengths-based; they assume Indigenous people as agents of knowledge and recognise the criticality of Indigenous strengths, capacities, and voices.

Relationality

Aunty Mary Graham (2014) articulates that "Aboriginal relationality – traditionally the foundation of the Law – is an elaborate, complex and refined system of social, moral, spiritual and community obligations that provided an ordered university for people" (p. 17). Relationality is a core concept that informs all Indigenous knowledge paradigms and is expressed in every aspect of Indigenous ways of being, knowing, and doing (Dudgeon & Bray, 2019). Indigenous relationality is more than emphasising the importance of relationships. It is the premise that all is connected: physical, temporal, material, or spiritual (Macdonald et al., 2023) and relationality exists between people, land (Country), plants, animals, and spirits (Dudgeon & Bray, 2019). Place and belonging are all connected to land or Country, and relationships are governed by protocol, diplomacy, and kinship systems (Graham, 2014).

Martin (2008) explains that relatedness in her Quandamoopah paradigm means that no single entity (people, plants, animals, Country) is greater or of more importance than another. Moreton-Robinson (2016) supports this tenet and discerns that, in the setting of knowledge production, relational knowledge is holistic and interconnected between all living things and Country. Recognition of the criticality of Indigenous relationality within the realms of knowledge production, much less within practice settings, has been an ongoing challenge. There is an increasing recognition and call for Western researchers and knowledge institutions (including schools and universities) to embrace Indigenous concepts of relationality as the world faces unprecedented and existential challenges. Macdonald et al. (2023) argue that the academy (and indeed society more broadly) can benefit from engaging with diverse knowledge and that operationalising Indigenous relationality in research means engaging in collective processes that recognise and embrace the interconnectedness between entities.

Strengths-Based Approaches and Theories

SBA are a philosophical way of working with people to bring about change. McCashen (2005) highlights that the basis for implementing SBA relies on positive views of individuals' dignity, abilities, rights, distinctiveness, and shared characteristics. The entrenched nature of deficit discourses in Indigenous education has been analysed extensively (Sarra & Shay, 2019; Vass, 2012). As policy reform in Indigenous education has gradually strengthened to require individual and systemic changes in the quest to deliver more equitable outcomes for Aboriginal and Torres Strait Islander people and communities, rigorous educational frameworks alternative to pathogenic approaches of the past are scarce. As much as the aim of "Closing the Educational Gap" and finding "strategies to effectively teach Indigenous students" are at the forefront of the minds of educators, so too is the idea that Indigenous students remain a problem to be fixed.

The field of Indigenous education has, like many areas of Indigenous affairs, been swept up in a broader fascination with problems and the pathologising of wicked problems (Saleeby, 2013). The pervasiveness of deficit discourses in Indigenous education has been well acknowledged within the field, with Vass (2012) outlining the devastating impact of deficit thinking as potentially leading to "lowered expectations of Indigenous students academically and behaviourally in the classroom; poor education policies that fail to negotiate systemic concerns; and inadequate education research that is responsive to these concerns" (p. 88). The effects of deficit thinking and ideologies extend to a broader understanding of Indigenous people. McCallum et al. (2022) report on an analysis of the way that Indigenous students are reductively represented in numerically ranked statistics in comparison to their non-Indigenous peers. They further outline that, as this is the dominant narrative told via the media, these representations of failure and inferiority contribute to entrenched deficit discourses. Therefore, all Australians absorb these ideas.

SBA is a radically different approach to closing gaps and applying quantitative measures of how education systems deliver on current Indigenous education policy imperatives. SBA first originated in the social work literature as a promising framework that enabled practitioners to focus on the strengths and capacities of clients and to mobilise these in pursuit of changing their situation (Saleeby, 2013). SBA seeks to attend to power differentials and dynamics in addressing social, political, and institutional constraints through an ecological lens. It concerns social justice, centring agency, and self-determination (Saint-Jacques et al., 2009). Elements and principles of SBA have found their way into research paradigms through various theories across diverse fields, including appreciative inquiry (AI), asset-based theories, funds of knowledge (FOK), funds of identity (FOI), and salutogenic theory. We propose that SBA is also inherently entwined with Indigenous theories and knowledge paradigms. SBA theorists assert that Indigenous ways of being, knowing, and doing are valid and robust (Martin, 2008; Shay & Oliver, 2021). They emphasise transformative knowledge production that is grounded in Indigenous peoples as knowledge holders and authorities of Indigenous knowledge (Tuhiwai Smith, 2021).

The following sections will briefly overview extant theories that include aspects of SBA. There is still debate within the literature about how SBA is defined and whether it is a theory, philosophy, practice, or framework. However, these are established strengths-based theories that researchers use across various disciplines to produce knowledge and will inform the development of SBA in the field of Indigenous education.

Appreciative Inquiry

AI emerged from the field of organisational development (Watkins et al., 2011). Theorists are focused on inquiry and change through a lens that emphasises existing strengths over articulating problems, particularly within organisations (Ludema et al., 2006). Informed by social constructivism (Bergmark & Kostenius, 2018) AI theorists are transformative in asking participants and research partners to have a vision for their aspirations (Willoughby & Tosey, 2007). Some authors propose AI as a methodology (Robinson et al., 2013), while others categorise AI as an established theory (Kaminski, 2012). Watkins et al. (2011) assert that AI is fundamentally about collaborative and participatory approaches and proactively seeking positive potential. It deliberately steers away from diagnosis, criticism, and negativity. Tschannen-Moran and Tschannen-Moran (2011) developed a model for AI application in organisational research that provides researchers with a model called the 5D cycle, which consists of a generative phased process: define, discovery, dream, design, and destiny.

Grant and Humphries (2006) acknowledge that critical theory and AI share epistemic roots of social constructionism and grapple with theoretical paradoxes. They further share their concern for the limited evaluation of how AI is applied and whether it does deliver on its ambition to affect change. Since this critique in the mid-2000s, AI scholarship has increasingly included investigating the impact of AI applications in various settings. For example, Robinson et al. (2013) reflected on applying AI as a methodology in a probation setting. The authors report that using AI meant they could generate high-quality data around aspects of culture that they believe would have remained hidden had they not used AI. In a further example, Hung et al. (2018) reported on the use of AI in a study with staff in a hospital unit exploring how to bridge research and practice in a clinical health setting. Their key findings resulted in understanding ten key enablers and a conceptual tool. The authors concluded that AI was useful in this study as problem-focused approaches had failed to deliver success in improving outcomes for patients in the same settings previously. The authors were optimistic about the application of AI and its ability to engage staff in the research process.

Asset-Based Community Development (ABCD)

Asset-based community development (ABCD henceforth) was "originally created by John McKnight and Jody Kretzmann as a development strategy to support disinvested city populations in the United States in 1988" (Aoki Yamashita, 2023, p. 12). Asset-based approaches are primarily used in community development (hence the ABCD model dominant in the literature) but are used across contexts, including education and health. Community development historically assumed a position of deficit when working with communities labelled as being of high poverty, high unemployment, and lacking in education, for example (Missingham, 2017). The adoption of a more strengths-based approach means that the use of ABCD in practice requires community development practitioners or researchers to recognise that every community – no matter how disadvantaged – possesses skills, gifts, capital, and resources that can be used to change a situation (Forrester et al., 2020).

Older literature, such as a paper by Ennis and West (2010), outlines that ABCD is not a theory of practice but more of an approach or attitude. In more contemporary literature, while Forrester et al. (2020) assert that ABCD is a conceptual framework or strategy, Yamashita (2023) states that "ABCD is a theory of practice that emphasizes what is currently present in the community, the capacities of the residents or workers, and the relationships built between people, associations, and institutions" (p. 5). Missingham (2017) concludes that ABCD is becoming an influential theory and practice. While there are marginally different ways that contemporary scholarship is defining ABCD, there is consensus that the use of ABCD requires a focus on strengths and a shift in power relations (facilitators must work collaboratively rather than assuming the position as experts)

(Forrester et al., 2020; Missingham, 2017). In education, schools are increasingly being recognised as community assets (Forrester et al., 2020), as well as contexts where the use of ABCD can benefit the micro-school environment, particularly for students from minority backgrounds (Flint & Jaggers, 2021).

Similarly to other theories, critiques include concern that there is a lack of adequate recognition of structural inequalities and root causes of issues that people experience, such as poverty and intergenerational disadvantage (Forrester et al., 2020; Missingham, 2017). Like other SBA theories, limited examples in the literature have evaluated or examined in depth the application of ABCD and whether it was successful in achieving its intent. However, Mathie and Cunningham (2003) developed a conceptual framework and, through their analysis of existing literature, propose great potential for different outcomes to those of needs-based approaches.

Funds of Knowledge

FOK was first developed in the late 1980s and, since then, there have been many developments in its concept and application (Llopart & Esteban-Guitart, 2018). FOK is an educational theory developed from a need to shift research inquiry from highlighting deficit ideologies that blame students from minorities to recognising the strengths or assets they bring to classrooms (Hogg, 2011). FOK researchers seek to identify existing knowledge from family homes, communities, peers, or other social contexts (Velez-Ibanez & Greenberg, 2005). Gonzalez et al. (2005) affirm the importance of positioning culture as a lived experience, creating space by applying FOK to ensure the voices of students, their families, and communities are central to knowledge production. Zipin (2009) defines FOK as "culturally developed and historically accumulated bodies of skills and knowledge" (p. 317). Llopart and Esteban-Guitart (2018) reiterate the importance of culture being recognised as living, evolving, and hybrid, not static and fixed.

The essence of FOK is similar to other theories discussed in this chapter; it was born out of a need to discontinue reinforcing deficit thinking and problematising cohorts who most need support and policy reform. In applying FOK in a school-based project, Castillo et al. (2023) shared findings from a study that used dialogical journals from students exploring their FOK. Castillo et al. (2023) report that applying FOK revealed information about the students' backgrounds that could inform teachers to support them in classrooms better. Furthermore, exploring students' communities helped teachers better understand the significant resources within their communities, which can assist in providing better support for their students. Students expressed motivation and confidence in the project process, demonstrating that making space for students to talk about their lives outside of school and what is positive about it is an important practice.

Funds of Identity

Funds of identity (FOI) originated from funds of identity where scholars built on the concept that skills and existing knowledge students bring from their homes, families, and communities are a strength (Hogg, 2011). FOI is concerns student voices in developing a deeper understanding of their lived experiences, cultures and community context (Gonzalez et al., 2005). FOI advocates identities as fluid, dynamic and complex (Esteban-Guitart & Moll, 2014). It aims to counter deficit discourses that build on the types of knowledge developed from FOK (family, community, culture, for example) and ensure there is space for students to express these identities positively (Hogg & Volman, 2020). Advocates of FOI conceptualise identity within a sociocultural (Vygotsky) and ecological (Bronfenbrenner) framework. This framework enables them to explore the concept of identities, especially through the lived experiences of children and young people.

An example of FOI and its application in research is reported by Hedges (2021) in a qualitative case study in New Zealand. Hedges found very young children in prior-to-school settings can draw on FOI. They found that the child in the case study has a clear learner identity developed from her influence at home to read frequently. In another study, Zhang-Yu et al. (2021) aimed to understand identity through a concept they refer to as dark FOK, created through experiences of poverty, violence, or racism. Despite the strengths-based orientation that informs FOI, Zhang-Yu et al. (2021) specifically engaged with dark aspects of FOK that have contributed to shaping the identities of the cohort they worked with. Several key findings emerged, including the shared experience many young people have when they are experiencing similar issues (such as racism).

Salutogenic Theory

The concept of salutogenesis was developed over four decades ago by Antonovsky (Bauer et al., 2020). Antovsky's salutogenic model devised a core concept, "sense of coherence", which is about understanding how individuals cope with stressors and stay healthy (Sagy & Mana, 2022). Like many strengths-orientated theories, salutogenic theory emerged from a need to shift away from biological models of health (only looking at scientific measures of physical health) as this reinforced deficit views and ideologies about health and wellbeing (Brolin et al., 2018). Salutogensis is an umbrella concept underpinned by a positionality that health and disease are a continuum (Eriksson, 2022). In other words, it is based on the premise that no individual should be categorised as only diseased or healthy, as everyone is on a spectrum between these two categories (Drageset et al., 2023). Developments of the theory over time include broadening the paradigm to interdisciplinary research and for application in other disciplines (Sagy & Mana, 2022).

As the theory sits within the health sciences, more empirical evidence is available to test causation and correlation. For example, in a study on the well-being of nursing home populations who were characterised as having chronic illnesses and impairments that could not be cured, the research examined how nurses could apply principles of salutogenic theory to promote well-being among this population (Drageset et al., 2023). Drageset et al. (2023) reported that using the sense of cohesion concept was helpful "to make the NH context and its culture consistent as far as possible, with underload-overload balance, and participatory for residents, health care staff and visitors, could be an adequate argument and way to make NHs generally more salutogenic driven" (p. 4). The authors further found that applying a sense of cohesion approach at an institutional level strengthens how practitioners encourage people towards well-being and better health.

Back to Epistemology

How and what we think we know about Indigenous peoples, cultures, and histories is of great significance in moving Indigenous education forward in this country. We know that perceptions, perspectives, and even facts are reproduced through particular discourses reinforcing dominant cultural hegemonies. The way knowledge has been produced and reported has caused consequential harm to Aboriginal and Torres Strait Islander peoples. However, we argue that it also harms non-Indigenous peoples as they, too, are fed mistruths and are robbed of understanding the tens of thousands of years of culture, knowledge, and history of this place they now call home.

> The collection and documentation of Indigenous Knowledge by the development and scientific communities is a very partial enterprise, selecting and privileging some Indigenous Knowledge while discarding and excluding others.
>
> (Nakata, 2007, p. 187)

Epistemology matters because educational sites produce and (re)produce knowledge, and whether it is perceived as legitimate or rigorous. An example of the overwhelming impact of epistemology and its impact on understanding complex topics from new perspectives is research by Walpiri and Murinpatha Professor Peter Anderson. Anderson et al. (2023) present a sophisticated analysis of how close the gap continues to frame its failure to deliver on outcomes on Indigenous deficit. They turn the gaze onto schools and systems to understand causes of failure. Anderson and colleagues outline findings from a meta-synthesis of the challenges in schools to deliver education to Indigenous children. Their analysis identified lack of teacher, curriculum, pedagogical and school environment and culture readiness. This analysis demonstrates the possibilities of new knowledge and ways of understanding problems through applying SBA in understanding the problems. The authors emphasise schools and systems and their practices and capabilities to deliver Indigenous education imperatives rather than Indigenous students and their ability to fit into a system that may not be equipped to provide an environment for Indigenous students to excel at school.

This chapter outlines some key Indigenous knowledge theories: Indigenous standpoint, Indigenist knowledge paradigms, and relationality. These are distinct from Aboriginal and Torres Strait Islander people and are yet to be perceived broadly as a distinct knowledge paradigm, as Nakata (2007) outlined above. Contrastingly, we explored key theories informed by strengths approaches, and this body of scholarship has grown and developed rapidly within the academy. Although these theories may incorporate elements of Indigenous knowledge or have been applied by Indigenous researchers, they are very much framed within Western constructivist paradigms.

The epistemic implications for how these theories have developed over time in Indigenous education are twofold. Research plays a key role in how knowledge is produced. The limited growth, acceptance, and diversity of Indigenous theories and paradigms means all researchers have limited options regarding the conceptual and methodological lens they use to undertake research that involves Indigenous peoples or is of significant interest to Indigenous peoples. Moreover, SBA theories are often discipline or context-based (for example, AI for community development and salutogenic theory in health sciences). While some of the principles and underlying ideas might work for aspects of Indigenous research, they are not developed in such a way that recognises the criticality of centring Indigenous knowledge within the colonial context that recognises the social, cultural, political, historical, and economic discourses that continue to shape policy, research and practice in Indigenous education. Having conceptual tools that support new knowledge production that serves the interests of Indigenous people is now vital as we continue to grapple with improving educational outcomes for our people in this country.

How knowledge is produced impacts every aspect of Indigenous education – from policy development to the nationwide everyday practices of education settings. Developing new ways of producing knowledge that attend to discipline and professional nuances and recognising Indigenous knowledges is the primary aim of this book. In future chapters, we provide practical examples through case studies of how we have applied Indigenous and SBA-based theories in our work as researchers and educators in developing a conceptual lens for SBA approaches in Indigenous education.

References

Anderson, P. J., Yip, S. Y., & Diamond, Z. M. (2023). Getting schools ready for Indigenous academic achievement: A meta-synthesis of the issues and challenges in Australian schools. *International Studies in Sociology of Education, 32*(4), 1152–1175.

Aoki Yamashita, E. (2023). *ABCD + E: The evolution of asset based community development to address equity and displacement.* ProQuest Dissertations Publishing.

Bauer, G. F., Roy, M., Bakibinga, P., Contu, P., Downe, S., Eriksson, M., Espnes, G. A., Jensen, B. B., Juvinya Canal, D., Lindström, B., Mana, A., Mittelmark, M. B., Morgan, A. R., Pelikan, J. M., Saboga-Nunes, L., Sagy, S., Shorey, S., Vaandrager, L., & Vinje, H. F. (2020). Future directions for the concept of salutogenesis: A position article. *Health Promotion International, 35*(2), 187–195.

Bergmark, U., & Kostenius, C. (2018). Appreciative student voice model – Reflecting on an appreciative inquiry research method for facilitating student voice processes. *Reflective Practice, 19*(5), 623–637.

Brolin, M., Quennerstedt, M., Maivorsdotter, N., & Casey, A. (2018). A salutogenic strengths-based approach in practice - An illustration from a school in Sweden. *Curriculum Studies in Health and Physical Education, 9*(3), 237–252. https://doi.org/10.1080/25742981.2018.1493935

Castillo, K., Cárdenas, L. D., & Lastra, S. (2023). Constructing community knowledge by exploring a group of high school students' funds of knowledge. *Profile Issues in Teachers' Professional Development, 25*(2), 129–146. https://doi.org/10.15446/profile.v25n2.102348

Drageset, S., Ellingsen, S., & Haugan, G. (2023). Salutogenic nursing home care: Antonovsky's salutogenic health theory as a guide to wellbeing. *Health Promotion International, 38*(2), daad017. https://doi.org/10.1093/heapro/daad017

Dudgeon, P., & Bray, A. (2019). Indigenous relationality: Women, kinship and the law. *Genealogy, 3*(2), 23. https://doi.org/10.3390/genealogy3020023

Ennis, G., & West, D. (2010). Exploring the potential of social network analysis in asset-based community development practice and research. *Australian Social Work, 62*(4), 404–417.

Eriksson, M. (2022). Key concepts in the Salutogenic Model of Health. In M. B. Mittelmark, G. F. Bauer, L. Vaandrager, J. M. Pelikan, S. Sagy, M. Eriksson, B. Lindström, & C. Meier Magistretti (Eds.), *The handbook of salutogenesis* (2nd ed., pp. 59–60). Springer. https://doi.org/10.1007/978-3-030-79515-3

Esteban-Guitart, M., & Moll, L. C. (2014). Lived experience, funds of identity and education. *Culture & Psychology, 20*(1), 70–81.

Flint, A. S., & Jaggers, W. (2021). You matter here: The impact of asset-based pedagogies on learning. *Theory into Practice, 60*(3), 254–264. https://doi.org/10.1080/00405841.2021.1911483.

Forrester, G., Kurth, J., Vincent, P., & Oliver, M. (2020). Schools as community assets: An exploration of the merits of An asset-based community development (ABCD) approach. *Educational Review, 72*(4), 443–458. https://doi.org/10.1080/00131911.2018.1529655

Gonzalez, N., Moll, L. C., & Amanti, C. (2005). *Funds of knowledge: Theorizing practices in households, communities, and classrooms.* Routledge.

Graham, M. (2014). Aboriginal notions of relationality and positionalism: A reply to Weber. *Global Discourse, 4*(1), 17–22.

Grant, S., & Humphries, M. (2006). Critical evaluation of appreciative inquiry: Bridging an apparent paradox. *Action Research, 4*(4), 401–418.

Hogg, L. (2011). Funds of knowledge: An investigation of coherence within the literature. *Teaching and Teacher Education, 27*(3), 666–677. https://doi.org/10.1016/j.tate.2010.11.005

Hogg, L., & Volman, M. (2020). A synthesis of funds of identity research: Purposes, tools, pedagogical approaches, and outcomes. *Review of Educational Research, 90*(6), 862–895.

Holstein, J. A., & Gubrium, J. F. (Eds). (2013). *Handbook of constructionist research.* Guildford Publications.

Hung, l, Phinney, A., Chaudhury, H., Rodney, P., Tabamo, J., & Bohl, D. (2018). Appreciative inquiry: Bridging research and practice in a hospital setting. *International Journal of Qualitative Methods, 17*(1). https://doi.org/10.1177/1609406918769444

Kaminski, J. (2012). Appreciative inquiry theory. *Canadian Journal of Nursing Informatics*, 7(1). http://search.proquest.com/docview/1699227760/

Llopart, M., & Esteban-Guitart, M. (2018). Funds of knowledge in 21st century societies: Inclusive educational practices for under-represented students. A literature review. *Journal of Curriculum Studies*, *50*(2), 145–161. https://doi.org/10.1080/00220272.2016.1247913

Ludema, J. D., Cooperrider, D. L., & Barrett, F. J. (2006). Appreciative inquiry: The power of the unconditional positive question. *Handbook of action research: The concise paperback edition* (pp. 155–165). Publisher.

Macdonald, M., Gringart, E., Garvey, D., & Hayward, K. (2023). Broadening academia: An epistemic shift towards relationality. *Higher Education Research and Development*, *42*(3), 649–663. https://doi.org/10.1080/07294360.2022.2087602

Martin, K., (2008). *Please knock before you enter Aboriginal regulation of outsiders and the implications for researchers*. Post Pressed.

Mathie, A., & Cunningham, G. (2003). From clients to citizens: Asset-based community development as a strategy for community-driven development. *Development in Practice*, *13*(5), 474–486.

McCallum, K., Ryan, T., & Caffery, J. (2022). Deficit metrics in Australian indigenous education: Through a media studies lens. *Discourse: Studies in the Cultural Politics of Education*, *43*(2), 266–281.

McCashen, W. (2005). *The strengths approach: A strengths-based resource for sharing power and creating change*. St Luke's Innovative Resources.

Missingham, B. D. (2017). Asset-based learning and the pedagogy of community development. *Community Development*, *48*(3), 339–350. https://doi.org/10.1080/15575330.2017.1291528.

Moreton-Robinson, A. (2013). Towards an Australian Indigenous women's standpoint theory: A methodological tool. *Australian Feminist Studies*, *28*(78), 331–347. https://doi.org/10.1080/08164649.2013.876664

Moreton-Robinson, A. (2016). Relationality: A key presupposition of an Indigenous social research paradigm. In *Sources and methods in Indigenous studies* (pp. 69–77). Routledge. https://doi.org/10.4324/9781315528854

Nakata, M. (2007). *Disciplining the savages, savaging the disciplines*. Aboriginal Studies Press.

Norris, C. (2005). *Epistemology: Key concepts in philosophy*. A&C Black.

Paris, D. (2019). Naming beyond the white settler colonial gaze in educational research. *International Journal of Qualitative Studies in Education*, *32*(3), 217–224. https://doi.org/10.1080/09518398.2019.1576943

Park, Y. S., Konge, L., & Artino, A. R. Jr (2020). The positivism paradigm of research. *Academic Medicine*, *95*(5), 690–694.

Rigney, L. I. (1999). Internationalization of an Indigenous anticolonial cultural critique of research methodologies: A guide to Indigenist research methodology and its principles. *Wicazo sa Review*, *14*(2), 109–121.

Rigney, L. I. (2001). A first perspective of Indigenous Australian participation in science: Framing Indigenous research towards Indigenous Australian intellectual sovereignty. *Kaurna Higher Education Journal*, *7*, 1–13.

Robinson, G., Priede, C., Farrall, S., Shapland, J., & Mcneill, F. (2013). Doing 'strengths-based' research: Appreciative inquiry in a probation setting. *Criminology & Criminal Justice*, *13*(1), 3–20. https://doi.org/10.1177/1748895812445621

Saarela, S.-R. (2019). From pure science to participatory knowledge production? Researchers' perceptions on science–policy interface in bioenergy policy. *Science & Public Policy*, *46*(1), 81–90. https://doi.org/10.1093/scipol/scy039

Sabzalian, L. (2018). Curricular standpoints and native feminist theories: Why native feminist theories should matter to curriculum studies. *Curriculum Inquiry*, *48*(3), 359–382. https://doi.org/10.1080/03626784.2018.1474710

Sagy, S., & Mana, A. (2022). Salutogenesis beyond health: Intergroup relations and conflict studies. In M. Mittlemark, G. Bauer, L. Vaandrager, J. Pelikan, S. Sagy, M. Eriksson, B. Lindstrom, & M. Magistretti (Eds.), *The handbook of salutogenesis* (pp. 225–231). Springer International Publishing. https://doi.org/10.1007/978-3-030-79515-3_22

Saint-Jacques, M., Turcotte, D., & Pouliot, E. (2009). Adopting a strengths perspective in social work practice with families in difficulty: From theory to practice. *Families in Society, 90*(4), 454–461. https://doi.org/10.1606/1044-3894.3926

Saleebey (2013). *The strengths perspective in social work practice* (6th ed.). Pearson.

Sapfo Malaspinas, A., Westaway, M., Muller, C., Sousa, V. C., Lao, O., Alves, I., Bergström, A., Athanasiadis, G., Cheng, J. Y., Crawford, J. E., Heupink, T. H., Macholdt, E., Peischl, S., Rasmussen, S., Schieffels, S., Subramanian, S., Wright, J. L., Albrechtsen, A., Barbieri, C., Dupanloup, I., & Willersley, E. (2016). A genomic history of Aboriginal Australia. *Nature, 538*(7624), 207–214. https://doi.org/10.7892/boris.108876

Sarra, G., & Shay, M. (2019). Indigenous education, critical perspectives to enhance learning practices. In M. A. Peters (Ed.), *Encyclopedia of teacher education* (pp. 1–8). Springer. https://doi.org/10.1007/978-981-13-1179-6_195-1

Shay, M., & Oliver, R. (2021). *Indigenous education in Australia: Learning and teaching for deadly futures*. Routledge.

Shay, M., Sarra, G., & Lampert, J. (2023). Indigenous education policy, practice and research: Unravelling the tangled web. *The Australian Educational Researcher, 50*(1), 73–88.

Silverman, D. (2013). *Doing qualitative research* (4th ed.). SAGE Publications Ltd.

Simpson, J., & Wigglesworth, G. (2019). Language diversity in Indigenous Australia in the 21st century. *Current Issues in Language Planning, 20*(1), 67–80. https://doi.org/10.1080/14664208.2018.1503389

Smith, L. T. (2012). *Decolonizing methodologies: Research and indigenous peoples* (2nd ed.). Zed Books.

Steup, M., & Neta, R. (2002). Epistemology. *Stanford Encyclopedia of Philosophy*. Retrieved from https://plato.stanford.edu/entries/epistemology/?utm_medium=podcast&utm_source=bcast&utm_campaign=gold-exchange-with-keith-weiner

Tschannen-Moran, M., & Tschannen-Moran, B. (2011). Taking a strengths-based focus improves school climate. *Journal of School Leadership, 21*(3), 422–448.

Tuhiwai Smith, L. (2021). *Decolonizing methodologies: Research and indigenous peoples* (3rd ed.). Zed Books.

Vass, G. (2012). "So, what is wrong with indigenous education?": Perspective, position and power beyond a deficit discourse. *The Australian Journal of Indigenous Education, 41*(2), 85–96. https://doi.org/10.1017/jie.2012.25

Velez-Ibanez, C., & Greenberg, J. (2005). *Formation and transformation of funds of knowledge*. In N. González, L. Moll, & C. Amanti (Eds.), *Funds of knowledge theorizing practice in households, communities, and classrooms* (pp. 47–69). L. Erlbaum Associates.

Watkins, J. M., Mohr, B. J., & Kelly, R. (2011). *Appreciative inquiry: Change at the speed of imagination* (2nd ed.). Wiley.

Willoughby, G., & Tosey, P. (2007). Imagine "Meadfield": Appreciative inquiry as a process for leading school improvement. *Educational Management Administration & Leadership, 35*(4), 499–520. https://doi.org/10.1177/174114320708105

Zhang-Yu, C., García-Díaz, S., García-Romero, D., & Lalueza, J. L. (2021). Funds of identity and self-exploration through artistic creation: Addressing the voices of youth. *Mind, Culture, and Activity, 28*(2), 138–151.

Zipin, L. (2009). Dark funds of knowledge, deep funds of pedagogy: Exploring boundaries between lifeworlds and schools. *Discourse, 30*(3), 317–331. https://doi.org/10.1080/01596300903037044

3 Theoretical Underpinnings for a Stronger Smarter Philosophy of Learning

Grace Sarra, Marnee Shay, Gary MacLennan, and Ian Mackie

Introduction

We believe that a strengths-based approach to Indigenous Education and Affairs must be based not just on "Indigenous epistemologies" but also on a turn to ontology and, as part of that turn, we must recognise the crucial role of the emotions. In addition, we argue, in what follows, that an engagement with the Stronger Smarter Pedagogy and other aspects of Dr Sarra's thinking is important because Sarra does ontology in that his primary concern is with Indigenous being (Bhaskar, 2024; Sarra, 2011a, 2011b, 2012, 2014, 2015, 2016a, 2016b; Sarra et al., 2018).

We follow Bhaskar (2008a, 2008b, p.34) here in stressing that the epistemological is contained within the ontological. How could it not be? Accordingly, to do ontology is also to do epistemology, but from a standpoint that is based on ontological realism, epistemological relativism, and judgemental rationality (Bhaskar, 2008a, 2008b). In what follows, we seek to show that a strengths-based approach should be grounded firstly in a recognition of the truth that Indigenous Australians are strong. We also advocate that a strengths-based pedagogy must also have an affective strategy. Considerations of space do not permit us to expand fully on the role of the emotions, especially Joy and Sadness, but this is a topic to which we hope to return.

It is, then, our contention that because current Indigenous thinkers have been primarily concerned with Indigenous epistemologies, they have been unable to argue for the relevance of an understanding of Indigenous being for First Nations People. Moreover, we would also maintain that a preoccupation with Indigenous epistemologies does not address or ameliorate the multiple crises that affect all humanity.

This chapter consists of the following:

- An overview of the Critical Realist Ontology;
- Towards an Affective Strategy: The Education of Desire;
- The Philosophical Discourse of Modernity and the Indigenous Gift; and
- Time in Indigenous and Non-Indigenous being.

DOI: 10.4324/9781003372783-3

A Critical Realist Ontology: A Brief Overview

Ontological Realism

In this section, we draw heavily upon Dr Chris Sarra's account of the Critical Realist (CR) ontology in his doctoral thesis. Sarra (2011b) tells us that:

> In his revolutionary work, *Realist Theory of Science*, Roy Bhaskar re-positioned the philosophy of science by restoring and vindicating ontology (Bhaskar, 1978). The purpose of this was to 'underlabour' for science by clarifying the theoretical issues surrounding science. Most important here was Bhaskar's insistence that the Critical Realist ontology, as a layered depth ontology, was the only ontology which was capable of accounting for the successive nature of the progress of science.
>
> (p. 16)

This layering of reality can be described as in Table 3.1.

Reading Table 3.1, we can see that reality consists of three domains. The first of these is the Real and it encompasses the other two domains. The Real consists of underlying structures, mechanisms, and tendencies. Some of these are manifested or actualised as events, and some of these events are experienced.

Epistemic Relativity

An important corollary to ontological depth is epistemic relativism. If we think of the creation of knowledge in terms of digging down through the layers of reality, we can see that at any one stage in the dig, it is possible for someone else to dig further. That is, the knowledge we create can always be surpassed. It is this notion of epistemic relativism that provides at least a partial antidote to the sort of epistemological triumphalism rightly targeted by the Indigenous thinker Linda Tuhiwai Smith (1999).

Judgemental Rationality

Although epistemological relativism is acknowledged, Critical Realism rules out judgemental relativism (Bhaskar, 2010, p. 106). Critical Realism holds that we can have good reasons, based on a scientific approach to physical

Table 3.1 The domains of reality

	Domain of real	*Domain of actual*	*Domain of empirical*
Structures and mechanisms	√		
Events	√	√	
Experiences	√	√	√

Sarra (2011b, p. 16).

and social reality, for judging one account is superior to another. It is worth stressing that if one accepts the argument for judgemental rationality then one is opposed to the judgemental relativism of neo-Nietzschean thought and the perspectivalism of the Indigenous epistemologies approach.

For instance, consider the argument that the lives of First Nations people were nasty, brutish, and short (Johns, 2010). We have good grounds for rejecting this account because the survival of Indigenous culture over the millennia would only have been possible if their life was ordered and controlled by law and ceremony (Stanner, 2014).

Emergence

The existence of ontological depth precludes approaches that reduce reality to knowledge of reality. Social being contains the possibility of the emergence from the lower depths of transformative practices. To see this in action in the colonial context, we turn to the writing of Simone de Beauvoir (1908–1986), who, following a visit to the then French Colony of Algiers, wrote:

> Yet, with all this sordid resignation, there were children who played and laughed; and their smile exposed the lie of their oppressors: it was an appeal and a promise; it projected a future before the child, a man's future. If, in all oppressed countries, a child's face is so moving, it is not that the child is more moving or that he has more of a right to happiness than the others: it is that he is the living affirmation of human transcendence: he is on the watch, he is an eager hand held out to the world, he is a hope, a project. The trick of tyrants is to enclose a man in the immanence of his facticity and to try to forget that man is always, as Heidegger puts it, "infinitely more than what he would be if he were reduced to being what he is;" man is a being of the distances, a movement toward the future, a project.
>
> (De Beauvoir, 1949, p. 143)

The above quote is from Simone De Beauvoir's book on ethics. De Beauvoir is working with two notions, that of transcendence and that of immanence. The transcendent is what might be. In Bhaskarian terms. it is a real possibility in process, which forms the grounding of concrete Utopianism (Bhaskar, 2008a, 2008b, p.294). Immanence is the status quo, that which is the actual.

Mackie (2019) has coined the term "awfulizing" to describe the reduction of the possible to that which is, especially when poverty and social deprivation are being described. "Awfulizing" denies the reality of the possibility of change and feeds into sayings such as "We have tried everything and nothing works". As such, in Spinozian terms, it spreads despair and misery and so reduces the power of those being described (Schmitter, 2021). Contra the practice and the expectations of "awlfulizing", we maintain that in the faces of young Aboriginal children, we can see the possibility of emergence and the transcendence of the actual, that which is.

In the following section, we turn to the role of desire and how Sarra sought to encourage and to educate it.

The Education of Desire

In his doctoral thesis, Sarra (2011c, p. 5) explains the necessity to begin his dissertation with an autobiographical moment. What emerges from the narrative is a moving portrait of what it would feel like emotionally to be a small country town First Nations boy, who drew upon strong family support to forge a career as one of Australia's leading educators and thinkers. Along the way, he also learned to tap into the massive resource that is Indigenous culture. That has given him reserves of dignity and courage, which have stood him in good stead in his time as Principal as Cherbourg, Director of the Stronger Smarter Institute at QUT, and Director General of the Department of Aboriginal and Torres Strait Islander Partnerships.

Firstly, we would like to address the moment of desire in Sarra's pedagogy. Desire was one of Spinoza's three basic emotions (Desire, Joy, and Sadness), from which he claimed all other emotions could be derived. Crucially, for Spinoza, Joy and [informed] Desire make one more powerful and stronger. Sadness reduces one's power (Adkins, 2017; Casey, 2022; Schmitter, 2021). Within the Dialectical Critical Realist tradition, desire is seen as important, but it must be educated and function as part of the drive towards universal emancipation. We believe that Sarra, especially perhaps in his Strong and Smart approach, amply demonstrates the relevance of the feelings of the oppressed to the project of their seeking emancipation. In addition, we make the claim that the Strong and Smart Approach, and Sarra's thinking generally, can be understood as a pedagogy of the Education of Desire, where he seeks to build desire in his students and his Indigenous audience in the realisation of the necessity to shape that desire to improve their lived experiences.

We should note, in this context, the contrast with the Pedagogy of Desire approach championed by Deleuze and Guattari (Zembylas, 2007). For these authors, desire is a productive force which is in a permanent state of becoming. Here, in their descriptions of the working of desire, they seem to us to be drawing on a Heraclitean approach, especially perhaps Fragment 20 where Heraclitus says

> This world, which is the same for all, none of gods or man has made; but it was ever, is now, and ever shall be an ever-living Fire, with measures of it kindling, and measures going out.
>
> (as cited in Warner, 1958, p. 25)

Contra this notion of perpetual flux, we note Bhaskar's (2008a) point that there has to be both "fundamental constants" and "sufficient change" for the constants to become known so Heraclitean caricatures cannot apply (p. 75).

However, Deleuze and Guattari's emphasis on becoming leads them to celebrate constant change, as well as call for a freewheeling individualistic politics of desire, where the student refuses all subjectivities and becomes instead a desiring "nomad, a schizoid, [and] a vagabond" (Zembylas, 2007, p. 336). Here, Butler's (2006) point that Deleuzians "for the most part wish to root negativity out of their conception of individuality and sociality alike" seems particularly astute (p. 112).

By contrast with the libertarian Deleuzian approach, Sarra's doctoral thesis and his autobiography record Sarra's struggle to awaken and then educate desire in his students at Cherbourg. Moreover, it is difficult to see how Deleuze and Guattari's pedagogy of desire can escape the charge of encouraging atomic individualism. By contrast, Sarra's (2011, pp. 129–131) programme, with its emphasis on social ethics, is committed to the development of social and community solidarity. For us, the key to understanding Sarra's approach to the education of desire is to grasp that, in Judith Butler's (2006) words, for Sarra "to persevere in one's own being is...to live in a world that not only reflects but furthers the values of other lives as well as one's own" (p. 112).

Our interest in the role of desire in education was sparked initially by E. P. Thompson's (1976, p. 27) reading of the French philosopher Miguel Abensour's (1939–2017) comment on Utopian thought in the work of the poet, designer, artist, and political activist William Morris (1834–1896). Abensour addressed the criticism that Utopian thought was wedded to model-building or the production of the blueprint of an ideal society and so could be quite restrictive and oppressive. The kind of Utopian thinking that has been rejected is that thinking that concentrates on the form rather than the function of Utopias (Levitas, 2013). The critics of Utopian thought went so far as to argue that the eventual end of the Utopian impulse was the emergence of the dystopia (Mumford, 1962; Nadir, 2010). Such criticism of immature abstract Utopian thinking is easily criticised. But as Bloch (1986) points out, there are dangers in abandoning Utopian longing to the "way-of-the-world philistine"...the "fat bourgeois and the shallow practicist" (p. 186). For Levitas (2013), the critics of Utopian thinking were operating from a "pro-capitalist ideological position" and they were "too cautious, [and] insufficiently Utopian" (p. 122). A notorious instance of what can happen if we abandon Utopian longing is, surely, Fukuyama's (1989) proclamation of the end of history and his confident assertion of humanity's inability to imagine anything beyond the present (Webb, 2009).

Nevertheless, Abensour seems to have accepted much of the criticism of Utopian thought, and, as an antidote, he emphasised the need to educate desire, thus making the Utopian project an open one. He wrote that we must "teach desire to desire, to desire better, to desire more, and above all to desire in a different way" (Abensour as cited in Thompson, 1976, p. 791). We will return to the question of Utopian longing in Section Four, where we discuss Sarra's concept of Thriving Communities when he was Director General of the Department of Aboriginal and Torres Strait Islander Partnerships, Queensland, where it will be helpful, we believe, to think of Sarra's policy programme as part of the general revival of Utopian thought (Webb, 2009).

Using the notion of the education of desire as a lens, one is struck when rereading Sarra's (2012) description of his first encounters with the staff and students of Cherbourg State School by the absence of educated desire. Sarra details how the students and the teachers had come to a modus vivendi that accepted that they would all inhabit a place of filth and acceptable levels of lawlessness and, unsurprisingly, desperately poor educational outcomes. For Sarra, this was low expectations (i.e., the absence of informed desire) at work, and he contrasts the attitude of the teachers and students with that of the parents. In his discussions with parents and community elders, Sarra discovered that they desired much better outcomes for their children, but were not empowered to make that desire clear to the staff.

The following anecdote shows that Sarra (2011b) had to strive to create desire and then educate it. He tells us:

> In the first few weeks as principal at Cherbourg State School I was dissatisfied with the lack of urgency of children getting to class after the bell rang. In response I instigated a very simple process whereby there would be two bells to indicate the resumption of class. The first bell would be a warning and by the time the second bell rang I expected every child to be in class and ready to learn. After several days with this arrangement, one student who had been away for several days asked me why there were two bells before class time. I explained the purpose to him. Interestingly he responded by saying with a tone of displeasure "You're trying to run this school like a white school." Somewhere in his mind he had established that even characteristics like getting to class on time was "a white thing", and taking your time and getting to class late was somehow "an Aboriginal thing".
>
> (p. 11)

The student in question had interiorised and sought to act out White notions of Indigenous being. This had led him into the state of anti-desire and clearly the student was not on the path to emancipation, because he had interiorised too many harmful notions of what Indigenous being entailed. In the following section, we seek to show that contemporary being is dominated by the Philosophical Discourse of Modernity. We try to show, via a brief study of the work of the Navajo intellectual Vincent Werito, that the Indigenous Way of Being contains an antidote to the toxicity of capitalistic modernity.

The Philosophical Discourse of Modernity and the Indigenous Gift

The Philosophical Discourse of Modernity

It is our firm belief, and one, we would argue, shared by Bhaskar (2016), that, in a liberated Indigenous consciousness, we can find at least part of the way to a more productive alternative to the exhaustion of the neoliberal project (Crouch, 2011; Gerbaudo, 2021; Gerstle, 2022). What we need, as Bhaskar (2016) pointed out, is an humane alternative to the collapsing hegemony of neoliberal modernity. We follow Bhaskar in attributing many of these problems to what he termed the philosophical discourse of modernity (PDM). As Hartwig (2011) points out, this phrase was first used by Habermas. Briefly, we agree with Bhaskar (2016) and also with Hartwig (2011) that we must reject PDM and find an alternative as a matter of urgency. We raise this issue here because we believe that the Indigenous way of thinking and being in the world is fundamentally a challenge to the dominance of the PDM and that, for us, constitutes much of the value in the turn to ontology that we believe is represented by Sarra's work.

In his posthumously published book, Bhaskar (2016) gives a very succinct critique of PDM. He takes the Cartesian text *cogito ergo sum* as representative of the central thrust of PDM. Bhaskar begins by arguing that the cogito ("I think, therefore I am") represents the prioritisation of the epistemological over the ontological. As such, it commits the epistemic fallacy which:

> consists in the view that statements about being can be reduced to or analysed in terms of statements about knowledge, i.e., that ontological questions can always be transposed into epistemological terms.
>
> (Bhaskar, 2008b, p. 36)

We have here the source for at least part of our plea for a turn to ontology, a turn which encompasses, and indeed provides, the rational ground for an epistemological approach. We would also repeat that we find the turn to ontology exemplified in Sarra's thinking and work.

Bhaskar's second point is that Descartes's cogito prioritises thought and, at the same time, gives thought more importance than entities such as the body, emotions, or the spirit. The way is open here for the positing of an abstract limited notion of the human. What is very important for us is that the dominance of the cogito delayed consideration of the affective basis of human behaviour.

The key element in the PDM is the egotistical and atomistic individual who views and acts on the world from his own impulses. All around him are objects and he is the lone subject. There is no recognition, Bhaskar points out, of the subject-subject relations that characterise society. The atomistic egotistical individual relates to the objects around "only by means of desire or fear, attachment or aversion" (Bhaskar, 2016, p. 177). This couple of the atomistic ego and abstract universality has dominated the discourse of modernity from the outset (Bhaskar, 2016). We would stress here that the strength of Indigenous culture is that it has not been based around the ego and the abstract universal.

However, what has also been exposed by recent events is the failure of PDM to underlabour for human emancipation by articulating a vision of a eudaimonian or thriving society. Here, Hartwig (2011, p. 488) argues that:

> A eudaimonian society... would be fully historicized, combining an awareness both (a) of radical departure from the past and (b) of future change as necessary and desirable for human flourishing with a (re-) enchanted view of the cosmos as the unfolding of Being and of its own continuity and connectedness with this process – 'embracing process and change, openness to the future as an essential part of our being'. We would live our lives in the moment, but in the full presence both of the past and of the future, such that the distanciated present was present to itself – not absent, as in the 'fast-twitch' punctualist here-now of market societies.

The vision that Hartwig articulates here is that of a society that is worthy of the name of the good society. We turn now to our brief study of the Navajo (Diné) educator Dr Vincent Werito (2014). We intend this study as an illustration of the strengths and values intrinsic to Indigenous being and how that very strength constitutes the Indigenous Gift to the non-Indigenous world in these troubled modern times.

Gergory Cajete, in his *Foreword* to Lee (2014a, 2014b), discusses the role of epistemology or how we come to know what we know. For him, this provides the foundation that constructs our perspectives on the world, and this, in turn, guides our behaviour, be it individual or collective. He then employs the term "metaphor" to describe the Diné saying *Sa'a̠h Naaghái Bik'eh Hózhó̠o̠n* (SNBH). Lee cites former Vice-President of the Navajo Nation Rex Lee Jim's account of the meaning of each word in SNBH. Jim writes:

> Literally, *sa̠* means old age, *ah* means beyond, *naa* means environment, *ghái* means movement, *bi* means to it, *k'éh* means according, *hó* means self and that sense of an ever-presence of something greater, *zhóón* means beauty, *nishłóo* means I will be, *naasháa doo* means I walk. This may be stated in the following way. "May I walk, being the omnipresent beauty created by the one that moves beyond old".
>
> (as cited in Lee, 2014a, p. 7)

It is true that SNBH does seem to be constructed, at least partially, around the metaphorical construct of life as a journey. Certainly, that is how it is seen by Cajete and others of the contributors to Lee's book. In his contribution to Lee (2014b), the Navajo scholar Vincent Werito (2014) sets himself on the particular task of understanding the concept of the *Hózhó* (beauty) element in SNBH. This, he assures us, is not an easy task because the concept of *Hózhó* is "intangible", "hard to understand", "multi-facetted", and "contradictory". Significantly, Werito begins his exegesis with an anecdote. He is awakened on an early cold morning by his grandfather. He and his siblings stumble outside in the dawn cold to greet the morning with a prayer. As we read Werito's account of his family prayer ceremony, the feeling that we are in the presence of something good is a very strong feeling indeed. It is important to acknowledge here, also, that prayer tends to shape or nudge the behaviour of the supplicant.

There is no doubting Werito's (2014) passion or enthusiasm or total belief in the importance of *Hózhó* for the Navajo people. He tells us:

> For Diné peoples or Ni'hookaa' Diyiin Diné'e—the five-fingered Earth-surface spiritual beings—SNBH is who we are; it is part of our thought processes and everyday lives. SNBH is what we strive for, hope for, and pray for, because we believe that its essence and meaning lie at the base of our language and cultural identity and traditional cultural knowledge and teachings. Also, SNBH is an intangible idea that is often evoked and referred to in many aspects of our lives, especially in the ceremonial and personal contexts. Thus, as a Diné, whether I am at home, in school, driving on a road, lying awake at night, sitting in a prayer meeting, or out in the early dawn praying, I have to remind myself and think of how I want to live my life in a better and more harmonious and peaceful way.
>
> (p. 26)

A means for us to understand *Hózhó* is to think of it not as a noun but as a verb. It is a way of acting and being beautiful in the world. Therefore, it is inherently social. One must show respect for nature, for oneself, others, and the land. As well, one must nurture one's spiritual faith. If we understand *Hózhó* is this way, we are, Werito tells us, engaging in critical thinking. We move to a decolonising framework that includes reviving language and revitalising communities. That in turn enables us to develop critical consciousness and to come to an understanding of others who face oppression based on race, class or gender. Here, the aesthetic intent to live in "beauty and harmony" (Werito, 2014, p. 25) has taken on a moral and ethical tone. This enables us to universalise from the particular of the experience of the Diné. Thus there are interesting possible connections at this juncture with the thought of the Tongan intellectual Tevita O. Ka'ili (2017) and the theologian Hans Urs von Balthasar (Bychkov, 2011; Voiss, 2007), both of whom place the transcendental or the beautiful at the centre of their thinking.

As well as evoking a world based on a turn to the beautiful, Werito is very conscious of the need to confront the operations of power in the world that Indigenous people must now inhabit. Bhaskar (2008a) championed freedom from what he termed the totality of master-slave relations based on "power₂", that is, the subset of power relations that is expressed in "structures of domination, exploitation, subjugation and control" (p. 60). Werito (2014) too seeks freedom from what he names as the exercise of colonisation and he seeks to decolonise. A part of the project of decolonisation is to reclaim intellectual sovereignty through the development of an indigenous intelligentsia. Werito always returns to what it means to centre one's life on Hózhó. He lists four principles that he internalises and on which he acts. which he internalises and acts on.

The first of these principles is conceptualisation or how Werito thinks himself as "a child of Earth and the sky" [and as] part of a larger and more complex spiritual, natural world" (Werito, 2014, p. 34). Here, Werito has inserted himself into a totality that consists of his family, language, and relations. The relations include spiritual beings, birds, and animals. For instance, Werito (2014) tells us that his "prayers, stories, songs, and cultural traditions are central" to his survival (p. 34).

The second principle is actualisation or coming to realise who one is. But this is a feat of self-recognition which acts as a spur to improve oneself, so that one can oppose the structures of colonisation. Necessarily, this entails an engagement with non-Indigenous thinkers and paradigms.

The third principle involves action. Having come to see himself as part of the totality, which has been colonised and oppressed, Werito is now committed to the task of helping his people achieve freedom from colonial oppression. This commitment means that, as a teacher, he will be an advocate for his people, his community, and his students. This is the manifesto of someone who feels called to be a teacher and called to work for his people. We are a long way here from the acquisitive individualism of the neoliberal subject (Friedman, 1970; MacPherson, 1977).

The fourth and final principle is named as "reflection". To his task of being an educator he brings the qualities of "hope, faith, respect, and reverence for life" (Werito, 2014, p. 35). His determination as a Diné man is to stay on the SNBH path. Werito (2014) also connects with other Indigenous and ethnic groups and traditions that share his commitment to "faith and love for self, others, and the natural world" (p. 35).

Werito's meditation on Hozho provides us then with an inspiring portrait of an "organic intellectual" (Gramsci, 1971) committed to the cause of the betterment of the life of his people. As part of that process, he is also dedicated to self-improvement guided by the petitional prayer SNBH. Werito confronts the challenges of modern living from within traditional Navajo spirituality. There is a lesson for all of us here, as we too face the multiple crises that plague humanity in these modern times.

We suggest that we in Australia would do well to ponder the lessons of the gift of Diné spirituality for non-Indigenous and Indigenous Australians. The spurious alternative, pute Indigenous Australians are supposed to be grateful for the experience of being colonised by White Settlers. The spokesperson for the gratitude squad was Senator Jacinta Price (McIlroy, 2023). Our argument here rejects the suggestion that the First Nations people should embrace the "White Gift". In the next section, we seek to show how a different approach to time can enable the Indigenous student to access levels of strength and endurance in the lived reality of their people.

Time in Indigenous and Non-Indigenous Thinking

As with his mentor, Roy Bhaskar, time for Sarra is real and tensed. The tenses are the past, the past in the present, the present, the future in the present, and the future (Bhaskar, 2008). It is important to grasp the break with the standard linear time model, where time is merely one event following another (McTaggart, 1993). For Bhaskar, as for Bloch (1986), Benjamin (1977), H. E. Hau'ofa (2008), and Ka'ili (2017), time is not linear. At any one moment, other time tenses can be present.

Concerning time, Jameson (2005, pp. 6–7) points out that the Utopian impulse is either centred on the past or on the future. The Indigenous intellectuals and educators Sarra, Hau'ofa (1994) and Ka'ili (2017, 2019, 2022a, 2022b) seem to provide clear examples of thinkers who turn to the past to discover and draw upon what Jameson (2005) termed a "standing reserve" of personal and political energy (p. 7) to guide their practice as educators. They also represent examples of educators who desire and imagine for their people a collective future that liberates them from the legacies of colonial dominance. These legacies include over-representation in the Justice System.

The thousands of Indigenous youth experiencing or facing incarceration must find the path to self-esteem and *amour de soi* by accessing their ground states of love and solidarity (Bhaskar, 2002a, 2002b). As we saw in Section Three, this is the necessary first step. Perhaps a route to achieving this can be found in Sarra's (2016a) speech at the NAIDOC awards. On that occasion, Sarra talked of a time in his life when he was at a low ebb. He told his audience how his faith in his people gave him the strength to recover. He said:

> For tens of thousands of years, our sovereign nations shared borders, trade and travel. Our laws were strong. Our faith was deep. And our songs enchanted. Culture enlightened our souls, and dreamings lit the way.
>
> (Sarra, 2016a, para 31)

Equally vital is Sarra's (2016a) expression of his self-esteem and the mutual esteem of his people. He said "We are more than victims and mere survivors. The scars we carry aren't who we are" (para 39).

For us, it is also important to grasp that here, Sarra is attempting to break free from linear notions of time (Traverso, 2017). To understand what we feel he is undertaking we turn to Benjamin's (1977) *Theses on the Philosophy of History* thesis XIV where revolution is described as "the tiger's leap into the past" (p. 261). Sarra turned to the "old people" — his ancestors in his hour of need. Benjamin too advocated a turn to the prehistoric past where relations he argued were characterised by "harmony, reciprocity and complicity between man and nature" (as cited in Löwy, 2017, p. 19). The feelings that the turn to the past can find include strength and pride.

It is important to stress that, in this visit of the past, we feel that Sarra is not advocating a return to what was. Instead, like Bloch, the thrust of Sarra's speech in particular, and his life work in general, is towards changing the world. To that end, he visits the past and selects what can help the process of the emancipation of his people. Hence, his emphasis on the recovery of a strong and smart Indigenous identity can enable the Indigenous child to function in the world of contemporary Australia (Sarra, 2011b).

What we are suggesting here is that Sarra, when he makes a tiger's leap into the past, is uttering both a prayer and making an act of revolt. It is a prayer because he is seeking to move beyond the here and now; that is, striving for transcendence. It is also a revolt because he is fighting the dominant ideology that the life of pre-historic Indigenous people was fundamentally "nasty brutish and short" and that traditional culture is both inferior and a barrier to modernity (Hasluck, 1970; Johns, 2010; Moore, 2011, 2012; Partington, 2007, 2012; Sutton, 2009).

The recent exhibition (Saines, 2024) of the work of the Indigenous artist Judy Watson at the Queensland Art Gallery contained a piece that spoke to a uniquely Indigenous approach to the politics of time. It is worth pointing out that the exhibition was thoroughly Indigenous in that it was embedded in deep and "historical" times and in country and community in a way that no non-Indigenous artist could emulate. Using the phrase "Indigenous Excellence" is inadequate, but this was Indigenous excellence writ large.

Much of the exhibition was very confronting. The "40 Pairs of Black-fellows Ears" installation, for instance, was particularly harrowing (Saines et al., 2024, pp. 54, 125). This was to commemorate the ears that were cut off the Indigenous people and exhibited at Lawn Hill Station. We seek to write very briefly about this piece entitled "Pale Slaughter" (Figure 3.1).

To grasp the message of Figure 3.1, we need to understand the differing attitudes of the Indigenous and the non-Indigenous Australians towards time. We base this account on Bhaskar's critique of MacTaggart's work on time (Bhaskar, 2008a, pp. 250–258). We can view time as a series of events – that was then; this is now, or we can see time as tensed and the tenses as real. For, the former Prime Minister, John Howard the *time* of Gallipoli is sacred. It is a past, which he feels should still live on in the present (Howard, 2005)

But for Howard, the time of the Indigenous people belongs to the "That was then, and this is now" series. Thus he refused to apologise for what was done to Indigenous Australians (Davies, 2008). For Howard, and it must be said for many Australians also, when it comes to Indigenous matters time is simply a succession of events. Talk of massacres of Indigenous people raises indifference, confusion, and even frustration among (many?) white Australians. "Mistakes" were made we are told. Now "get over it" seems to be the

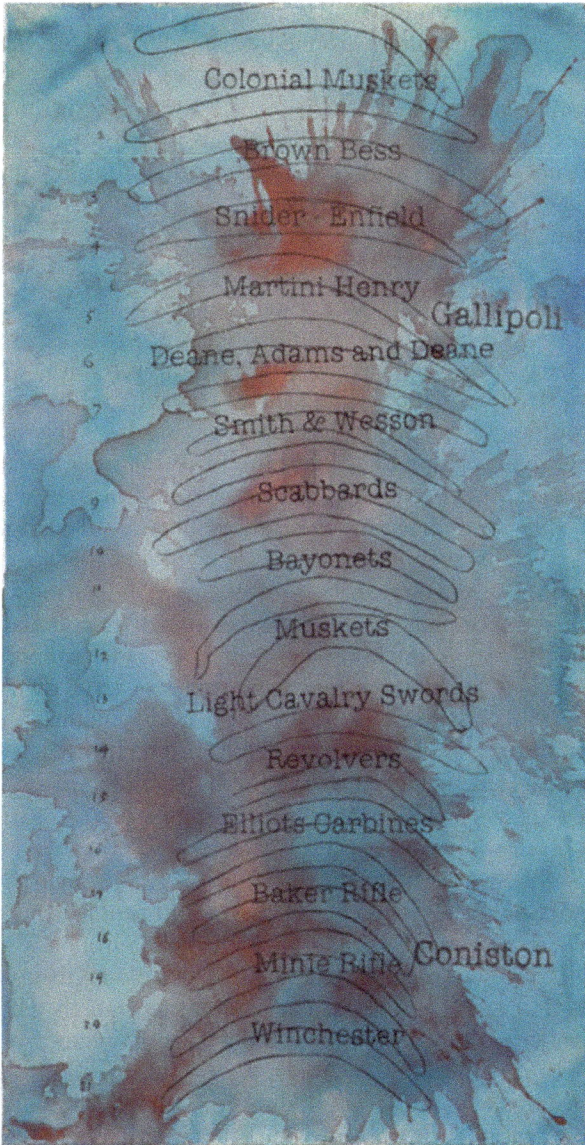

Figure 3.1 Pale Slaughter

message There is little or no consciousness or even contemplation of the truth that massacres are intrinsic to the process of settler colonialism (Wolfe, 2008).

In her work *"Pale Slaughter"*, Judy Watson directly confronts the Howard view of time head-on. She lists weapons and mentions two sites, Gallipoli and Coniston. Thus, in one artwork, we have two specific historic times. There is the time of Gallipoli and, for Indigenous Australians, the time of Coniston, where in 1928, an official death squad led by Constable William George Murray (1884–1975) roamed the country around Coniston Station, NT, massacring the Indigenous Australians they found. There is a difference though between these times. For Howard, and most non-Indigenous Australians, the time of Gallipoli is sacred and every death is, as Judith Butler puts it "grievable" (Butler, 2009). However, the same cannot be said for the massacres at Coniston. It is only when White Australians fully absorb the message of "*Pale Slaughter*" that we will have a reconciled nation.

Conclusion

In this chapter, we seek to engage with the philosophical thinking of Dr Chris Sarra. We also strive to make the engagement meaningful by ranging widely among his work and areas and topics that his work has suggested. We have done so because, as we sought to indicate, his primary concern is with Indigenous Being and in so engaging, he aspires to indicate the path to emancipation, not only for Indigenous Australians but for all who seek a more harmonious and reconciled nation.

Ultimately, in any emancipatory project for First Nations people, one must confront the workings of the dialectics of settler colonialism (Wolfe, 2008). Indigenous people must resist the affect of sadness expressed in the omnipresent push to make them feel responsible for their own oppression. First Nations people must also resist the effort to dehumanise them. Rather, they must turn to the joy and pride in being Aboriginal, which will give them the strength to forge a reconciled nation for all Australians.

We believe that it is fitting that we leave the final word to Sarra (2016b):

> The truth is this: we are stronger than we believe and smarter than we know. For 50,000 history-making years, our old people lived like kings in lands where camels die of thirst. They stood as ironbark – upright, strong, tall, standing and unbreakable. Their lessons, their songlines, their legacy and their dreamings. They are our true north. They are the truth not only of who we were, but who we can be again. My brothers and sisters, believe me when I say this. We are stronger than we believe. And smarter than we know. Solidly anchored by an honourable past, more than any other human beings on the planet, we can take our place in an honourable future. We have survived – and now we must thrive.

References

Adkins, B. (2017). Spinoza: Emotions and freedoms (ethics, parts 4 and 5). In *A guide to ethics and moral philosophy* (pp. 45–56). Edinburgh University Press.
Benjamin, W. (1977). *Illuminations*. Fontana.
Bhaskar, R. (2002a). *Meta-reality: The philosophy of meta-reality*. Sage.
Bhaskar, R. (2002b). *Reflections on meta-reality: A philosophy for the present*. Sage.
Bhaskar, R. (2008a). *Dialectic: The pulse of freedom*. Routledge.

Bhaskar, R. (2008b). *A realist theory of science*. Routledge.

Bhaskar, R. (2010). *Plato etc.: The problems of philosophy and their Resolution*. Routledge.

Bhaskar, R. (2016). In M. Hartwig (Ed.), *Enlightened common sense: The philosophy of critical realism*. Routledge.

Bhaskar, R. (2024). Racism, identity, and education: Bhaskar's report on the PhD thesis 'Strong and Smart' by Chris Sarra. *Journal of Critical Realism*, 23(3), 245–257.

Bloch, E. (1986). *The principle of hope* (N. Plaice, S. Plaice, & P. Knight, Trans. Vol. 1). MIT Press.

Butler, J. (2006). The desire to live: Spinoza's ethics under pressure. In V. Kahn, N. Saccamano, & D. Coli (Eds.), *Politics and the passions, 1500-1850* (pp. 111–130). Princeton University Press.

Butler, J. (2009). *Frames of war: When is life grievable?* Verso.

Bychkov, O. V. (2011). The aesthetic in theology. Hans Urs von Balthasar *aesthetic revelation* (pp. 51–77). Catholic University of America Press.

Casey, E. S. (2022). Emotion everywhere. Spinoza. *turning emotion inside out* (pp. 56–73). Northwestern University Press.

Crouch, C. (2011). *The strange non-death of neoliberalism*. Polity Press.

Davies, A. (2008, March 12). Nothing to say sorry for: Howard. *Sydney Morning Herald*. Retrieved from https://www.smh.com.au/national/nothing-to-say-sorry-for-howard-20080312-gds4t6.html

De Beauvoir, S. (1949). The ethics of ambiguity. *Citadel*.

Friedman, M. (1970, 13th September). The social responsibility of business is to increase its profits. The New York Times Magazine.

Fukuyama, F. (1989). *The end of history and the last man*. Free Press.

Gerbaudo, P. (2021). *The great recoil: Politics after populism and pandemic*. Verso.

Gerstle, G. (2022). *The rise and fall of the neoliberal order: America and the world in the free market era*. Oxford University Press.

Gramsci, A. (1971). *Selections from the prison notebooks*. International Publishers.

Hartwig, M. (2011). Bhaskar's critique of the philosophical discourse of modernity. *Journal of Critical Realism*, 10(4), 485–510.

Hasluck, P. (1970). *Black Australians: A survey of native policy in Western Australia, 1829-1897*. Melbourne University Press.

Hau'ofa, E. (1994). Our sea of islands. *The Contemporary Pacific*, 6(1), 148–161.

Hau'ofa, E. (2008). *We are the ocean: Selected works*. University of Hawai'i Press.

Howard, J. (2005, April 25). *Transcript of the Prime Minister, the Hon. John Howard at ANZAC Day Dawn Service Gallipoli*. Retrieved from https://pmtranscripts.pmc.gov.au/release/transcript-21719

Jameson, F. (2005). *Archaeologies of the future: The desire called utopia and other science fictions*. Verso.

Johns, G. (2010). Debate response: Reply by Gary Johns to Richard Trudgen's article. *Viewpoint*, (2), 17–19. Retrieved from http://www.viewpointmagazine.com.au/download/viewpoint_issue2.pdf

Jones, G. S., & Patterson, P. (Eds.). (2006). *Fourier: The theory of the four movements*. Cambridge University Press.

Ka'ili, T. O. (2017). *Marking indigeneity: The Tonga art of sociospatial relations*. The University of Arizona Press.

Ka'ili, T. O. (2019). *In the beginning was the ocean: Pacific cosmogany in Epeli Hau'ofa's Oceania and Disney's Moana*. Retrieved from https://www.youtube.com/watch?v=eLVdSosIBY

Ka'ili, T. O. (2022a, 13th June). I hope that the people of Oceania are benefiting financially from the growing number of kava bars in Lakeland, Florida. Retrieved from https://www.facebook.com/tevita.kaili

Ka'ili, T. O. (2022b, 9th June). Is it time to legally protect Tongan culture, such as dances, geometric patterns, legends, music, garlands, carvings, architects, mats, tapacloths. Retrieved from https://www.facebook.com/tevita.kaili

Lee, L. L. (2014a). Diné perspectives. Introduction. In L. L. Lee (Ed.), *Diné perspectives: Revitalizing and reclaiming Navajo thought* (pp. 3–13). The University of Arizona Press.

Lee, L. L. (Ed.) (2014b). *Diné perspectives: Revitalizing and reclaiming Navajo thought*. The University of Arizona Press.

Levitas, R. (2013). Discourses of risk and utopia. *Journal of Architectural Education (1984)*, 67(1), 122–128.

Löwy, M. (2017). *Redemption and utopia: Jewish libertarian thought in Central Europe: A study in elective affinity* (Kindle ed.). Verso.

Mackie, I. (2019). *Innovation and reform in Queensland Indigenous educational policy: A critical analysis* [Unpublished doctoral thesis]. Southern Cross University.

MacPherson, C. B. (1977). *The political theory of possessive indvidualism*. Oxford University Press.

McIlroy, T. (2023, 14th September). Colonisation had "a positive impact": Jacinta Price. *Financial Review.* Retrieved from https://www.afr.com/politics/federal/colonisation-had-a-positive-impact-nampijinpa-price-20230914-p5e4mh#:~:text=Leading%20No%20campaigner%20Jacinta%20Nampijinpa%20Price%20says%20the,a%20second%20referendum%20if%20the%20Voice%20campaign%20fails.

McTaggart, J. M. E. (1993). The unreality of time. In R. Le Poidevin, & M. MacBeath (Eds.), *The philosophy of time* (pp. 23–34). Oxford University Press.

Moore, T. (2011). Misadventures with Aboriginalism. *Social Identities: Journal for the Study of Race, Nation and Culture*, 17(3), 423–441. http://dx.doi.org/10.1080/13504630.2011.570979

Moore, T. (2012). Policy dynamism: The case of Aboriginal Australian education. *Journal of Social Policy*, 41, 141–159. http://dx.doi.org/10.1017/S0047279411000584

Mumford, L. (1962). *The story of utopias*. The Viking Press.

Nadir, C. (2010). Utopian studies, environmental literature, and the legacy of an idea: Educating desire in Miguel Abensour and Ursula K. Le Guin *Utopian Studies*, 21(1), 24–56.

Partington, G. (2007). *Thoughts on Terra Nullius*. The Samuel Griffith Society. Retrieved from http://www.samuelgriffith.org.au/papers/html/volume19/v19chap11.html.

Partington, G. (2012). *Hasluck versus Coombs*. Quakers Hill Press. Retrieved from http://www.quadrant.org.au/Partington%20Hasluck.pdf

Saines, C. (2024). Judy Watson: mudunama kundana wandaraba jarribirri. Brisbane: QAGOMA.

Sarra, C. (2011a). Not the only way to teach Aboriginal youngsters. *National Indigenous Times.* Retrieved from http://chrissarra.wordpress.com/2011/05/26/not-the-only-way-to-teach-indigenous-students/

Sarra, C. (2011b). *Strong and smart - towards a pedagogy for emancipation: Education for first peoples*. Routledge.

Sarra, C. (2011c). Strong and smart: Towards a pedagogy for emancipation—Education for first peoples [Doctoral dissertation, Murdoch University]. Murdoch University Research Repository. https://researchrepository.murdoch.edu.au/id/eprint/3373/

Sarra, C. (2012). *Good morning, Mr Sarra: My life working for a stronger, smarter future for our children*. UQP.

Sarra, C. (2014). *Beyond victims: The challenge of leadership*. Paper presented at the Griffith Review Annual Lecture Sate Library Queensland Brisbane.

Sarra, C. (2015). *Chris Sarra's "Delivering beyond Indigenous policy rhetoric" lecture: Full text and key quotes*. SBS.

Sarra, C. (2016a, 8 July). Chris Sarra: "We are stronger than we believe and smarter than we know", NAIDOC Person of the Year – 2016. *All speeches great and small*. Retrieved from http://speakola.com/ideas/chris-sarra-naidoc-person-of-year-2016

Sarra, C. (2016b, 10 July). We Indigenous people are stronger than we believe, and smarter than we know. *The Guardian*. Retrieved from https://www.theguardian.com/australia-news/2016/jul/10/chris-sarra–indigenous-people-are-stronger-than-we-believe-and-smarter-than-we-know

Sarra, C., Spillman, D., Jackson, C., Davis, J., & Bray, J. (2018). High-expectations relationships: A foundation for enacting high expectations in all Australian schools. *The Australian Journal of Indigenous Education*, 49(1), 32–45. https://doi.org/10.1017/jie.2018.10

Schmitter, A. M. (2021). 17th and 18th century theories of emotions. In E. N. Zalta (Ed.), *The Stanford encyclopedia of philosophy* (Summer ed.).

Stanner, W. E. H. (2014). *On aboriginal religion*. Sydney University Press.

Sutton, P. (2009). *The politics of suffering*. Melbourne University Press.

Thompson, E. P. (1976). *William Morris: Romantic to revolutionary*. Pantheon.

Traverso, E. (2017). *Left-wing melancholia: Marxism, history, and memory*. Columbia University Press.

Tuhiwai Smith, L. (1999). *Decolonizing methodologies: Research & indigenous peoples*. Zen Books.

Voiss, J. (2007). Rahner, von Balthasar and the question of theological aesthetics: Preliminary considerations. In M. Bosco & D. Stagaman (Eds.), *Finding God in all things: Celebrating Bernard Lonergan, John Courtney Murray, and Karl Rahner* (pp. 167–181). Fordham University Press.

Warner, R. (1958). *The Greek philosophers*. Mentor.

Webb, D. (2009). Where's the vision? The concept of utopia in contemporary educational theory. *Oxford Review of Education*, 35(6), 743–760.

Werito, V. (2014). Understanding Hózhó to achieve critical consciousness: A contemporary Diné interpretation of the philosophical principles of Hózhó. In L. L. Lee (Ed.), *Diné perspectives revitalizing and reclaiming Navajo thought* (pp. 25–38). University of Arizona Press.

Wolfe, P. (2008). Structure and event: Settler colonialism, time, and the question of genocide. In D. Moses (Ed.), *Empire, colony, genocide: Conquest, occupation, and subaltern resistance in world history* (pp. 102–132). Beergahn.

Zembylas, M. (2007). Risks and pleasures: A Deleuzo-Guattarian pedagogy of desire in education. *British Educational Research Journal*, 33(3), 331–347.

4 Applying SBA in Research and Practice

Grace Sarra and Marnee Shay

Introduction

Theoretical underpinnings in any research or practice setting can provide a robust lens or way of looking at problems, solutions, analysis, problem-solving, and re-imagining. In applying strengths-based approaches in Indigenous education, this chapter explicitly unpacks how SBA principles can inform our thinking and actions. This chapter addresses the process of conceptualising "problems", exploring existing SBA and frameworks, and reflecting on the importance of grounded ways of working within the context of Indigenous education.

There is a persistent mythology that those in need can only be fixed by experts rather than being a source of expertise with feasible solutions to persistent problems (Maton et al., 2004). The notion of being a problem to fix has hindered progress in many circumstances in Indigenous education, where well-intentioned non-Indigenous educators believe they have the answers and solutions to "fixing" the problems. In many years of working in Indigenous education in various roles, we have observed the frustrations experienced when good intentions fail to translate to the intended outcomes. Instead of reflecting on how the work was approached, the frustrations about the lack of progress can often be attributed back to Indigenous students, their families, and communities. There is a tendency, then, for people to believe that the problem is so unsolvable that they give up on trying to improve things (Chapin, 2011).

In Chapter 3, the trailblazing work of Dr Chris Sarra and the enduring legacy of Stronger Smarter set the foundations to build on the possibilities of strengths-based approaches in transforming outcomes for Indigenous children, young people, families, and communities. We further explore existing applied strengths-based approaches, including the Stronger Smarter meta-strategies, culturally responsive pedagogy (CRP), high expectations and relationships, and Engoori.

Established Strengths-Based Approaches in Indigenous Education

Strength-based approaches in Indigenous education acknowledge and build on the strengths, aspirations, resilience, skills, and abilities of individual students, people, families, and their communities rather than the deficits.

DOI: 10.4324/9781003372783-4

Furthermore, it entails an approach that respects the cultural knowledges and values of Aboriginal and Torres Strait Islander people. It focuses on the positive attributes of students and communities and their willingness to work with educators to facilitate meaningful changes that will enhance learning opportunities in education and employment. McCashen (2005) identified seven key principles of a strengths-based approach that encompassed respect, social justice, sharing of power dynamics, importance of the strengths and capacities of people to facilitate change and growth, inclusion, transparency, and self-determination.

These principles align quite closely with a holistic and inclusive understanding and belief that Indigenous students and communities come from diverse backgrounds and experiences, which must be valued. Furthermore, it draws on the cultural resources of Indigenous communities, which Yosso (2005) identifies as "community cultural wealth" (p.70). Yosso (2005) introduces the concept of community cultural wealth within the framework of critical race theory (CRT), which redefines traditional views of cultural capital. CRT redirects the focus from seeing communities of colour as lacking cultural resources to recognising and valuing the diverse cultural knowledge, skills, abilities, and networks that marginalises groups possess, which are often overlooked and unacknowledged (Yosso, 2005).

It provides a space that empowers communities to recognise the wealth they have and use it to rebuild an education system that is imperfect and works to exclude them (Ewing & Sarra, 2023). Strength-based approaches entail looking for the strengths that exist in students, families, and communities and working in collaborative partnerships that value and appreciate Indigenous knowledges and perspectives. As explored earlier by McCashen (2005), the seven key principles are a way to work together to enable individuals and communities to be their own agents of change through growth and self-determination and a change to the power dynamics in educational institutions.

Sarra (2014) penned *Strong and Smart – Towards a Pedagogy for Emancipation – Education for First Peoples*, which examined his work as the principal at Cherbourg State School. The Strong and Smart approach is grounded in a strengths-based approach that articulates five meta-strategies to ensure success in learning. These strategies included: "acknowledging, developing, and embracing a positive sense of Aboriginal identity; acknowledging and embracing Aboriginal leadership in schools and school communities; having leaders who have high expectations of teachers, which in turn, have high expectations of students; innovative and dynamic school models in complex social and cultural contexts; and innovative and dynamic school staffing models" (Sarra, 2022, pp. 284–287). These strategies encompass a belief that positive change is possible when Aboriginal and Torres Strait Islander students are proud of their identity – who they are and where they come from, strong in their hearts, solid in their community and smart in the way they do things when they are focused on high expectations and achievement to succeed.

Strengths-based approaches and high-expectation relationships are connected and must go hand in hand. Otherwise, educators are at risk of developing low expectations of their students. In an inclusive supporting learning environment, the key to embracing a student's Aboriginal and/or Torres Strait identity and culture is through a positive school culture and leadership that ensures it is part of whole school agendas and curriculum planning that is visibly recognised and seen by everyone. In turn, students can see that their school values and respects who they are and their culture thus leading to a positive attitude to their engagement in learning (Ewing & Sarra, 2023).

As Indigenous researchers, we believe it is important to uncover the ways in which identity matters in the Indigenous Australian context, as expressed by Indigenous peoples. A project that we conducted, *Our stories,* "Our way: Cultural identities and health and wellbeing of Indigenous young people in diverse school settings" explored the meanings and significance of identity specifically among Indigenous young people because identity formation is a key developmental task of adolescence. Groome (1995) highlights the significant challenges facing Indigenous adolescents in having to navigate predominantly negative messages about their identity, which are reproduced in educational environments. Given that young people spend most of their formative years in school contexts, this research project was specifically located in high school settings. It recognised and honoured the diversity of Indigenous peoples, cultures, and identities by examining meanings of Indigeneity among young people in urban, rural, and remote communities and in public, private, and alternative educational institutions. The task here was not to inadvertently dichotomise Indigenous identities between these settings but rather to recognise the vitality of Indigeneity and engage comprehensively with the multiplicity of identity expressions.

Shay et al. (2021) examined how Aboriginal and Torres Strait Islander young people viewed culture and identity and the implications for their health and well-being. Furthermore, the research explored the importance of cultural identity to the health and well-being of Aboriginal and Torres Strait Islander young peoples. It used strengths-based approaches that co-constructed spaces where the physical/cultural/social/emotional and spiritual well-being of Indigenous young peoples were supported and their voices centred. In having a strengths-based approach to underpin the study design and research workshops with young people, young people were asked what their perspectives were on what is good about being Aboriginal and or Torres Strait Islander, what positive relationships they had with non-Indigenous peoples; what their strengths are (individually and collectively) and what their aspirations are in relation to wellbeing and schooling outcomes. Indigenous young people in this study clearly identified a range of characteristics and attributes they felt should be connected to Indigenous identities. An example of these included how young people valued and respected teachers who affirmed their identities in their classrooms and in their schools. In addition, television and social media were places that young people identified as being sources of identity affirmation, conveying the importance of seeing black people on TV and on social media platforms, and talked about the visibility of other black people as being a way of affirming who they are.

Despite these findings, Bodkin-Andrews and Carlson (2014, p. 784) report that Indigenous identity research from a Western perspective, which embraces Indigenous ways of being, is deeply interwoven within the undertones of epistemological racism that is still prevalent in society today. Pursuing this further, the perpetuation of lifelong inequalities exists within the systemic education facilities that should be designed to redress these inequalities for Aboriginal and Torres Strait Islander students. Epistemological racism refers to the phenomenon where research methodologies, theories, and knowledge systems are rooted in the social history of the dominant group. This often leads to the marginalisation and dismissal of minority groups, cultures, and researchers (Moreton-Robinson, 2011; Tuhiwai Smith, 2012). Furthermore, Lachaud (2020) identified that epistemological racism is an ongoing practice that occurs in learning institutions and includes colonising the minds of the oppressed, people of Colour, which has been a practice that has existed since colonisation by oppressors. Therefore, it is important that this form of racism is contested in the areas of teaching, learning, and pedagogy for Indigenous Australian students.

Culturally Responsive Pedagogy (CRP)

CRP is a way of life that is grounded in an understanding that regardless of students' cultural background, all children have the right to an inclusive learning environment that empowers, values, and honours their Indigeneity, languages, cultures, and worldviews. Put simply, for a child to enjoy success in any classroom or school, they must be able to see themselves in it and feel like they have a sense of place in the teaching and learning context. Here, learners are provided with different opportunities for pedagogical experiences that require educators to think differently about how they can empower, teach, and engage with their students. Gay (2018, p. 1) recognises CRP can reverse the underachievement of students of colour and improve educational outcomes for marginalised students if the knowledge surrounding their lived realities and experiences is considered in the planning of teaching practices, curriculum development and in their high expectation teacher/student relationships and interactions. CRP recognises that culture is dynamic, complex, interactional and constantly changing and can offer opportunities for deep learning if students' worldviews and ways of knowing that are honoured and embedded in learning and teaching practices rather than seeing it as a barrier to learning (Gay, 2018).

Walter et al. (2017) acknowledge that Aboriginal and Torres Strait Islander people have been occupying the lands in Australia for approximately 65,000 years and are considered the oldest living culture in the world. However, throughout this time, our people have been subjugated to experiences of racism, which is a social construct that is designed to disempower Indigenous peoples by devaluing their identity – negatively labelling them (Bodkin-Andrews et al., 2021; Perso, 2012) and meeting out harsh mistreatment since the time of invasion in 1788. Similarly, Jones (1972) states "Racism results from the transformation of race prejudice and/or ethnocentrism through the exercise of power against a racial group defined as inferior, by individual and institutions with the intentional or unintentional support of the entire culture" (p. 117). Consequently, racism has amplified and polarised paternalistic views anchored in low expectations, negative perceptions and stereotypes and biased assumptions towards the representation of Aboriginal and Torres Strait Islander peoples, cultures, and worldviews (Shay et al., 2023).

However, teaching can be most rewarding and valuable when the cultural, social, political, and historical factors of students are embedded into teaching and learning practices. Often, teaching has been taught from middle class, Eurocentric structures that influence and shape school practices. Gay (2018) explains this as cultural blindness, in which there is a disconnect between what is taught and how, on the one hand, and the lived realities and cultures of minority students, on the other hand. Rather than seeing students' cultural backgrounds, culture, and individuality as a deficit or weakness, which is used to blame the victim, one must consider the strengths of these individuals and their Indigenous communities, which can encompass rich cultural learning practices that can educate and enhance success in their learning opportunities.

> Success does not emerge out of failure, weakness does not generate strength, and courage does not stem from cowardice. Instead, success, begets success.
>
> (Gay, 2018, p. 31)

Sisson et al. (2024) assert that adopting CRP refutes deficit views of Indigenous students and is an approach to decolonise educational settings. It refers to pedagogical practices that both value the lifeworlds and lived realities and encompass the cultural knowledge and ways of knowing that Aboriginal and Torres Strait Islander students bring with them to their learning relationships. This process reflects a strength-based approach that acknowledges and attends to power inequities that educators, students, and communities must consider through critical reflections in order to decolonise pedagogy.

CRP is achieved by supporting individual students and recognising their cultural knowledges, practices, and learning abilities. This is further reinforced by Ewing and Sarra (2021, p. 51), who identified the taken-for-granted assumptions that Western knowledge and ways of teaching are the norm and the merging of learning different knowledge and perspectives, such as Indigenous knowledge are considered outside the norm. CRP attends to this issue by reinforcing the importance of privileging Indigenous voices in these spaces to recognise the lived realities and Indigenous knowledges of students in teaching and learning pedagogical practices.

Some examples of CRP and the importance of privileging Indigenous voices in the research work conducted across three specific projects are briefly discussed. The first of these three projects is an Australian Institute of Aboriginal and Torres Strait Islander Studies (AIATSIS) project, The "Binung Ma Na Du: Cultural stories and living histories on Wakka Wakka Country" led by Associate Professor Marnee Shay (UQ), Professor Grace Sarra (QUT), Mr Fred Cobbo (Adjunct researcher UQ), and Professor Margaret Kettle (CQU). This project is covered in depth in Chapter 7 but we discuss here within the context of this chapter. Second is an Australian Research Council (ARC) Centre of the Digital Child project, "Early Years Language: Cultural Stories and Living Histories on Country", led by Professor Grace Sarra and Associate Professor Marnee Shay. The final example of a project that included CRP was an ARC Indigenous Discovery project, "Unlocking the learning potential of incarcerated and low SES young people", led by Professor Grace Sarra and Adjunct Associate Professor Bronwyn Ewing (QUT).

The "Binung Ma Na Du: Cultural stories and living histories on Wakka Wakka Country" was an amazing example of a codesign project with Indigenous students, families, schools, and the Indigenous community in Cherbourg and Murgon. One of the aims of this project was to develop a series of digital and written stories to embed in the curriculum learning and pedagogy from Wakka Wakka Country to enhance a Wakka Wakka language teaching programme that is being implemented at the local high School. The creation of these local curriculum digital stories was developed and produced to assist in teaching language and Indigenous knowledges from Indigenous students, Wakka Wakka traditional owners, Cherbourg historical Elders, and community members of the local area. If schools are to embed Indigenous perspectives or teach Indigenous languages in their schools, then it is vital that they have access to high-quality local Indigenous curriculum resources which have been codesigned with the local community in which they teach. This project had been conceptualised with strong local leadership from the community of Cherbourg and Wakka Wakka traditional owners.

There are limited examples of research that centre Indigenous voices on what successful, reciprocal partnerships with schools to achieve outcomes such as creating local curriculum materials look like. This means there is very little evidence from which policymakers can draw (Gillan et al., 2017). However, by prioritising the voices of local Indigenous people in decision-making processes that impact their lives and communities, educators developed a deeper understanding of the intricate relationships between communities, schools, and policy during the resource development process. Additionally, this Indigenous-led initiative of creating stories to aid in teaching a locally driven curriculum and serving as a community resource resulted in tangible outcomes. It showcased the successful codesign with local Indigenous communities and the effective application of CRP in student learning.

Through this collective partnership, the Cherbourg local Council now displays the digital resources on their Cherbourg website for not only schools and early years learning centres in the local area to access but also provides open access for members of the local and broader communities. These video stories have now been published on the Cherbourg Council website. This project demonstrates how applying strengths-based approaches through codesign can enhance the pedagogical practices for educators who want to embed local Indigenous knowledges and perspectives.

Another codesigned project is the ARC Centre of the Digital Child project, "Early Years Language: Cultural Stories and Living Histories on Country". This codesign research project involved remote and regional Indigenous Communities with staff, educators, Elders, and the community to lead the development of written and digital stories to enhance cultural language in the early years. This project has aimed to document the process and experiences of Indigenous peoples, including stories for young children of the local area to embed Indigenous knowledge and perspectives in the early years. The focus of this study has been providing opportunities for young children to explore their views and reflections of their Country/Place through the use of culturally appropriate digital resources that embrace and value Indigenous cultures. An example of the resources developed includes the development of culturally appropriate bot mats of the local area and mats that represented early years counting. The codesign processes in this early years project were similar to the previous example with the "Binung Ma Na Du: Cultural stories and living histories on Wakka Wakka Country" project that engaged with children, families, communities, and educators.

Finally, the ARC Indigenous Discovery project, "Unlocking the learning potential of incarcerated and low SES young people", aimed to develop new knowledge concerning the mathematics learning potential of incarcerated Indigenous and low socio-economic status young people (10–17 years). This project designed and developed a tailored mathematics intervention that was culturally responsive and embedded Indigenous perspectives to unlock and support the mathematics learning potential for young incarcerated people. In addition, the curriculum content relied on the inclusion of three vitally important domains: students' knowledge and experiences of their lived experiences of everyday contexts, interesting and engaging learning activities, and CRP. This CRP intersects culture with teaching and the curriculum. It made visible students' culture and represented cultural funds of knowledge and experiences to inform and guide teachers' planning and instruction (Ladson-Billings, 1995; Lewthwaite et al., 2014).

By understanding their students' cultural backgrounds, teachers were able to link the mathematics curriculum to student's experiences, making the learning of mathematics more relevant within their cultural contexts. This approach engages students in meaningful and challenging tasks, accessible to all regardless of their prior knowledge. It also provides opportunities for high achievers to extend their thinking and be challenged (Boaler et al., 2018).

Sarra's (2014) Stronger Smarter framework was incorporated in the professional development with educators to gain an understanding of Aboriginal perceptions of being Aboriginal. Similarly, we included an understanding of Torres Strait Islander perceptions of being Torres Strait Islander and school strategies to reinforce Aboriginal and Torres Strait Islander identity and the impact of strategies that reinforced Indigenous identity, which contributed to unlocking young people's potential to learn. Of profound importance here is the need and ability of the teacher to reflect on how one thinks, feels, and self reflects on their own perceptions and understandings of what it means to be Aboriginal and/or Torres Strait Islander. The ability to do this authentically will take us to the essence of "who am I?" in this very important relationship with Aboriginal and Torres Strait Islander learners, and indeed all learners. The stronger smarter approach requires teachers to understand very well the profound importance of the notion of "the relationship" and, more profoundly, "who am I?" in this relationship. With this better understood, a teacher can reflect on a range of important elements that have the potential to positively or negatively impact upon the teacher-student relationship, and ultimately, the student's ability to enjoy success. Put simply, an Aboriginal and Torres Strait Islander child's success in any classroom is not only dependent on all of the variables and elements of the child, but, rather, is more likely to be influenced positively or negatively by the variables and elements of "the relationship" with their teacher. This profound insight allows the teacher (who is paid to be in the relationship) to reflect more honestly on things in the relationship, including:

- the power imbalance;
- unconscious biases;
- rapport with student, and
- adequate insight into the social and cultural context of students.

Ewing and Sarra (2023) identified that a key component of engaging with CRP is that it provides for two-way learning approaches that privilege the voices of Aboriginal and Torres Strait Islander people. Consequently, a series of CRP posters had been developed as part of this project.

Engoori

A strengths-based framework named "Engoori" was developed by Gorringe and Spillman (2008) with the Mithaka and Tjimpa people. The three-staged cyclic phase provides an open and informal conversational process for addressing complex intercultural challenges. This framework was created to explore local leadership in cultural renewal by respecting and recognising the history of Indigenous people while also contemplating future progress. Furthermore, this Indigenous way of addressing complex inter-cultural challenges begins with the first stage posing questions related to identity – Who are we? How do we do things? It is a relational process that requires people to remember and reconnect how they should be together as individuals and as a collective group. The second phase requires people to consider what patterns, behaviours, and practices we need to change? It focuses on re-examining and re-learning, enabling discussions that identify and affirm individual and collective patterns of perceiving, thinking, judging, responding and behaving. The final phase of "Engoori", asks the question, what behaviours do we need to embed? (Gorringe, 2012).

As part of the ARC-funded project, "Unlocking the learning potential of Indigenous and low SES young people in mathematics education", conducted professional development training in schools with maths educators and the "Engoori" framework was adapted to provide opportunities for schools and organisations to engage with a specific key curriculum learning area that required aspects of improvement. In this instance, it was mathematics.

Using the "Engoori" framework, educators centred and focused in "Mathematics for cultural renewal". Often, Aboriginal and Torres Strait Islander students are confronted with a Eurocentric mathematics curriculum, which is quite abstract with little to no connection to the culture and world views of these students. The "Engoori" framework was a tool that reinforced and demonstrated to educators that mathematics could be presented in a way that contextualised the learning through CRP to relate to the culture of Aboriginal and Torres Strait Islander young people. This, in turn, valued their world views and Indigenous knowledges that these students would bring into their schools and classrooms.

The Cycle of School Change and Leadership complemented the "Engoori" process and provided educators with new skills and knowledges that would encourage them to shift their thinking, individually and collectively, for the young Indigenous and low SES students in their schools. The Cycle of School Change and Leadership was embedded in the "Engoori" process to recognise and ensure community capacity within their schools to empower and privilege Aboriginal and Torres Strait Islander voices from the local community. Furthermore, a cultural lens was used that included the six elements as part of the "Engoori" process to support teachers to consider cultural renewal in mathematics, that identified their strengths and areas of improvement in their teaching and learning pedagogy (Ewing & Sarra, 2023). An important factor was identified, these elements must be considered across each of the three "Enoogri" stages, which provided opportunities for educators to reflect on their individual and collective practices critically. These elements included:

- *Identities, Relationships and Diversity* – understanding who you are, how you interact and the importance of valuing and embracing diversity.

- *Multiple Perspectives* – encouraging a variety of ideas and valuing them without criticism.
- *Collective Sense Making and Buy In* – engaging those experiencing challenges in a collaborative process to drive change.
- *Narratives and Stories* – using personal stories to highlight diversity and foster relationships and understanding.
- *Challenging Assumptions* – rethinking our thought processes and avoiding past assumptions.
- *Multiple Initiatives* – realising that there is no single solution or answer (Gorringe & Spillman, 2008).

The framework is designed in a way that allows for cross-cultural competency training that engages with communities, school leaders, educators, and organisations to develop an understanding of how Indigeneity is perceived and how they might think about what patterns, behaviours, and practices are needed to change. Furthermore, what they might do to embed these changes through an understanding of CRP (Rigney et al., 2020). Within the context of working with schools and educators, it is a framework that reinforces positive Indigenous identity through acknowledging and embracing Aboriginal identity and acknowledging and embracing Torres Strait Islander identity to contribute to positive learning for young people (Ewing & Sarra, 2023).

In addition to this work, Schein (2004, p. 26) developed a framework that identified three levels of Culture. These included Artefacts, Espoused values and beliefs and Underlying Assumptions that can be viewed within our awareness and outside of our awareness. If we were to unpack these levels within the context of a school culture, the first level relates to what he refers to as Artefacts. These are the visible organisational structures and processes that are seen within the school environment. As an example, if a new teacher was commencing at a new school, it would relate to what one would be able to hear, see, and feel. Such as the type of language being used, the style of the school uniform being displayed, or the visible mission and value statements often located when entering the school office. These artefacts are very easy to observe but can be quite difficult to decipher and make meaning of. Secondly, Espoused Beliefs and Values refer to the mission statements, vision, rules, mottos, etc., that espouse justifications for the school culture and its environment. These espoused beliefs and values refer to the values and beliefs of the school and what is expected within this school culture. Finally, Underlying Cultural Assumptions refer to the unconscious taken for taken-for-granted beliefs and perceptions that a new teacher might encounter within the school.

Schein (2004) states, "Basic assumptions are extremely difficult to change and to learn something new requires us to resurrect, reexamine, and possible change some of the more stable portions of our cognitive structure".

(p. 31)

Conclusion

This chapter has highlighted the importance of codesign practices that acknowledge strengths-based approaches and integrating CRP into Indigenous educational practices that embrace Indigenous identities of young people. Furthermore, fostering high-expectation relationships in a supportive and inclusive environment in which Aboriginal and Torres Strait Islander students and their communities feel respected and valued can empower students to succeed.

Reciprocity and respect are fundamental principles emphasised by the NHMRC. According to the AIATSIS ethics guidelines for Indigenous research, "at every stage, research with and about Indigenous peoples must be founded on a process of meaningful engagement and reciprocity between the research and Indigenous peoples" (Australian Institute of Aboriginal and Torres Strait Islander Studies, 2012, p. 1). Additionally, the AIATSIS guidelines frequently highlight respecting Indigenous knowledge, rights, practices, and innovations. These research projects included Indigenous and non-Indigenous researchers who were highly experienced in conducting research and upholding these ethical values and practices. The expertise of the team ensured that the research conceptualisation, design, and approaches throughout the projects considered Indigenous participants experts in their own lives. The approach used is built on the strengths of the Indigenous students and communities.

The research projects discussed in terms of strengths-based approaches in research and teaching practices demonstrate an understanding of and respect for the knowledge systems, cultural practices, heritage, beliefs, experiences, and values of Aboriginal or Torres Strait Islander students and communities. Through these strengths-based approaches, Aboriginal and Torres Strait Islander students and communities can flourish in a more equitable and responsive education system that acknowledges, embraces, and honours the holistic development of Indigenous learners.

References

Boaler, J., Munson, J., & Williams, C. (2018). *Mindset mathematics, grade 5.* John Wiley & Sons, Incorporated.

Bodkin-Andrews, G., & Carlson, B. (2014). The legacy of racism and Indigenous Australian identity within education. *Race Ethnicity and Education, 19*(4), 784–807. https://doi.org/10.1080/13613324.2014.969224

Bodkin-Andrews, G., Foster, S., Bodkin, F., Foster, J., Andrews, G., Adams, K., & Evans, R. (2021). Resisting the racist silence: When racism and education collide. In M. Shay, & R. Oliver (Eds.), *Indigenous education in Australia learning and teaching for deadly futures* (pp. 21–37). Routledge.

Chapin, R. K. (2011). *Social policy for effective practice: A strengths approach* (2nd ed.). Routledge.

Ewing, B., & Sarra, G. (2021). Culturally responsive pedagogies and perspectives in mathematics. In M. Shay (Ed.), *Indigenous education in Australia* (pp.148–161). Routledge.

Ewing, B., & Sarra, G. (2023). *Educating Indigenous children in Australian juvenile justice systems.* https://doi.org/10.1007/978-981-19-8684-0_1

Gay, G. (2018). *Culturally responsive teaching: Theory, research, and practice* (3rd ed.). Teachers College Press.

Gillan, K., Mellor, S., & Krakouer, J., & Australian Council for educational research. (2017). *The case for urgency: Advocating for Indigenous voice in education.* Australian Council for Educational Research.

Gorringe, S. (2012). *Engoori: A strength based approach to complex intercultural challenges* [DVD]. MurriMatters.

Gorringe, S., & Spillman, D. (2008). Creating stronger smarter learning communities: The role of culturally competent leadership. In *World Indigenous peoples conference: Education.* Conference Proceedings, 7–11 December 2008. Melbourne.

Groome, H. (1995). *Working purposefully with Aboriginal students.* Social Science Press.

Jones, J. (1972). *Prejudice and racism.* Addison-Wesley.

Lachaud, Q. (2020). *Combatting epistemological racism: Critical race participatory action research toward the promotion of faculty critical race conscience and transformative practice* [Unpublished doctoral dissertation]. University of Pittsburgh.

Ladson-Billings, G. (1995). Toward a theory of culturally relevant pedagogy. *American Educational Research Journal, 32*(3), 465–491. https://doi.org/10.3102/00028312032003465

Lewthwaite, B., Owen, T., Doiron, A., Renaud, R., & McMillan, B. (2014). Culturally responsive teaching in Yukon First Nation settings: What does it look like and what is its influence? *Canadian Journal of Educational Administration and Policy, 155*, 1–34.

Maton, K. I., Schellenbach, C. J., Leadbeater, B. J., & Solarz, A. L. (2004). *Investing in children, youth, families, and communities: Strengths-based research and policy.* American Psychological Association. https://doi.org/10.1037/10660-000

McCashen, W. (2005). *The strengths approach.* St Lukes Innovative Resources.

Moreton-Robinson, A. (2011). The white man's burden: Patriarchal white epistemic violence and Aboriginal women's knowledges within the academy. *Australian Feminist Studies, 26*(70), 413–431.

Perso, T. (2012). *Culturally responsiveness and school education: With particular focus on Australia's First Peoples. A review and synthesis of the literature.* Menzies School of Health Research, Centre to Child Development and Education, Northern Territory.

Rigney, L., Garrett, R., Curry, M., & MacGill, B. (2020). Culturally responsive pedagogy and mathematics through creative and body-based learning: Urban Aboriginal schooling. *Education and Urban Society, 52*(8), 1159–1180. https://doi.org/10.1177/0013124519896861

Sarra, C. (2014). *Strong and smart – Towards a pedagogy for emancipation: Education for First Peoples.* Routledge.

Sarra, C. (2022) Good Morning, Mr Sarra: My Life Working for a Stronger, Smarter Future for Our Children pp 284–287. Queensland: University of Queensland Press.

Schein, E. H. (2004). *Organizational culture and leadership* (3rd ed.). Jossey-Bass.

Shay, M., Sarra, G., & Woods, A. (2021). Strong identities, strong futures: Indigenous identities and wellbeing in schools. In M. Shay, & R. Oliver (Eds.), *Indigenous education in Australia: Learning and teaching for deadly futures.* Taylor & Francis Group. https://ebookcentral.proquest.com/lib/qut/detail.action?docID=6461787.

Sisson, J. H., Rigney, L. I., Hattam, R., & Morrison, A. (2024). Co-constructed engagement with Australian Aboriginal families in early childhood education. *Teachers and Teaching, 31*(1), 16–30. https://doi.org/10.1080/13540602.2024.2328014

Tuhiwai Smith, L. (2012). *Decolonizing methodologies: Research and Indigenous peoples.* Zed Books.

Walter, M., Martin, K. L., & Bodkin-Andrews, G. (2017). *Indigenous children growing up strong: A longitudinal study of Aboriginal and Torres Strait Islander families* (1st ed.). Imprint: Palgrave Macmillan.

Yosso, T. (2005). Whose culture has capital? A critical race theory discussion of community cultural wealth. *Race Ethnicity and Education, 8*(1), 69–91.

Yumi Deadly Centre (2019). *YuMi Deadly Maths: Overview – Philosophy, pedagogy, change and culture.* Queensland University of Technology.

5 Case Studies of Strengths-Based Approaches in Research

Marnee Shay and Grace Sarra

Introduction

This chapter shares two case studies of how strengths-based approaches (SBA) were applied across the design of Indigenous education research projects. The chapter aims to provide practical examples of research in Indigenous education underpinned by SBA and to share our experiences of what worked well, challenges, outcomes, and future opportunities. It is well established that research is inherently a problem-based effort. How we conceptualise research, design it, and approach it is founded on problems (and sometimes significant problems) that need solving. In Indigenous education, not solving these problems can have dire consequences. In this chapter, we share the significance of the process we used to solve our research problems. We highlight how, using a strengths-based lens, our thinking impacted how the knowledge was produced and the research outcomes. We illustrate that strengths-based research can start with identifying significant problems. However, problem-based inquiry is not the only way to understand the problem or the solutions to address the problems.

The field of Indigenous education, practice, policy, and research continues to be framed by deficit. As outlined in previous chapters, Closing the Gap has shaped national discourse about the priorities in Indigenous education and the immediate need to fix this dire problem. The trouble with framing Indigenous education through Closing the Gap is that it posits Indigenous students (and, by association, their families, and communities) as a problem. This individual problematising extends to broader societal blaming of many population groups that experience significant disadvantages. Understanding the cause of such disadvantage has resulted in many fields of studies and multiple theories, all of which are determined to understand what causes one to face significant disadvantage — individual choice and behaviour or systemic mechanisms (Oorschot & Halman, 2000). Alcañiz-Colomer et al. (2023) undertook a study in Spain that analysed the issue of poverty by comparing how poverty is perceived in crisis. The authors found that more favourable attitudes in policy were applied when there was a perception of poverty in crisis over circumstantial poverty. When understanding persistent poverty,

DOI: 10.4324/9781003372783-5

people were more likely to make individual attributions to experiencing poverty. This attribution, in turn, had a negative or deficit impact on how the issue was approached and on the policy responses.

Let us turn to Indigenous education and apply the lessons from the Spanish study. We can see that Indigenous education has always been framed as an underlying extant issue rather than an emergent crisis. There is a lack of studies that seek to make the empirical connection between the perception of the problem and how it impacts policy and practice in Indigenous education. Walter (2018) explains that there currently needs to be more contextual data to inform Indigenous policy. For Walter (2018), too much data includes an abundance of statistics about Indigenous people while simultaneously excluding either data from Indigenous people or critical data about institutions responsible for the outcomes that are the subjects of reports. We propose there is even less Indigenous-informed data that describes strengths-based aspects of Indigenous experiences and perspectives. Where studies are focused on the individual, an emphasis on understanding either counter-stories or Indigenous-informed data over quantitative measures of Indigenous lack is needed in developing new ways of understanding old problems. The case studies in this chapter share examples of individual and systemic-focused research that applies SBA to produce new knowledge in a field saturated in deficit.

We can see from the current body of literature on Indigenous education and policy responses that the business-as-usual approach is the collection of abstract statistical data that emphasises the individual, such as Indigenous student attendance rates and literacy and numeracy levels. The same data lacks context, Indigenous voices and aspirations, and systemic accountability. In this chapter, we argue that applying an SBA to research or knowledge production in Indigenous education means a shift from how data has informed evidence and understandings in the field of Indigenous education to date.

Case Study One: "Cultural Identities and Health and Wellbeing of Indigenous Young People in Diverse School Settings"

Research Overview

The "Cultural identities and health and wellbeing of Indigenous young people in diverse school settings" project was undertaken by the two authors of this book (Marnee Shay and Grace Sarra) and Annette Woods. The project aimed to privilege the voices of Aboriginal and Torres Strait Islander young people in understanding their perspectives on identity, wellbeing, and schooling. The study was underpinned by Rigney's (2006) Indigenist theory, which frames the study with three key principles: resistance as the emancipatory imperative, privileging the voices of Indigenous people, and political integrity. Fund of Identity (FOI henceforth) also framed this work. FOI theorises the criticality of students' lived experiences and stories in understanding identity (Gonzalez et al., 2005). FOI's foundational theorists frame the concept of identity through sociocultural (Vygotskian) and ecological (Bronfenbrenner) lenses (Esteban-Guitart, 2016). Being informed theoretically by Indigenist and FOI meant there was an emphasis on the voices of young people, holistic perspectives on what informs identity, recognising the role of family and community in identity development and grounding the study in Indigenous ways of being, knowing, and doing. We argue that these principles are inherently strengths-based.

This project was a collective case study of diverse Indigenous young people aged 12–18 from urban, regional, and remote Queensland and Western Australia communities. The research design included developing a series of workshops to explore the research topics by centring: local knowledge and perspectives; creative and cultural methods for data collection; and developing a creative artefact. These workshops included exploring the concept of identity, race, and culture; delving into what being healthy and well means to them in connection to identity; understanding how identities are constructed and expressed; and investigating belonging and identity in school settings. Although we (Marnee and Grace) are Indigenous researchers, we were researching in communities outside our own, and it was important to recognise local knowledge holders. In each community, we appointed local researchers in a paid capacity to work with the team in undertaking the research. We also ensured there was a budget to pay Elders and traditional owners to deliver workshops about the Country we were in and other aspects of culture related to the research project.

In 2021, we published a literature analysis on the voices of Indigenous young people on identity in Australia, framed by Rigney's Indigenist theory (Shay & Sarra, 2021). Our paper painted a stark picture of the lack of qualitative studies that included the voices of Indigenous young people. Despite an immense amount of government statistical data tracking Indigenous young people (Australian Government, 2023), contrastingly, there appeared to be limited published research that included primary data from Indigenous young people themselves. Developing a research design that ensured many ways for young people to express their perspectives and stories was paramount to this research. Data collection methods for the research workshops included collaborative yarning (Shay, 2019), drawing, painting, taking photographs, building Lego, cooking, and mapping (Shay et al., 2024).

At the end of the research workshops, which took place over several weeks, young people were given a budget to develop an artefact from the research. The only stipulation was that it must reflect their identities and show the positive aspects identified throughout the project. The inclusion of the artefacts served two purposes. The first was ensuring reciprocity through investing in the young people and providing an artefact they can keep and use in their communities. The second was to develop something tangible for young people to demonstrate their capacities and perspectives on a complex topic. This would support them in continuing conversations about identity in their schools and communities. However, it also assisted in communicating the research and its findings through the creativity and perspectives of young people.

Below are two examples of the artefacts. Image one shows the design by young men in one community that was developed with a male artist from the community to tell their story about the project. There was a long process behind the design; the young men talked with their families about their totems and family histories and, when they worked on the design, they included different totems to tell the story of their collective identities as young Aboriginal men. They also added the words "our pride our culture", which spoke to their sense of identity in being part of the project. Image two was from the same community but with the young women. A female artist from the community was engaged to work with the young women who also decided to do a design that told the story of them being part of the project. There are different images of people meeting and gathering and different totems. The young women titled their design "Strive with Pride". These designs were printed as posters and displayed throughout the communities, including schools, health centres, Indigenous knowledge centres, and local education centres. They were also printed onto shirts and hoodies. It was powerful to see the young people wearing their designs as the history of this community was one of brutal exclusion and discrimination. To have something designed by young people that spoke to their pride in their identities that they were able to wear demonstrated their agency and counter-narratives to those who continue to hold deficit views about Indigenous people (Figures 5.1 and 5.2).

We published the findings from this study in a key paper co-authored with local researchers in 2024 (Shay et al., 2024). Our paper outlined that young people in this study conceptualised identity through values including pride, respect, succeeding, collectivism, handshakes, responsibility, family values, and staying true. The further theme we reported was "where you are from", referring to family and Country connections people have. The theme of "culture" included many traditional and contemporary aspects of culture, including language, respect for Elders, ceremonies, history, community, clothing, stories, hunting, and being different. The "role models" theme emerged as young people talked about prominent Indigenous football players and singer Jess Mauboy. However, as prominently, young people talked about local people as role models, such as grandparents, parents, aunties, uncles, brothers, sisters, and other community people. Finally, the theme of physicality showed that race does impact how Indigenous young people conceive of their identities, as they regularly referred to skin colour, blackness, and facial features such as nose shape.

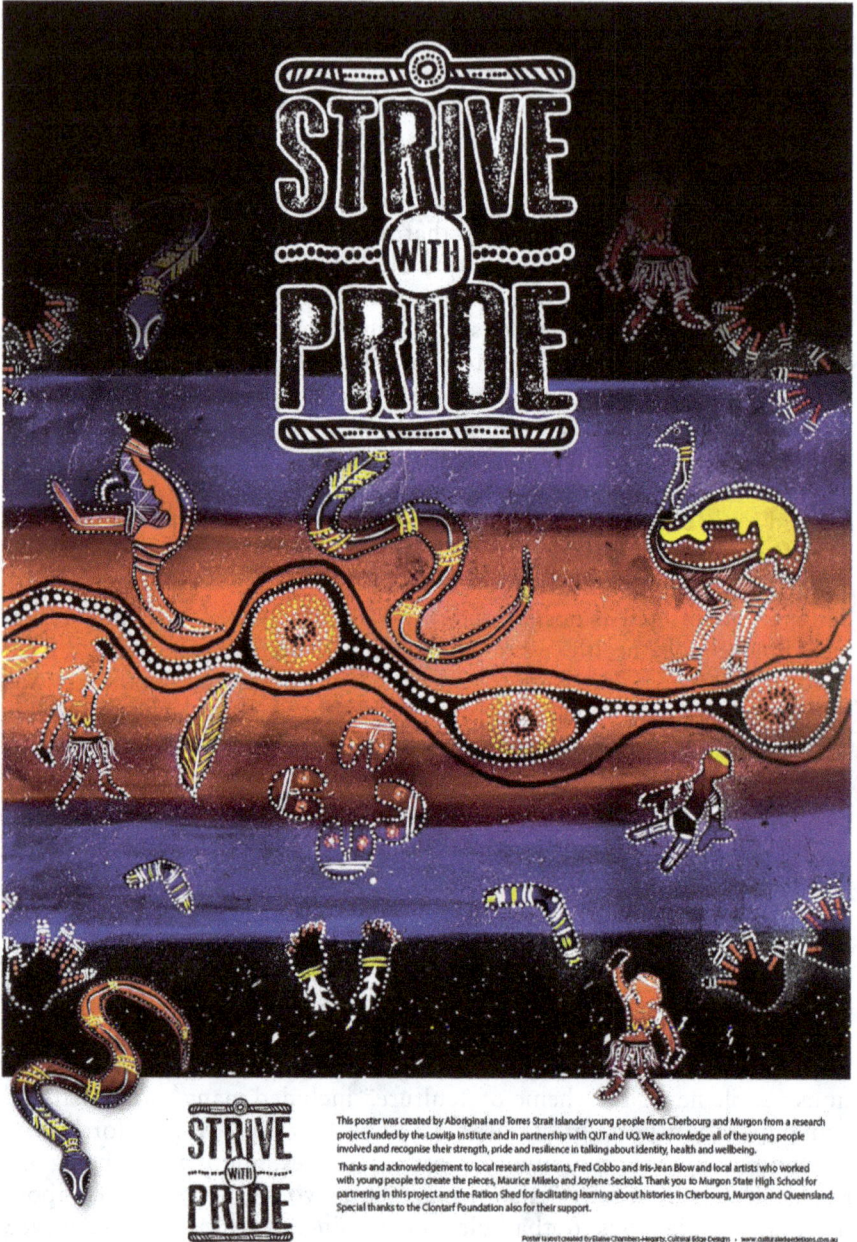

Figure 5.1 Our pride our culture.

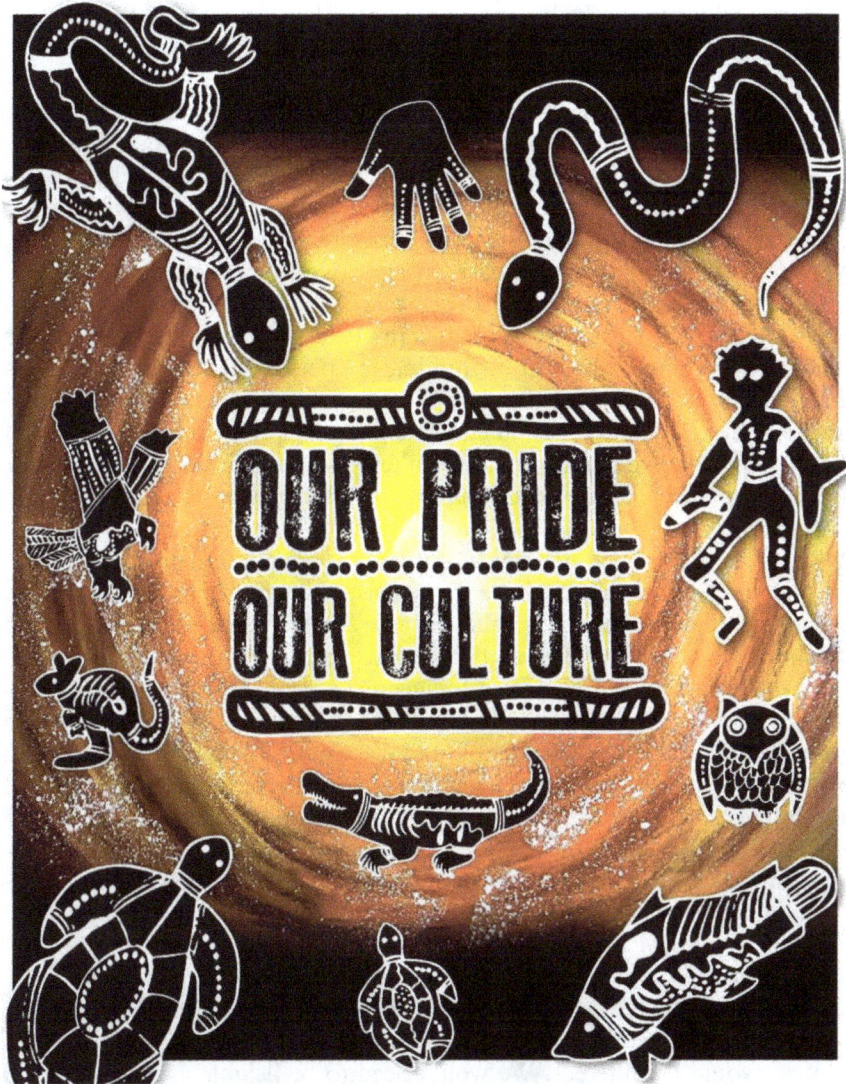

Figure 5.2 Strive with pride.

Applying Strengths-Based Approaches

From the conception of this project, the team was committed to applying SBA across the research design. We were all familiar with the persistent deficit ideologies that prevail with how Indigenous young people are perceived, portrayed, and represented – especially in the media, but in society more broadly. Providing a platform and opportunity for Indigenous young people to tell their stories about identity, wellbeing, and schooling their way was fundamentally a strengths-based undertaking. There were also different ways to apply SBA further across the research design to enable new findings to emerge.

The problem we identified at the commencement of the research was the lack of Indigenous young people's voices on identity and the topics of wellbeing and schooling. We deliberately did not presuppose that the identities of Indigenous young people are connected to poorer educational outcomes or poorer health, for example. Instead, in applying SBA in this research setting, we wanted to allow strengths-based perspectives to emerge. If we conceptualised the research problem through a deficit, the findings were destined only to tell a deficit-based story. For example, if our research problem were "Indigenous young people are achieving far poorer educational outcomes than non-indigenous young people", then our subsequent research questions and design would focus on understanding the problem from this lens. It would likely involve questions based on understanding individual behaviour and circumstances. This would result in reproducing what we already know through statistical data.

Theoretical and methodological design was equally important in applying SBA in this research. We have written elsewhere in Chapter 2 about how Rigney's Indigenist theory is inherently strengths-based, as it is premised on the notion that Indigenous people have capacity, agency, and aspirations through the need to centre Indigenous voices. FOI is also inherently strengths-based, also unpacked in Chapter 2 in understanding identity as an asset students bring to their schools and classrooms. Applying strengths approaches to the methods meant locating the young people's existing strengths and interests, and we achieved this by engaging local elders and people to facilitate understanding these quickly. For example, a traditional owner was appointed as a local research assistant at one site. This person was an active community member and already knew the young people well. They could provide expert advice about activities that were contextual for the cohort but would also support facilitating the research activities we needed to complete. We approached this by applying SBA because we recognised that each young person was different (as was each community) and that the strengths of each context would be different. We would need to be flexible as researchers to ensure we honoured our theoretical framing and commitment to applying SBA in practice.

Valuing local knowledge holders and community was a key aspect of how we applied SBA in this research. At each site, we appointed local Indigenous researchers (at some sites, as was culturally appropriate and under the guidance of local knowledge, a male and female) who worked alongside the research team. The principles of SBA recognise the capital and strengths within communities, which was highly visible to the young people we worked with in the project. It also demonstrated a commitment to sustainability as all local researchers contributed to many aspects of the research and were trained in data collection methods, analysis, and reporting.

The Outcomes

The effectiveness of applying SBA in this research was in the project's outcomes. Although we did not measure the impact and outcomes of applying SBA (something we are considering for future research), there are many positive outcomes to report from the project. It is clear SBA played a major role in achieving these outcomes. For example, at one secondary school in a regional community, the school had previously not had one Indigenous school captain or leader in its over 100-year history. The school is located within five minutes of an Aboriginal community. After Indigenous students were allowed to access secondary schooling opportunities, the school had significant numbers of Indigenous students enrolled. Our local researchers noticed an immediate effect on the young people involved in the project – some were growing in confidence, asking critical questions, and volunteering for roles within the school and the community. Since the project was undertaken with this school, it has had numerous Indigenous school and house captains for the first time in the school's history. The local researchers believe this is because the project not only built young people's confidence through using SBA to explore identity, but it also demonstrated the young people's capability to the school.

At the same site, when the project was completed, we had funding to hold a community and school forum to showcase the project and the artefacts designed by the young people. When we were organising the forum, which the young people decided would be at a local club, we noticed some school staff were doubtful about how many parents and community members would attend. Under the guidance of young people and local researchers, the forum was held on a weekday evening, and we had a packed room of over 100 Elders, parents, and family members of the young people. Representatives from the school leadership talked about their delight and surprise at seeing so many parents and families attend. They talked about how they found engaging with parents and attracting attendance at events difficult. We attribute the success to the local researchers who supported the young people in organising and delivering such a successful outcome. However, underpinning that, we also recognise the role of SBA in engaging young people and families in the project. We did not have the preconceived idea that parents and families would not attend. Rather, we understood that parents and families are interested in their children's schooling and activities and would want to attend the event if they could.

Applying SBA to this research produced new knowledge about Indigenous young people, identity, wellbeing, and schooling. In the abundance of research about Indigenous peoples, there was a dire lack of research that was Indigenous led; it deliberately included the voices of Indigenous people and used Indigenous methods in the research design. Moreover, and significantly in considering SBA and its application in knowledge production, purposefully and intently seeking data to understand the positives and strengths in the situation did allow new knowledge to emerge. We have published numerous peer-reviewed articles on the findings (For example, Shay et al., 2021; Shay et al., 2024). However, there has also been interest in the findings through publishing in *The Conversation*, a research-based media outlet with open access and a wide readership. The article is titled "The Imagination Declaration: Young Indigenous Australians want to be heard – but will we listen?" (Shay et al., 2019). At the time of writing this book, we had 18,000 reads of the article. We also did several radio interviews and other media engagements when the article was first published. We believe it interested a wider audience because it was a positive story – and a new story – about Indigenous young people that many Australians do not get to hear. When you consider the role of research (to produce new knowledge), it can impact social discourse, policy, and practice. This project demonstrates why some topics desperately need SBA in researching complex topics, as it provides a more holistic picture of the issues at hand.

Case Study Two: "Excellence in Indigenous Education"

Research Overview

Marnee conceptualised the Excellence in Indigenous Education project in 2018. She commenced a pilot study with her University of Queensland (UQ) colleague, Jodie Miller. After receiving further funding, they expanded the team to include UQ colleagues Suraiya Hameed and Danielle Armour. The idea for the research started with a simple observation. The word "excellence" is applied in many aspects of education policy and practice. It is used widely and freely in many educational contexts, including policy, classrooms, school policies, and awards. For example, the University of Melbourne has "A Framework for Educational Excellence", developed to identify key aspects that impact an excellent educational experience (University of Melbourne, 2024). Globeducate British International Schools defines educational excellence as a "fundamental objective in the formation of students, as a quality education has a positive impact on their academic, professional and personal lives" (Globeducate British International Schools, 2023). Taylor & Francis even have a peer-reviewed journal, *Equity & Excellence in Education*. It is used widely in almost every educational setting you can imagine. However, when the project started, a simple Google search of the terms "excellence" and "Indigenous education" showed very few results.

For conceptual clarity, the research focuses on what excellent educational provision could look like for Aboriginal and Torres Strait Islander people, not Indigenous excellence. The research team came from the position that Indigenous students are excellent; each student has their own strengths and capital (even if they are experiencing high levels of disadvantage circumstantially). Instead of researching Indigenous students, the study aimed to explore what to aspire to in aiming for excellence in Indigenous education. This may include the concept of Indigenous excellence. However, this was not the focus of the study. We commenced the pilot using a collective case study to explore the topic with Indigenous educators, non-Indigenous educators, and school leaders. The pilot study included three secondary schools, one in a regional, one in an urban, and one in a remote community.

One observation discussed early in the research was the reaction of participants (Indigenous and non-Indigenous) to the research topic. The researchers theorised early that people found it difficult because Indigenous education has always been framed in such a deficit way, with a focus on the students and their deficits, that people had yet to have the opportunity to consider Indigenous education in any other way. The data from the pilot study was rich and insightful. We yarned with 31 Indigenous and non-Indigenous educators, which were then analysed using qualitative thematic analysis. The key findings included that excellence in Indigenous education was fundamentally about nurturing the culture and identities of Indigenous students, school culture and leadership, and relationships. Close the Gap emphasises attendance rates, literacy and numeracy outcomes, and school completion rates. Using SBA at a conceptual level resulted in many new insights and affirmed the need to continue the research. It also importantly identified a divergence in government priorities in Indigenous education through policy and funding allocations and what experts from Indigenous communities and educational practitioners felt should be the priority in aspiring to excellence in Indigenous education.

After the pilot study, Edmund Rice Education Australia (EREA henceforth) commissioned the researchers to continue the research across all their 12 independent flexi schools in Queensland. The study's aims remained the same – to understand what excellence was or could be in the unique context of flexi schools. Flexi schools are for young people disenfranchised from mainstream schooling options (ref). As the data shows, Indigenous young people are excluded at higher rates than non-indigenous students (ref). As a result, disproportionately higher numbers of Indigenous students are enrolled in flexi schools (ref). Because of the higher enrolments and significant Indigenous staff numbers (ref), EREA recognised the need for research to understand flexi schools' role in Indigenous education. They were interested in how the flexi schools could contribute to excellence in education for Indigenous young people, their families, and communities. We interviewed x number of staff members, school leaders, and practitioners. We also created a professional development video series where filming occurred across the sites to share the many perspectives and practice exemplars across school practices. At the time of writing this book, we are finalising the analyses and publishing from this data. Similarly, to the pilot, we found many variances in what people identified we should be doing in practice in aspiring to excellence in Indigenous education to current Indigenous education policy imperatives.

Applying Strengths-Based Approaches

The way this study was conceptualised was an inherently strength-based approach. It was based on the presupposition that an alternative to the current status quo in Indigenous education is indeed possible; Indigenous excellence already exists, and it is time for educational systems to allow excellence to thrive. When exploring the topic with practitioners and community members, appreciative inquiry (AI) framed the research design. Chapter 10 outlines the 5 Ds: define, discovery, dream, design, and destiny (Tschannen-Moran & Tschannen-Moran, 2011). AI incorporates many elements of SBA, fundamentally asserting the premise that research must be based on a problem (Knibbs et al., 2012). AI also incorporates SBA through enabling "positive principle", "constructionist principle", "poetic principle", "principle of simultaneity", and "anticipatory principle" (Kumar et al., 2023, p. 1006). The positive principle engages positive attitudes needed for relationality for change, underpinning the approach to excellence in Indigenous education research. Further principles such as simultaneity and anticipatory incorporate inquiry and change as a way of guiding future actions. The poetic principle is outlined by Kumar et al. (2023) as a co-authorship of storied perspectives from people within an organisation.

This research commenced from the perspective that: (1) some good practices are happening in Indigenous education; and (2) space and resources are provided for all involved in the school to consider what needs to happen if the school aspires to excellence in Indigenous education. It is a well-recognised phenomenon that non-Indigenous educators are reluctant to enact some imperatives in Indigenous education policy, such as embedding Indigenous knowledge and perspectives (Riley et al., 2019). Using AI and an SBA approach, the research team had a significant uptake of participants at each site, and the data resulted in something new to contribute to the plethora of existing research in the field.

The Outcomes

The outcomes of this project are still emerging. An immediate outcome was developing a professional development film series, whereby films across each site explored various perspectives and examples, unpacking the research questions about excellence in Indigenous education. The resource was invaluable for this school network because each flexi school is often highly unique and operates in situ of the local culture and community context. Professional development modules were developed using the content and relating to key Indigenous education policies, including the Australian Institute of Teaching and School Leadership (AITSL) standards, particularly those related to Indigenous education. It also was shaped around the evidence in the field and reflective questions and processes for continual learning and growth in aspiring

https://education.uq.edu.au/Excellence-Indigenous-Education

Figure 5.3 QR code excellence in Indigenous education website.

to excellence in Indigenous education. The video material and professional development modules are all owned by EREA.

The team also felt it was necessary to be in line with AI and SBA to ensure that all the findings were open to access where possible. This project now has a website that is updated regularly with links to the researchers, peer-reviewed journal articles, shorter articles, and resources. Yanyuwa educator and artist Lauren Turner developed an Aboriginal design to represent the project. The design is the banner for the website but is also used when the researchers present the findings to the community, industry, governments, and schools. Incorporating Indigenous ways of telling stories, particularly in research where Western paradigms such as scholarly articles are predominant, is an SBA approach in Indigenous research. Shirts were printed incorporating the design on the front, with the QR code to the website on the back. The shirts are a walking way of communicating the research and inviting people to engage with the topic of excellence in Indigenous education (Figure 5.3).

Conclusion

Use of SBA approaches in Indigenous research is growing as there have been increasing calls from Indigenous leaders and advocates to move away from deficit discourses that continue to harm efforts to improve outcomes for our people. In 2018, the Lowitja Institute published a report to understand "how deficit discourses are produced and reproduced", as they propose that understanding how deficit discourses permeate thinking is "essential to challenging them" (Fogarty et al., 2018, p. vii). Many Indigenous thinkers and leaders have called for a move away from deficit diatribes to recognise the many strengths and positives that exist in Aboriginal and Torres Strait Islander families and communities nationwide. Mithaka man and educator, Scott Gorringe, wrote for *IndigenousX* in 2015:

> my strong belief is that there is no lack of passion, desire and resources to shift the struggle we have in Indigenous Australia. The problem is the way we frame these issues. We're all caught in this thing called a "deficit discourse" and we don't even know we are in it... we can change the deficit discourse by challenging the assumptions of the way people frame their approach to some of these big problems. I'm not denying the struggles that exist in Aboriginal communities and families. I see it nearly every day when I'm working in schools. But it shouldn't be the place where we start. It's a thing that we need to address but it shouldn't be the way we frame things.
>
> (Gorringe, 2015, Paragraphs 1–8)

In shifting the starting place in education away from deficit discourses, this should extend to how knowledge is produced. Policymakers and schools ostensibly base many of their programmes and practices on the evidence, much of which is produced via research. In Chapter 2, we discussed the significance of epistemology and subjectivities in how knowledge is produced and received, perceived, and taken up. The field of Indigenous health is much further advanced, and researchers recognise the need to balance the field with some much-needed counter-stories and strengths-based data. This chapter has provided two examples of our efforts to apply SBA in our research. We continue developing these ideas over time and encourage other researchers to consider the possibilities of SBA across the many dimensions of Indigenous education.

References

Alcañiz-Colomer, J., Moya, M., & Valor-Segura, I. (2023). Not all poor are equal: The perpetuation of poverty through blaming those who have been poor all their lives. *Current Psychology*, 42(31), 26928–26944.

Australian Government (2023). *Education of First Nations people*. Australian Institute of Health and Welfare. Retrieved from https://www.aihw.gov.au/reports/australias-welfare/indigenous-education-and-skills

Esteban-Guitart, M. (2016). *Funds of identity: Connecting meaningful learning experiences in and out of school*. Cambridge University Press.

Fogarty, W., Bulloch, H., McDonnell, S., & Davis, M. (2018). *Deficit discourse and Indigenous health: How narrative framings of Aboriginal and Torres Strait Islander people are reproduced in policy*. The Lowitja Institute.

Globeducate British International Schools (2023). *What we mean by educational excellence*. Retrieved from https://www.britishinternationalschool.com/blog/british-international-schools/news-british-international-school/~board/gbis-en/post/what-we-mean-by-educational-excellence

Gonzalez, N., Moll, L. C., & Amanti, C. (2005). *Funds of knowledge: Theorizing practices in households, communities, and classrooms*. Routledge.

Gorringe, S. (2015, May 15). Aboriginal culture is not a problem. The way we talk about it is. *IndigenousX*. Republished in *The Guardian*. Retrieved from https://www.theguardian.com/commentisfree/2015/may/15/aboriginal-culture-is-not-a-problem-the-way-we-talk-about-it-is

Knibbs, K., Underwood, J., MacDonald, M., Schoenfeld, B., Lavoie-Tremblay, M., Crea-Arsenio, M., Meagher-Stewart, D., Leeseberg Stamler, L., Blythe, J., & Ehrlich, A. (2012). Appreciative inquiry: A strength-based research approach to building Canadian public health nursing capacity. *Journal of Research in Nursing*, 17(5), 484–494. https://doi.org/10.1177/1744987110387472

Kumar, B., Suneja, M., & Swee, M. (2023). When I say... appreciative inquiry. *Medical Education*, 57(11).

Oorschot, W. V., & Halman, L. (2000). Blame or fate, individual or social? *European Societies*, 2(1), 1–28.

Rigney, L. (2006). Indigenist research and Aboriginal Australia. In J. E. Kunnie, & N. I. Goduka (Eds.). *Indigenous peoples' wisdom and power* (pp. 32–50). Ashgate Publishing.

Riley, T., Monk, S., & VanIssum, H. (2019). Barriers and breakthroughs: Engaging in socially just ways towards issues of indigeneity, identity, and whiteness in teacher education. *Whiteness and Education*, 4(1), 88–107.

Shay, M. (2019). Extending the yarning yarn: Collaborative yarning methodology for ethical Indigenist education research. *The Australian Journal of Indigenous Education*, 50(1), 1–9. https://doi.org/10.1017/jie.2018.25

Shay, M., & Sarra, G. (2021). Locating the voices of Indigenous young people on identity in Australia: An Indigenist analysis. *Diaspora, Indigenous and Minority Education*, 15(3), 1–14. https://doi.org/10.1080/15595692.2021.1907330

Shay, M., Sarra, G., Proud, D., Blow, I., & Cobbo, F. (2024). Strive with pride": The voices of Indigenous young people on identity, wellbeing and schooling in Australia. *International Journal of Qualitative Studies in Education*, 36(2), 327–341. https://doi.org/10.1080/09518398.2023.2233939

Shay, M., Sarra, G., & Woods, A. (2021). Strong identities, strong futures: Indigenous identities and well-being in schools. In M. Shay, & R. Oliver (Eds.). *Indigenous education in Australia: Learning and teaching for deadly futures* (pp. 63–75). Routledge.

Shay, M., Woods, A., & Sarra, G. (2019). The Imagination Declaration: Young Indigenous Australians want to be heard – But will we listen? *The Conversation*. Retrieved from https://theconversation.com/the-imagination-declaration-young-indigenous-australians-want-to-be-heard-but-will-we-listen-121569

Tschannen-Moran, M., & Tschannen-Moran, B. (2011). Taking a strengths-based focus improves school climate. *Journal of School Leadership*, 21(3), 422–448.

University of Melbourne (2024). *A framework for educational excellence*. Retrieved from https://melbournecshe.unimelb.edu.au/__data/assets/pdf_file/0004/4860058/Framework-for-Educational-Excellence.pdf

Walter, M. (2018). The voice of Indigenous data: Beyond the markers of disadvantage. *Griffith Review*, 60, 256–263.

6 Strengths-Based Codesign

Marnee Shay, Grace Sarra, Jo Lampert, and Jodie Miller

Introduction

Codesign is a buzzword that is attracting increasing interest. As governments, schools, and other organisations seek to use different approaches that incorporate marginalised voices, it is not surprising that codesign has rapidly become a commonplace language in policy and programme approaches involving Indigenous people. Like many, we too were sceptical about the ascension of codesign and its promise of different outcomes when it appeared to lack conceptual clarity or any clear explanation of what makes codesign different from terms such as consultation, coproduction, collaboration, community engagement, or other participatory approaches. As researchers, we became interested in asking complex questions, such as what effective codesign looks like for Indigenous people and how we move towards an evidence-informed framework for codesign, when we all come to the process with our own conceptions, expectations, and understandings.

This chapter will share key findings from a study on codesigning Indigenous education policy in Queensland. The research includes case studies with schools and communities, a large-scale community-based survey, and a systematic literature review. It became clear to the team across the research process that the data informed by Indigenous people incorporates strengths-based philosophies. If codesign is undertaken well, it is inherently a strengths-based approach. We will commence the chapter by sharing the background of the study and what we know about codesign so far, and we propose a framework for strengths-based codesign underpinned by our research. It is anticipated that the framework can be used for practice or research.

What Is Codesign with Indigenous People and Communities?

Codesign is a term used in policy studies from the 1960s (Mintrom et al., 2024). Increasing critical consciousness of the importance of lived experience and knowledge in developing programme and policy responses to address disadvantage resulted in a strong interest in methodologies and approaches that enable marginalised voices to be included (Chilisa, 2019). Codesign also draws from

DOI: 10.4324/9781003372783-6

participatory thinking and design literature (Blomkamp, 2018), emphasising the significance of working *with* people rather than doing things *to* people.

Although there is no consensus on codesign as a definition, there is a broader understanding that codesign should actively seek perspectives and input from people who have lived and contextual experience (Mintrom et al., 2024). The groups (often marginalised) are considered content experts and lived experience is accepted as a valid source of knowledge (Blomkamp, 2018). With these key elements in mind, understanding how codesign would work within the colonial context of Australia with Indigenous Australians, who still do not have a treaty, needs significant research and exploration.

In 2024, we published a systematic literature review on codesign in Indigenous education policy and practice in Australia to seek an evidence-informed understanding of the potential of codesign in transforming educational outcomes for Indigenous people (Shay & Lampert, 2024). We found only 15 papers relevant to codesign in Indigenous education. Our analysis focused on understanding codesign across three domains: conceptualisation, process, and evaluation. We found across the literature that codesign was not conceptualised clearly; however, two papers emphasised community engagement and working with the community. Three more papers relied on participatory design to underpin their conception of codesign with Indigenous peoples. A few papers were transparent about when the codesign process commenced and how it was applied across the life of the project. Only half of the papers showed evidence of clearly defined roles and, concerningly, just over one-third of papers reported clearly that Indigenous leadership supported the process.

Codesign with Indigenous peoples and communities in education contexts appears to be an emerging approach; the health discipline has quickly adopted codesign and is seeking an understanding of the effective elements of codesign. For example, Butler et al. (2022) identified key areas for successful evidence-based codesign in Indigenous health settings, including clear benefits to Indigenous people and communities, inclusive partnerships, evidence-based decision-making, respect, Indigenous leadership, and culturally grounded practices. King et al. (2022) reported that, while literature and evidence on successful codesign in Indigenous settings were limited, special attention should be paid to power and decision-making in the process.

Despite the promise of codesign, there is considerable concern about codesign from conception, process, and evaluation. For example, Driese and Mazurski (2018) warn that community members must know what codesign is and what is expected of them to take part if the process is to differ from consultation. Furthermore, they identify the risks when government officials are left to draw on their individual perspectives of local communities when they are often non-Indigenous and do not have the expertise to make such judgements. Akama et al. (2019) explain that design culture is underpinned by "west is best" notions, increasing the potential for codesign to reproduce Eurocentric ways of doing and colonial discourses. Despite these concerns, the Australian government has shifted to "codesign". It is unclear if this move is simply a shift in language rather than in ways of working with Indigenous people (Dillon, 2021). Our research, outlined in this chapter, explores some of the tensions and issues but also aims to contribute to a much-needed evidence base for understanding whether codesign can transform outcomes in Indigenous education or is just another buzzword of the day. While our research is still underway at the time of writing this chapter, our analysis of the data suggests that if key elements to the process are present, codesign does have the potential to shift educational outcomes for Aboriginal and Torres Strait Islander people.

Strengths Approaches and the Potential of Codesign with Aboriginal and Torres Strait Islander People and Communities

The model of consultation is a path well-trodden in Indigenous education. Holt (2021) outlines that the 1970s were a turning point for Indigenous education. The first official committees were established to provide Aboriginal and Torres Strait Islander voices at a national level to inform educational policies in progressing Indigenous participation and success in education. While these high-level committees were established to include a wide range of Indigenous voices and expertise, the model is one of consultation, as the government or bodies that establish such committees have no requirement to include advice, or act on the advice given, from Aboriginal and Torres Strait Islander people. We have published elsewhere about the slippery slope of how decisions are made about who the community is, whose voices count, and how they are included (Shay & Lampert, 2024). The issue of Indigenous voices in education remains an ongoing issue (Guenther et al., 2023), as yearly "Close the Gap" reports highlight the lack of real improvement in Indigenous education (Commonwealth of Australia, 2024).

Consultative bodies remain the status quo in having Indigenous voices in policy-making processes. As Indigenous education has lacked the growth of a large Indigenous community-controlled sector as seen in health, in 2024, governments across jurisdictions in Australia were still establishing Indigenous education groups and bodies to inform Indigenous education policy (Shay, 2024). For example, in Queensland, the Queensland Family and Child Commission outline plans for establishing the Queensland Early Childhood Education, Education and Training Consultative Body (Queensland Family and Child Commission, 2024). The committee is already positioned as "consultative", demonstrating a commitment to a consultative model whereby the government brings ideas to these committees and then chooses whether to action this advice. Critical questions must be asked in understanding the effectiveness of consultation to date. For example, when governments and departments establish bodies – they select and appoint (and nowadays pay) committee members; how does this impact the ability of members to critique policies and practices? What transparency is there about who is selected and what is the reason for it?

Flemmer and Schilling-Vacaflor (2016) reported findings from a study investigating consultative processes with Indigenous peoples in Bolivia and Peru in the context of extractive industries. They found that the consultation approach had limited Indigenous governance of the processes; Indigenous people struggled to be heard, which resulted in very few outcomes for these groups. In a further example from Canada, Youdelis (2016) critiques contemporary practices of consultation with Indigenous peoples as reproducing "unequal colonial-capitalist power dynamics, replying on antipolitical strategies to produce the appearance of inclusion" (Youdelis, 2016, p. 1374). In Australia, in 2023, there was a practical attempt to move away from consultation models to an enshrined Indigenous voice to parliament. In Cox's (2024) view, consultation alone would not get to the heart of the problem [disadvantage], which requires Indigenous leadership and an active and political voice. An enshrined voice was put forward to the Australian public for a vote as it involved a change to the Australian Constitution. Although most of the voting public voted "no", we know that the majority of Indigenous Australians were more likely to vote "yes" (Biddle et al., 2023). The reasons likely differ for individuals and communities, but the vote says clearly that Indigenous Australians are looking for new ways of working in shifting outcomes for future generations.

Consultation models differ, much like the lack of conceptual clarity in codesign. How one person conceives quality consultation differs from the next, depending on who they are and why they are coming to the process. A plethora of guides are available from government departments to non-government organisations on consulting with Aboriginal and Torres Strait Islander peoples and communities. For example, the New South Wales Government Family and Community Services Department published guidelines for consultation in 2011 that appear to still be active, as available on their webpage (Department of Family and Community Service, 2011). The consultation guide states that "Aboriginal consultation is an exchange or two-way flow of information. It is an important method that empowers Aboriginal families and communities to help make decisions on matters that affect the care and protection of their children and young people" (Department of Family and Community Services, 2011, p. 5). The guidelines further emphasise the importance of consultation, participation in decision-making, and enabling self-determination. While there may be many statements about what consultation with Indigenous people should be, the *Cambridge Dictionary* defines consultation as "a meeting to discuss something or to get advice" (Cambridge University Press, n.d.).

Throughout our professional careers in education, we have observed cycles of consultative models in Indigenous education be implemented and withdrawn as spontaneously as they were conceived. In understanding the key differences between consultation and codesign, we developed a comparative framework that outlines key principles and practices to distinguish ideological and practical patterns of differentiation in moving towards an evidence-based understanding of codesign in Indigenous education. Figure 6.1

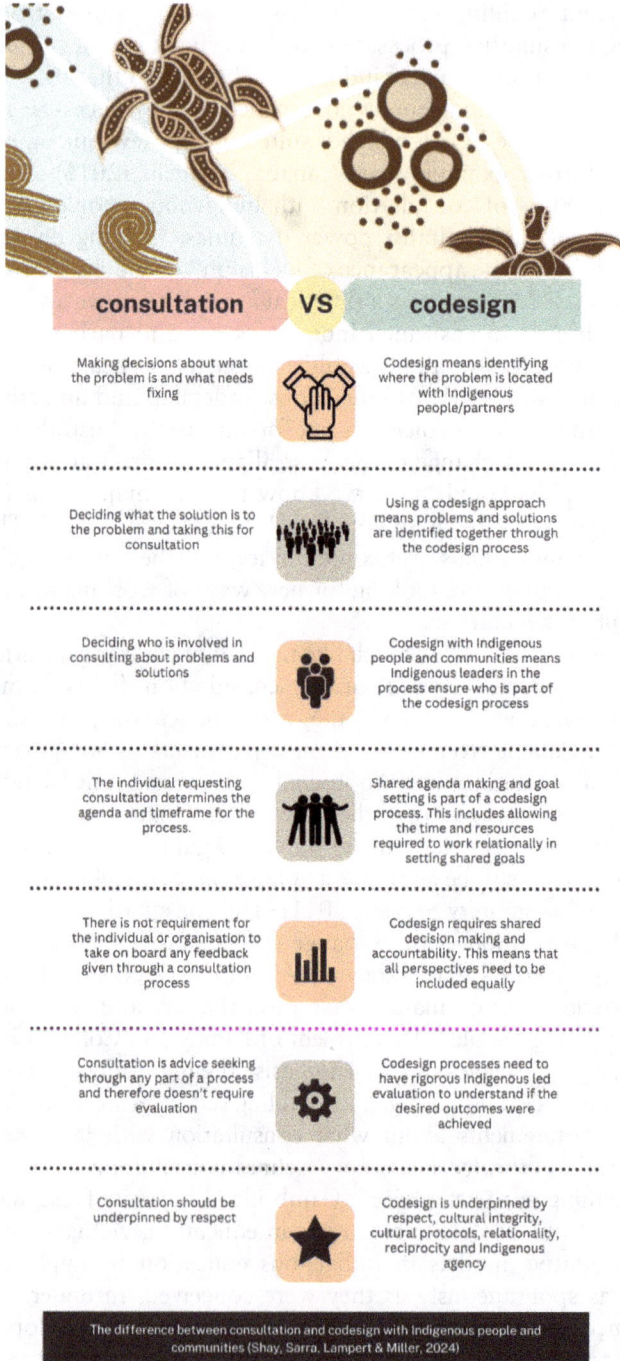

consultation	VS	codesign
Making decisions about what the problem is and what needs fixing		Codesign means identifying where the problem is located with Indigenous people/partners
Deciding what the solution is to the problem and taking this for consultation		Using a codesign approach means problems and solutions are identified together through the codesign process
Deciding who is involved in consulting about problems and solutions		Codesign with Indigenous people and communities means Indigenous leaders in the process ensure who is part of the codesign process
The individual requesting consultation determines the agenda and timeframe for the process.		Shared agenda making and goal setting is part of a codesign process. This includes allowing the time and resources required to work relationally in setting shared goals
There is not requirement for the individual or organisation to take on board any feedback given through a consultation process		Codesign requires shared decision making and accountability. This means that all perspectives need to be included equally
Consultation is advice seeking through any part of a process and therefore doesn't require evaluation		Codesign processes need to have rigorous Indigenous led evaluation to understand if the desired outcomes were achieved
Consultation should be underpinned by respect		Codesign is underpinned by respect, cultural integrity, cultural protocols, relationality, reciprocity and Indigenous agency

The difference between consultation and codesign with Indigenous people and communities (Shay, Sarra, Lampert & Miller, 2024)

Figure 6.1 The difference between consultation and codesign with Indigenous people and communities.

provides an overview of established principles about consultation practices in Indigenous contexts. The codesign design principles are outlined specifically for Indigenous contexts and are informed by the literature on codesign (Shay & Lampert, 2024) and new data generated from our current research.

Figure 6.1 was designed to demonstrate the importance of conceptual clarity when approaching partnership and working collaboratively with Indigenous peoples and communities. Conceptual clarity is important in social policy because it helps define the concepts to support cohesive conception and application (Magnoli, 2011). It was the aim of the study we share in this chapter not only to provide conceptual clarity for policymakers and practitioners about what codesign is and how it might support the advancement of Indigenous education but also for it to be underpinned by a strong evidence base that is rigorous and Indigenous-informed.

Our Findings to Date

Our research includes a published systematic literature review (Shay & Lampert, 2024), case studies including interviews and yarning unpacking codesign in Indigenous education and an Indigenous community-based survey. The two latter data are still being collected; however, we have significant data from the research to support the codesign framework presented in this chapter. Our work is underpinned theoretically by Rigney's (2006) Indigenist principles, privileging Indigenous voices, resistance as the emancipatory imperative, and political integrity.

Case studies were undertaken at two primary school locations (one regional and one remote) and three secondary school locations (one regional, one remote, and one urban). Case studies allowed us to work closely with each site to support and document the process along the way and at the end interviewing people directly involved in the process. The research questions were designed on the three key aspects of the process that we also used to frame the systematic literature review – conceptual, process, and evaluation. We have undertaken preliminary thematic analysis of the interview and yarning data (40 in total at the time of writing this chapter), along with our research notes from the process at each of the case study site, in developing the strengths-based codesign framework we present in this chapter.

The cohorts of participants are diverse and include: Aboriginal and Torres Strait Islander Elders, community members, parents and staff; school principals and leaders; teachers; Department of Education staff; and support staff. Research questions asked through yarning or interviews unpacked how people conceived of impactful codesign across the process from the beginning to evaluation phases. The case studies allowed us to undertake deeply reflective analysis through practical examples in practice, including a funded codesign project at each case study site. This aspect of the research provided rigorous, and practice supported, data to support the development of the codesign framework in this chapter.

Preliminary analysis of the data includes reflexive thematic analysis, which included many reflective conversations about the case study data (by Shay and Sarra), as well as reading transcripts from the interviews/yarns. The inclusion of principles and practices was not weighted by frequency (as seen in quantitative methodologies) but rather by significance in the role it played in the case studies, the depth in which it was discussed in the interviews/yarns, and evidence generated from the systematic literature review. The development of the framework is a result of many conversations with community members, policymakers, educational leaders, and practitioners who expressed the need to develop a framework for codesign. Our data support that where people were unsure of the process created a sense of hesitancy in getting involved. The creation of a framework supported by data is an attempt to address some of the concerns raised in the data.

Codesign in Indigenous Education Framework

Figure 6.2 presents an infographic of the principles and practices informed by our data. Indigenous leadership, Indigenous agency, shared power, and relationality feature in our data, but were strongly underpinned by the principles for successful codesign with Indigenous people outlined in the systematic literature review. Indigenous leadership is regularly outlined as being a required ingredient of codesign in Indigenous contexts, meaning Indigenous people must have distinct ways of leading across all aspects of the process.

Listen: Indigenous Leadership – Problem Location

It became very clear in the early phases of the research that there were differences in: (1) people's expectations of Indigenous leadership in the codesign process; and (2) how problems or projects are identified for codesign. There were, however, some data that raised the issue of listening and Indigenous leadership. The practice of listening is aligned with the principle of Indigenous leadership and how problems are located. The issue of listening and Indigenous leadership surfaced regularly across all data from both Indigenous and non-Indigenous participants. For example, when asked how they defined codesign with Aboriginal and Torres Strait Islander communities, a Torres Strait Islander school staff member responded, "Genuinely listen, working with, exploring and learning about communities - what they deem important and how that can be implemented in a school context". A school principal from one of the remote community sites echoed the importance of listening: "... it's the respect for others, of treating others as you'd like to be treated yourself, of not dominating the conversation of sitting back and listening".

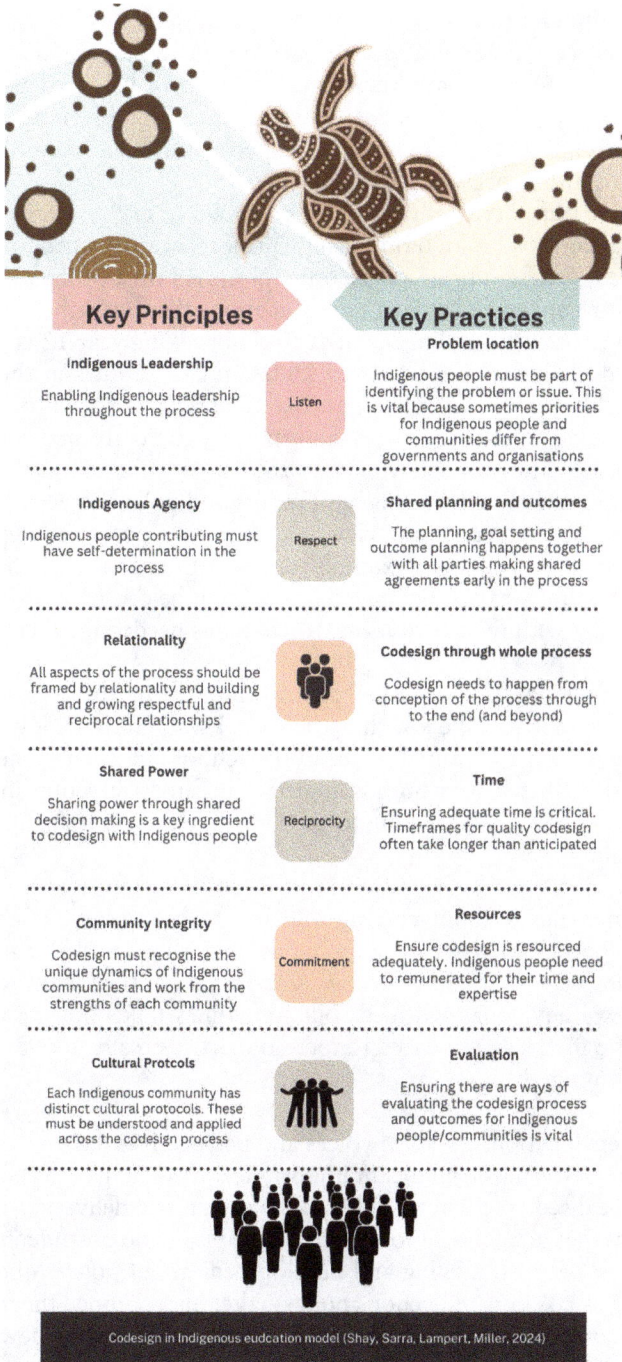

Figure 6.2 Codesign in Indigenous education framework.

One parent/Indigenous community member reflected on the concept of power and listening: "I think people [are] not listening. People that don't listen. The people that have the power that don't listen to people who know in community". These data demonstrate that listening must play a key role in all aspects of codesign, especially the earlier phases when relationships and processes are established.

The earlier phase critically includes what we term "problem location". Problem location is a broad term for how projects are identified for codesign. Like research, codesign projects are often premised on a problem that needs addressing or solving. In Indigenous education, there may be a number of issues, such as attendance, engagement, and improving year 12 completions. Our data and being immersed in the codesign case studies in this research showed quickly that problem location is a pivotal part of the process. Often, those attempting to codesign with Indigenous people are not conscious or aware of the need to codesign from the problem location phase. This is often because governments and schools have remits and policy objectives that they are trying to achieve, and they view codesign as a potential vehicle to do this more collaboratively. For example, one non-Indigenous principal from a regional community explained that they came to the codesign process in this project initially with their own ideas of what was needed for their school:

> It is that collaboration with key people and hearing the voices of everyone there that was the key thing because I wanted to see it go in one direction for what I wanted to see in the school but hearing the voices around the table it went in a completely different direction in a way that I didn't think it was going to go but it filled a gap that I didn't see in the school.

> Codesign is really about coming together to hear everyone's voice... really important that we get our Indigenous Elders and parents in to make sure we hear their voice and what direction they want to go in. Because we have our own ideas but sometimes that's not the way we need to go in or what we need to focus on. So, it's really about that collaboration together.

In problem location, it is local voices and perspectives that our data identified as being of the most significant importance. One Indigenous policymaker shared, "Localised voices at the table in the design and delivery of policy and or programs that impact their localised communities and or students. Equality and equity in decision making and development about polices about us and that impact us". A non-Indigenous policymaker also outlined the importance of Aboriginal and Torres Strait Islander perspectives in seeking new ideas and identifying issues that governments, schools, and policymakers may not even be aware of: "If done well and properly, it [codesign] creates the opportunity for Aboriginal and Torres Strait Islander communities and government to build a shared vision, walk together and grow trust. It may identify issues and find solutions that governments may not have previously considered. It should be more than just seeking perspectives, input, and consultation".

In seeking Indigenous perspectives in problem location also means seeking Indigenous leadership. Indigenous leadership was outlined as one of the key contributing factors to codesign with Indigenous people from our systematic literature review (Shay & Lampert, 2024). Indigenous leadership further features in all data from this research from both Indigenous and non-Indigenous cohorts. One Aboriginal school staff member reflects, "Everything around codesign can be positive, but if it is not led by your First Nation team/staff, how can they speak about us without us? We know and understand the students/families, this is the first priority to best help/support the students/families". Indigenous leadership starts with schools recognising the skills and expertise their Indigenous staff possess. One example was a principal from a remote school who shared that he had to "walk hand in hand with my deputies, with my HODs, with my teachers as well, because teachers are leaders back in the classroom. But so is Uncle Frank* and Aunty Ella* in our school. They're all in leadership roles".

Respect: Indigenous Agency – Shared Planning and Outcomes

Respect is a foundational value that needs to be present throughout a codesign process with Indigenous people. A subjective term that, again, each person brings their own meanings and expectations to is still recognised throughout the existing literature and is featured throughout the data from this project, particularly from Indigenous contributors. One Aboriginal community member explains "Our mob to see the schools are wanting to form genuine respectful connections with our mobs....our mobs are human just like everyone else that walks through their gates and our mobs just happen to be the Traditional Owners (TOs) of this Country and other mobs are wanting to know about how our mobs are treated and respected in this country cos if our mobs are not respected and valued as TO's in our own country then how will visitors be treated as visitors to this country". Another Indigenous community member shared the importance of not homogenising Indigenous people and to recognise and understand the distinctness of cultural differences: "understanding and showing that respect towards the two different cultures – Aboriginal and Torres Strait Islander being two distinctive cultures". The experience of consultation over many years has been shown to impact the expectations of many Indigenous people coming to the process. One Elder and community member shared, "to me the importance is respecting, valuing, and not just... not just saying 'tick the box because I've consulted', but let's see it by implementing in... in your reconciliation action plans or implementing it in the curriculum".

Indigenous agency is interrelated to all principles and practices in Figure 6.2. One Aboriginal community member felt that "Most school staff struggle with codesign when they come from a classroom background of dictate, control and limited meaningful, genuine connections with First Nations community". Although the term "Indigenous agency" was not explicit throughout the data, the need for agency in shifting to codesign featured across the data from Indigenous and non-Indigenous participants. One Aboriginal community member was emphatic about the role of agency "I believe that First Nations peoples should have a voice in everything that directly affects them. They should be treated as the experts in their own lives". Some of these quotes serve as a reminder that historically and for many Indigenous people contemporaneously, agency is not a privilege that has been afforded.

In approaching codesign underpinned by the value of respect and Indigenous agency, shared planning and outcomes emerged in the data as being a key ingredient to successful codesign with Indigenous people. One non-Indigenous staff member articulated that part of developing shared outcomes is developing shared understandings, "providing a safe environment to identify the views of Aboriginal and Torres Strait Islander communities in respect of the project and practices. Finding out what is important and what are the parameters or non-negotiables to be able to develop a shared understanding". Developing shared outcomes and goals also surfaced as a finding in the systematic literature review (Shay & Lampert, 2024), revealing that this aspect of codesign is significant in codesigning with Indigenous people across contexts.

Relationality – Codesign through Whole Process

Moreton-Robinson (2016) outlines that "relationality is grounded in a holistic conception of the inter-connectedness and inter-substantiation between and among all living things and the earth, which is inhabited by a world of ancestors and creator beings" (p. 71). She further explains that relationality is a core way of being, knowing, and doing – which has many implications for a codesign process with Indigenous peoples. Indigenous relationality is more than having good relationships, as conceived in Western cultures. Kombumerri Elder and philosopher, Mary Graham (2014), outlines that Aboriginal relationality attributes are framed by empathy and ethics, identity and place, autonomy and balance. She further articulates that relationality is underpinned by stewardship, being, belonging, identity and connectedness, conduct and stand, perspective and sovereignty, decision-making, conflict management, and social order. Graham (2014) conveys that these benefit the whole of community for coherence, as well as for spirit and human agency.

The data featured many dimensions of relationality from many perspectives. An Aboriginal school staff member emphasised the need for "genuine and sustainable relationships", while another Aboriginal community member highlighted the importance of "allowing our mobs to have a genuine opportunity to have a say in matters of concern". Ensuring relationships are not centred on one or two key voices was identified by one Aboriginal policymaker: "true codesign is engaging people from a cross section of the community, not just the few that always put their hands up. Creating the trust first before engagement of the codesign to ensure it's not just ticking and flicking either". Relationships and Indigenous relationality may be something that needs to be taught explicitly through codesign training. One Aboriginal community suggested that we must "empower the next load of teachers graduating [to] graduate with more First Nations knowledge of how to work, communicate, interact and form genuine relationships".

Reciprocity: Shared Power – Time

Dillon (2021) warns that, while codesign with Indigenous communities has some potential strengths, critical questions must be addressed about codesign with Indigenous people. Dillon (2021) proposes that key questions about who is included and excluded must be asked, as well as how power is (re) distributed through the process. If power is to be redistributed, reciprocity is ostensibly a way of moving past old models of transactional relations and seeking knowledge from Indigenous people without any material recognition for obtaining such knowledge. Although there is wider recognition now for basic reciprocity such as remunerating people for their time, the practice of governments and schools expecting Indigenous people to give up their time altruistically to address the myriad of systemic issues that continue to disadvantage Indigenous people is ongoing. Continued frustration surfaced on many levels across this research, particularly from Indigenous perspectives, but increasingly, non-Indigenous leaders who wish to compensate Indigenous people for their time and expertise and but experience systemic barriers in doing so.

There were many examples in the data of why reciprocity is important in shifting practices that are at the forefront of the memories of many Indigenous people whereby they would generously give up their time and knowledge only for there to be no tangible outcomes. For example, one person who is an Elder, community member and staff member shared:

> I think the reason why some people may not want to be involved in codesign would be going back to years ago when they... when people would have meetings and nothing would happen, and they think that this is going to be the same where there's no outcomes. Secondly, that they're not being listened to. And thirdly, because they shy away from government institutions, like school.

Another Aboriginal and Torres Strait Islander parent and community member shared a further example of how some Indigenous people continue to experience an imbalance around what schools expect and what they are getting back:

> I've got children in high school as well and I find that with the high school there's not as much involvement where they're asking parents for their participation. It's more so that we're getting...whether it's newsletters or contacted to advise this is what's happening. These are the events that are going to take place. So, there's not as much, I suppose, asking parents, you know, what they think should happen on NAIDOC Week or just asking for parental views.

Other participants felt reciprocity should be a foundational question when approaching codesign. One Aboriginal community member stated, "I would speak to the Elders, build rapport with them, and come in with reciprocal, you know, relationships. Not just [what] you want [for] the codesign. No, like I said before, what are you giving back?".

Sharing power is particularly significant in using codesign in Indigenous contexts (Dreise & Mazurski, 2018). Australia's colonial history has a dark shadow of paternalism, violence, and exclusion of Indigenous people (Fricker et al., 2024). An Aboriginal community member explains the significance of this history and its role in contemporary relations:

> there's other institutional and societal... sort of institutional bias I mean in policy sort of settings. I always yarn about that's our mob that's still dealing with that collective intergenerational trauma, which speaks to the last 250 odd years. Oh, when it comes to the Constitution, it's about 130 odd years ago where we've had foreign... foreign government and governance systems imposed upon us. And it's not the system that really speaks to how we've done business on this country for 65,000+ years. That speaks... to patriarchy, matriarchy. It speaks to empowering communities. But in the main, we need to really provide and empower a lot of our community... our local communities. And a lot of them do have that.

> We've got to decolonise all the things we do. And that's a very... I mean, that's the word of a lot of people are now using. Decolonisation of these... these spaces and these conversations and these platforms and these approaches. But you've got to truly understand what that actually means. So, I used to always take it back to the premise in the approach that what we do is about that shared value.

Shifting to codesign and approaching the process relationally rather than transactionally requires different conceptions of time concerning project planning and establishing expectations about time. In the case studies undertaken as part of this research, every site did not deliver the project within the timeframes they anticipated at the beginning of the process. One school principal said the most important leadership skill in doing codesign with Indigenous people and communities is their "commitment to time". An Aboriginal community member explained the importance of time in the process:

> Have respect if someone's saying, "oh they don't understand". Take that time. Don't say 'oh we're on a timeframe here. We can't stop now'. You've gotta stop and you've gotta give that time and you gotta make sure everybody's on the same page about everything.

Time may seem like an obvious factor to consider. Our data suggests it is even more significant for all parties (Indigenous people and the bodies codesigning with them) for a multitude of reasons including, respect for people's time; the ability to listen properly; and to allow for a process that is not fixed and may change considerably throughout the process.

Commitment: Community Integrity – Shared Resources

Community integrity was a nuanced concept to emerge from the data, particularly from Indigenous people. It must be stressed that every Indigenous community has its own microcosm of politics, histories, cultures, and dynamics. Community integrity includes honouring the diversity of voices in Indigenous communities and translating these perspectives into practice. For example, one Aboriginal school staff member shared:

> Codesign would ensure the diverse voices, knowledge, experiences, and perspectives of Aboriginal and Torres Strait Islanders contribute to creating effective education experiences for Indigenous students. This would ultimately assist with fostering a culturally relevant curriculum, improving student engagement, and enhancing educational outcomes that respect and reflect Indigenous identity and heritage.

Shared resources embrace the concept of reciprocity, but it is much more tangible from the data. Most Indigenous participants, in particular, addressed why codesign must incorporate resourcing into the entirety of the process. One Aboriginal school staff member explained that listening to Indigenous people about what resourcing is required is the first step as "It will enable better understanding of the issues that face First Australians and assist in deploying resources where they are really required". Another Aboriginal staff member explained that resourcing for codesign in Indigenous education should be considered in the current context of teacher shortages in Australia, which impact everything from funding to time allocated to codesign:

> Everybody is keen, but teacher shortages and continued increases to workload make teachers time poor. In this same context, where many teaching staff and school leaders are already overworked and overwhelmed, there is also an increasing number of consultants and new policy imperatives pitching or requiring the adoption of new programs and materials. School staff get weighed down with having to spend time wading through all the programs to determine which one is best suited for their context.

A non-Indigenous policymaker reflected on the possibilities of codesign but outlined that the biggest barrier was allocating appropriate resourcing:

> Codesign can provide opportunities for policy and decision makers (e.g. school leaders) to work collaboratively with Aboriginal and Torres Strait Islander Peoples to identify issues impacting their communities and find solutions that prioritise the self-determination and outcomes of Aboriginal and Torres Strait Islander Peoples. Unfortunately, government systems rarely allow the time (from identification to implementation and evaluation), funding or space for policy and decision-makers to engage with and appropriately remunerate Aboriginal and Torres Strait Islander Peoples for their time and cultural knowledge throughout a co-design process.

Our data suggests that material resources not only include funding but mechanisms to allow those funds to get to Indigenous people contributing to the process of codesign. These lessons are helpful for governments and organisations to ensure these processes and allocations are in place before commencing a codesign process with Indigenous people and communities.

Cultural Protocols – Evaluation

Cultural protocols were extensively discussed in the data from Indigenous people. The biggest lesson is again to understand the uniqueness and diversity of each community and understand that this has implications for how cultural protocols are understood and enacted. One Aboriginal and Torres Strait Islander community member emphasises this importance, "make sure that, you know the communities you go to, they're not all the same. So be specific around, you know, how you will engage and, you know, get to that codesign outcome". One Aboriginal community Elder explains what this means for his community, "there's certain protocols in... certain communities – I think people need to be made aware of that. But I also think sometimes, especially in my place here at [place redacted], you know we... just got to read the room sometimes". Other Indigenous voices from the data shared what cultural protocols mean in action in their communities. These data are valuable because our data from school leaders (who are all non-Indigenous) suggests a limited understanding of cultural protocols and how to work with these in a codesign process.

The data that provide examples of how to observe cultural protocols demonstrates the diversity across communities. For example, in one remote location that is a discrete Aboriginal community, one Elder explains that enacting cultural protocols in their community looks like:

> the first point of call would be our Council. It would be to talk to them, to let them know, and I think to get their permission because they are still trustees to this land. And then ask the Council then who they might suggest as an appropriate people to be talking to and stuff like that. I think a lot of people don't do that.

A further example is an Aboriginal and Torres Strait Islander community member from a regional community who outlines:

> it's also going through the protocols. So doing a bit of desktop analysis around the demographics. Who are the key people? Your Traditional Owner groups? Looking at key people. So not just Elders, but even young people that have influences in… in their sort of sphere. But just trying to get everybody and being very inclusive. So, it's not just a… matter of going to the leaders itself that are probably in high positions, but also going out into the community and profiling the project itself to go, "Hey, we're here for this project". Because other people that mightn't be leaders… as in … out in the community. There's a lot of people that probably have hidden messages that they need to talk about through their own lived experiences. They can bring some really good insights into a project as well.

Cultural protocols and evaluation are linked when we analysed the data because in honouring cultural protocols, evaluation is a key mechanism in valuing Indigenous input and contribution to the process. Evaluation may seem like an obvious practice in any process where there is an ambition to achieve different outcomes. There was agreement from all participants that evaluation is important. One non-Indigenous Principal in a regional community shared "anything should be evaluated to know if you've been successful… what you should repeat, what you should change next time, or add, to make sure you are successful in the future". However, it is well-recognised that Indigenous policy and programmes have generated significant data about Indigenous peoples for many years but lacked meaningful Indigenous input and leadership in evaluating the effectiveness of such programmes (Productivity Commission, 2013). In line with observing cultural protocols and many other dimensions outlined in the codesign framework, evaluation is fundamentally about respecting everyone's time and commitment to a codesign project. Without rigorous and Indigenous-informed evaluation, there will be ambiguity about the outcomes of the codesign project. Moreover, it is a missed opportunity to develop a strong evidence base for shifting outcomes in Indigenous education, which is sorely needed.

Ensuring Indigenous voices and leadership are strong in any evaluation is critical. As one non-indigenous regional Principal shared, "Sometimes it is what we don't see as leaders in the school that community are wanting to see". One Aboriginal policymaker explained that, to her, local voices are key, "Increased inclusion of localised people. Increased ownership and transparency of locally developed policies and programs. Increased ownership and accountability of local solutions driving local outcomes". Many people felt the importance of evaluation was in understanding what went well and where things need to be improved. One Aboriginal community member shared his perspective on evaluation "you might get things wrong and you might have to tweak the measures you know? And then go back to, oh okay, how do we fix that part, you know? And you wanna... you wanna give the best back to community too and to the program and the project". An Elder in a remote community cautions that evaluation should not just be at the end of projects where there are celebratory moments:

> evaluation has gotta be over a period of time as well. You know, we tend to do a lot of the... the evaluation around the launch of things and everybody is happy and whatever, and then we get into the nitty gritty of it and that's the real test of... of whether our co-design is going to work or not. But I... I think our evaluation has got to be realistic as well. You know, it can't be just again have this very high level of achievement when we know we have to do some steps to get there. And I think at each step it needs to be evaluated.

Strengths-Based Codesign

Strengths-based approaches underpin the codesign framework presented in this chapter. Each element is developed to elevate the voices, strengths, and aspirations of Aboriginal and Torres Strait Islander people. A codesign approach providing different outcomes for Indigenous people must recognise Indigenous identity and cultural resilience as a strength and protective factor to wellbeing and improve outcomes (Koch et al., 2023). There must also be recognition that Indigenous relationality can enhance a process like codesign and not hinder it. Indigenous relationality embraces and subsists well with complexities, dualities, and multiplicities (Dudgeon & Bray, 2019). It is these dynamics that some scholars warn have the potential to inhibit codesign or even reproduce negative outcomes. However, through embracing Indigenous knowledge, culture, leadership, and voices, our research-informed codesign framework aims to provide a strengths-based lens to codesign with Indigenous people and communities in education to improve educational outcomes.

An Aboriginal policymaker participant shared their optimism about codesign: "I feel very supportive of codesign. I feel it is organic in its approach and genuinely places localised voices in the design and delivery of policies that are for us". There are still many concerns and issues about codesign with Indigenous people that we may not have identified in this chapter. Conceptual clarity and a strong evidence base are key to moving codesign forward to generate new outcomes that potentially transform Indigenous education. We encourage future research and testing of ideas and approaches outlined in this chapter to generate change and improve educational outcomes for Aboriginal and Torres Strait Islander people and communities.

Conclusion

In this chapter, we shared key findings from our study on codesigning Indigenous education policy in Queensland. The findings from the data across the case studies, large-scale community-based survey and the systematic literature review, have underpinned the proposed strengths-based codesign in the Indigenous Education framework (see Figure 6.2). This framework intends to be used to guide practice or research that aims to undertake codesign with Aboriginal and Torres Strait Islander communities within education and across other fields. As our research continues, we will build a strong evidence base for the key principles and practices in the framework where future refinements may need to be made as we seek to understand how codesign is defined by Aboriginal and Torres Strait Islander people.

References

Akama, Y., Hagen, P., & Whaanga-Schollum, D. (2019). Problematizing replicable design to practice respectful, reciprocal, and relational co-designing with Indigenous people. *Design and Culture, 11*(1), 59–84.

Biddle, N., Gray, M., McAllister, I. & Qvortrup, M. (2023). Detailed analysis of the 2023 Voice to Parliament Referendum and related social and political attitudes. ANU Centre for Social Research and Methods. Retrieved from https://apo.org.au/node/325112

Blomkamp, E. (2018). The promise of co-design for public policy. *Australian Journal of Public Administration, 77*(4), 729–743.

Butler, T., Gall, A., Garvey, G., Ngampromwongse, K., Hector, D., Turnbull, S., Lucas, K., Nehill, C., Boltong, A., Keefe, D., & Anderson, K. (2022). A comprehensive review of optimal approaches to co-design in health with first nations Australians. *International Journal of Environmental Research and Public Health, 19*(23), 16166. https://doi.org/10.3390/ijerph192316166

Cambridge University Press (n.d.). Consultation. In *Cambridge Dictionary*. Retrieved January 7, 2025 from https://dictionary.cambridge.org/dictionary/english/consultation

Chilisa, B. (2019). *Indigenous research methodologies.* Sage Publications.

Commonwealth of Australia (2024). *Closing the Gap Annual Report.* Retrieved from https://www.niaa.gov.au/sites/default/files/documents/2025-02/NIAA%20CTG%20Combined%20Report.pdf

Cox, R. (2024). Political legitimacy and the Indigenous voice to Parliament. *Journal of Applied Philosophy, 41*(3), 423–441.

Department of Family & Community Services. (2011). *Aboriginal consultation guide.* Retrieved from https://dcj.nsw.gov.au/documents/children-and-families/adoption/aboriginal-consultation-guide.pdf

Dillon, M. C. (2021). *Codesign in the Indigenous policy domain: Risks and opportunities.* Centre for Aboriginal Economic Policy Research, ANU. Codesign in the Indigenous policy domain: Risks and opportunities | Centre for Aboriginal Economic Policy Research (anu.edu.au)

Dreise, T., & Mazurski, E. (2018). *Weaving knowledges: Knowledge exchange, codesign and community-based participatory research and evaluation in Aboriginal communities.* Aboriginal Affairs New South Wales. https://apo.org.au/sites/default/files/resource-files/2018-01/apo-nid261981.pdf

Dudgeon, P., & Bray, A. (2019). Indigenous relationality: Women, kinship and the law. *Genealogy, 3*(2), 23.

Flemmer, R., & Schilling-Vacaflor, A. (2016). Unfulfilled promises of the consultation approach: The limits to effective indigenous participation in Bolivia's and Peru's extractive industries. *Third World Quarterly, 37*(1), 172–188.

Fricker, A., Cairns, R., & Weuffen, S. (2024). The thin veneer of "the history wars" on unceded lands. In *Decolonising Australian history education* (pp. 1–15). Routledge.

Graham, M. (2014). Aboriginal notions of relationality and positionalism: A reply to weber. *Global Discourse, 4*(1), 17–22. https://doi.org/10.1080/23269995.2014.895931

Guenther, J., Rigney, L. I., Osborne, S., Lowe, K., & Moodie, N. (2023). The foundations required for First Nations education in Australia. In *Assessing the evidence in Indigenous education research: Implications for policy and practice* (pp. 265–284). Cham: Springer International Publishing.

Holt, L. (2021). *Talking strong: the National Aboriginal Education Committee and the development of Aboriginal Education policy.* Aboriginal Studies Press.

King, P. T., Cormack, D., Edwards, R., Harris, R., & Paine, S. J. (2022). Co-design for Indigenous and other children and young people from priority social groups: A systematic review. *SSM-Population Health,* 101077.

Koch, J. M., Townsend-Bell, E. E., & Hubach, R. D. (2023). *Identity as resilience in minoritized communities: Strengths-based approaches to research and practice* (1st ed.). Springer.

Magnoli, A. (2011). What Do You Mean?: Conceptual Clarity in Social Policy. In *Inter-American Development Bank eBooks.* Inter-American Development Bank. https://doi.org/10.18235/0012304

Mintrom, M., Goddard, P., Grocott, L., & Sumartojo, S. (2024). Co-design in policy-making: From an emerging to an embedded practice, *Policy Sciences, 57,* 745–760, https://doi.org/10.1007/s11077-024-09550-9

Moreton-Robinson, A. (2016). Relationality: A key presupposition of an Indigenous social research paradigm. In *Sources and methods in Indigenous Studies* (pp. 69–77). Routledge. https://doi.org/10.4324/9781315528854

Productivity Commission (2013). *Better Indigenous policies: The role of evaluation roundtable proceedings.* Productivity Commission. Retrieved from https://www.pc.gov.au/research/supporting/better-indigenous-policies/better-indigenous-policies.pdf

Queensland Family & Child Commission. (2024). *Listening and learning Aboriginal and Torres Strait Islander children, young people, and their families' aspirations within education.* Queensland Government. Retrieved from https://www.qfcc.qld. gov.au/sites/default/files/2024-08/QFCC%20Listening%20and%20Learning%20 Report%202024.pdf

Shay, M., & Lampert, J. (2024). Community according to whom? An analysis of how Indigenous 'community' is defined in Australia's *through growth to achievement* 2018 report on equity in education. In *Critical studies and the international field of Indigenous education research* (pp. 47–63). Routledge.

Shay, M., Sarra, G., Lampert, J., Jeong, D., Thomson, A., & Miller, J. (2024). Codesign in Indigenous education policy and practice—A systematic literature review. *Australian Journal of Social Issues*, *59*(4), 844–863. https://doi.org/10.1002/ ajs4.320.

Youdelis, M. (2016). "They could take you out for coffee and call it consultation!": The colonial antipolitics of Indigenous consultation in Jasper National Park. *Environment and Planning A: Economy and Space*, 48(7), 1374–1392.

7 Learning from Local Wisdom and Expertise in Applying Strengths-Based Approaches

Marnee Shay, Fred Cobbo, Grace Sarra, and Margaret Kettle

Introduction

Aboriginal cultures and communities and Torres Strait Islander cultures and communities are incredibly diverse. With many different languages pre-colonisation, each and every mob has its own lores, customs, histories, stories, totems, cultural practices, and politics. Of course, like many cultures, these have adapted to survive the aftermath of colonisation, and some cultural practices have modernised. However, the distinctness and uniqueness of each mob and community are sometimes overlooked as government policies and educational programmes have tended to refer to Indigenous Australians as one group. We have many commonalities as Indigenous Australians; however, a strengths-based approaches (SBA) must focus on the importance of diversity in local knowledge in all aspects of Indigenous education.

In this chapter, we demonstrate how schools and educational institutions can learn from local people and knowledge in applying SBAs. The topic of school and community partnerships has been featured in many Indigenous education guidelines and policies (Shay & Lampert, 2024). This chapter presents a case study from a research project in the communities of Murgon and Cherbourg in Queensland to provide an example of how SBAs in enhancing local stories, knowledge, and perspectives can enhance the learning experiences of all Australian students.

Local Voices as the Foundation for Indigenous Education

The dire need for Indigenous voices in education has been highlighted for many decades. More recently, Gillan et al. (2017) outline the development of practices, particularly by governments and policymakers, whereby a select group of Indigenous people are listened to and who might not reflect the views of the majority of Indigenous people. Ensuring Indigenous people have a voice in education may seem like an obvious element in moving Indigenous education forward. However, as schools and other educational settings are institutionalised, they re-produce power dynamics present within the dominant culture (Bourdieu & Passeron, 1990). In other words, schools,

DOI: 10.4324/9781003372783-7

as institutions, are actors for the state. Although there have been significant improvements in how governments recognise the rights of Indigenous people, they continue to perpetuate colonial discourses, which result in Indigenous people experiencing racism, discrimination, and exclusion (Bodkin-Andrews & Carlson, 2016).

The role of Indigenous voices provides a counter-narrative to prevailing negative stereotypes that continue to impact educational outcomes for Indigenous people. Over the past 15 years, Australia has emphasised the inclusion of Indigenous voices and knowledge, specifically by embedding Aboriginal and Torres Strait Islander knowledge and perspectives. Embedding remains a policy imperative supported by scholars such as (Bishop et al., 2021; McKnight, 2016; Murray & Campton, 2024). However, the inclusion of Indigenous voices in education is multifaceted. It raises issues such as power dynamics, inclusion, exclusion, and whether Indigenous voices will be listened to, even when they are present. Indigenous communities, like many communities, are complex and dynamic. Each community has its history, politics, and established relations with educational institutions. We know, as Indigenous women, educators, and scholars, how perilous it is to be part of meetings or projects whereby educational institutions say they are seeking Indigenous voices and yet implement practices when seeking these voices that dismiss those voices when they do not align with the school's goals or views.

Educational settings are busy places. From early childhood centres to schools to universities or even policy settings – educators and leaders are often time-poor and, even with the best intentions, can steer towards the easier path for seeking Indigenous voices. Rather, it is important to seek out Indigenous people who may have much knowledge but may not have a platform to contribute as part of forming SBAs to elevate local Indigenous knowledge. Understanding that all voices are not equal is also critical. There may also be other cultural dynamics at play that may not be visible to those seeking Indigenous voices. For example, in some communities, it may not be appropriate for men to speak freely in front of women and vice versa. In many communities, young people may also stay quiet if there are Elders present and speaking out of respect for them. These cultural dynamics are unique to each community, and applying a strength-based approach in seeking Indigenous voices requires a concerted effort to learn about these dynamics in seeking the best outcomes.

School and Community Partnerships

The context of Indigenous communities and how they are defined is unique to Australia. Shay and Lampert (2024) propose that how Indigenous communities have been described in educational policy over many years has caused confusion and a lack of direction for schools that want to connect with Indigenous peoples and communities. As outlined across the chapters in this book, given the diversity of Indigenous peoples and communities, it is critical to recognise that how each school and community will work together will differ depending on the local context.

Government policies and research have long emphasised the significance of strong relationships between schools and Indigenous communities, highlighting their role in fostering positive student outcomes and quality educational experiences (Gower et al., 2021; Lonsdale & Anderson, 2012). However, many dimensions have impacted these relationships, leading to mistrust and challenges in forming genuine partnerships (Lowe et al., 2019). Researchers have identified key factors that enable or restrict the sustainability of these collaborations, with successful partnerships requiring mutual commitment, cultural understanding, and shared problem-solving (Godinho et al., 2015; Lowe, 2011). The "What Works" project (Commonwealth of Australia, 2013) outlines essential elements such as strong leadership, accountability, cultural humility, and ongoing dialogue, which are crucial for maintaining effective school-community relationships (Langton, 1994).

Despite the recognised importance of community engagement in Indigenous students' success, deficit thinking and inconsistent partnership approaches remain significant barriers (Barr & Saltmarsh, 2014; Dockett et al., 2006). Studies indicate that institutional factors, including perceived hostility or ambivalence towards Indigenous peoples, deter parents from engaging with schools (Fricker et al., 2023; Lowe et al., 2019). Many Indigenous families associate schools with exclusionary past policies, colonial impacts, and tokenistic engagement, which further inhibits trust (Hayes et al., 2009; Woodrow et al., 2016). Additionally, disparities in educational knowledge and economic factors contribute to communication challenges, making it difficult to establish a shared understanding of the purpose and structure of these partnerships (Burgess & Evans, 2017).

However, several enabling factors can support the development of successful school-community partnerships established in the research literature. Schools that actively engage with Indigenous knowledge, practice respectful listening, and move beyond deficit-based narratives have seen positive outcomes (Godinho et al., 2015; Lowe et al., 2019). Programmes that involve Elders, incorporate Indigenous languages in the curriculum, and foster community-driven educational initiatives contribute to building trust and respect (Guenther & Osborne, 2017; Lea et al., 2011; Lowe, 2017). Effective partnerships also require strong leadership, clear communication, and power-sharing, ensuring Indigenous voices are central in decision-making (Godinho et al., 2015). Sustainable collaborations must adapt to local contexts, fostering cultural identity and recognising Indigenous "Ways of knowing, being, and doing" (Dockery, 2013; Martin, 2008). Schools can build lasting, respectful relationships with Indigenous communities by embedding Indigenous perspectives authentically into school structures rather than as add-ons (Riley & Genner, 2011).

Case Study – Binung Ma Na Du Cultural Stories and Living Histories on Wakka Wakka Country

The Binung Ma Na Du project centred on local Indigenous knowledge and wisdom. This project was initiated by Wakka Wakka Traditional Owners and aimed to understand how codesign from Indigenous perspectives can support schools and Indigenous communities in collaborating to develop localised cultural resources to support Aboriginal cultural and language revitalisation. The communities of Murgon and Cherbourg, both in Wakka Wakka Country, have rich histories and tapestries, and these were seen as untapped resources for learning for all students (Indigenous and non-Indigenous).

This project had two aims: (1) to document the process and experiences of Indigenous people and school staff in developing local curriculum resources using a codesign approach; and (2) to develop a series of digital and written stories from Wakka Wakka Country to enhance Wakka Wakka language teaching. The research explored the process of codesign through observing the process used in this project to develop and publish digital and written stories. It also entailed interviews/yarns that had conceptual and reflective questions aimed at unpacking how schools and communities can develop stronger partnerships to enhance local Indigenous knowledge in schools.

Our Team

The majority of the team that led this project was Indigenous. This team included Marnee Shay, Grace Sarra, Fred Cobbo, and Margaret Kettle. We were also very fortunate to have had three local Indigenous researchers who are based in Cherbourg work with the team: Iris-Jean Blow, Milbi Perrier, and Arlene Langton. Marnee, Grace, and Fred have collaborated on numerous other projects and have an established track record of delivering strong outcomes from previous research projects for the community. Margaret Kettle is a linguist who established relationships with Marnee and Grace, having previously worked at the same university. As the project developed, it became clear that there would be a significant focus on Aboriginal language revitalisation. It was identified that a linguist's expertise would strengthen the team, and it did. Marnee and Grace's positionalities are in the introduction chapter of this book. As Fred and Margaret co-authored this chapter, they are introduced to give readers a deeper understanding of the team who worked on this project.

Fred Cobbo

I am Fred Cobbo Wakka Wakka man. I'm the son of a railway labourer and domestic worker. I was brought up in the loving care of my social justice-caring grandmother and aunties. My Wakka Wakka ancestral connection and bloodlines trace back to apical ancestors on both sides of my family:

Jenny Lind/Mick Buck on mother's side and Boobyjah Cobbo on father's side. My father's mother is Stolen Generation. She came from the traditional lands of the Waramungu people of Northern Territory and was sent to Cherbourg in South East Queensland.

In my upbringing in Cherbourg, I lived under *The Aboriginals Protection and Restriction of the Sale of Opium Act, 1897 Qld*. Carrying permits and dog tags every time I left Cherbourg has caused intergenerational trauma to me. I'm the first of my family to graduate Year 12. A school Guidance Officer advised me that my people are good labourers and hands-on people; the guidance officer suggested I should aim to be a railway worker or a trade assistant. I aimed for something bigger by obtaining an apprenticeship to become an electrician and, after four years, I completed my apprenticeship.

I later found a passion for working with youth in a school setting environment. My passion in this space and working with young people is making them believe they can achieve their goals. Education has been a lifelong passion of mine. This led to me going to university to gain a bachelor's degree as a mature-aged student. Being only the second in my family to do so. I still want to climb the academic ladder, to achieve better educational outcomes for Aboriginal and Torres Strait Islander people. I have collaborated on numerous projects with researchers like Grace and Marnee and can see how research can help in improving outcomes for our people.

Margaret Kettle

I am Margaret Kettle, a Professor in the School of Education and the Arts at Central Queensland University based in Meanjin (Brisbane), Australia. My background is non-Indigenous, with the first member of my family sent as a convict from northern England to Sydney in 1821. I was raised in a settler family on a cattle station on Gangula Country in Central Queensland, the region where Gangalu was spoken. We were strongly aware of the Aboriginal presence on the land and the enduring paintings and artefacts in the area.

In my professional life, I have developed expertise in linguistics and the application of knowledge about language and language acquisition in communities, education, and employment. My work in applied linguistics has led to national, state-based, and university research projects including the Australian Institute of Aboriginal and Torres Strait Islander Studies (AIATSIS) project Binung Ma Na Da: Cultural Stories and Living Histories on Wakka Wakka Country, led by Associate Professor Marnee Shay.

The Binung Ma Na Da: Cultural Stories and Living Histories on Wakka Wakka Country project involved the development of bilingual storybooks for use in schools to teach cultural knowledge and the Wakka Wakka language. The Wakka Wakka language is currently preserved in the memories of Elders and community members, and in anthropological records, and there is a strong and urgent commitment to revitalising the language for use, particularly by young people. My role in the project was to work with Wakka

Wakka culture and language teachers and the project team to develop and produce the storybooks as resources for schools and also dissemination among community organisations.

Community History and Setting

Cherbourg Aboriginal community has a dark and unique history in the colonisation of Australia. The Barambah/Cherbourg Aboriginal community was set up by the Salvation Army at the beginning of the 1900s (Cherbourg Aboriginal Shire Council, 2025). The Queensland Government took control of the community and set it up as a Reserve or Mission under *The Aboriginals Protection and Restriction of the Sale of Opium Act, 1897 Queensland* (Queensland Government, 2015). Cherbourg was formally known as Barambah (westly winds in the Wakka Wakka language). Later, the name was changed to Cherbourg in the 1930s on the lands of the Wakka Wakka people. The township of Cherbourg is based on the banks of Barambah Creek in the rich farmlands of the South Burnett. The name was changed due to the confusion of a property name, Barambah Station, near the community. Resources meant for the community were sent to Barambah Station.

Cherbourg is approximately five kilometres from the rural township of Murgon. Most of the inmates of the community of Cherbourg during the early-mid 1900s came to the area by train; the nearest train station at the time was Murgon. Murgon and surrounding districts are made up of families, mainly European/German descendants. Murgon was predominantly a majority non-Indigenous town. However, it is increasingly diverse in contemporary times, with Aboriginal and Torres Strait Islander families now residing in Murgon.

Cherbourg has received its fair share of negative publicity and media. The foundational history is underpinned by race-based policies (such as *The Aboriginals Protection and Restriction of the Sale of Opium Act, 1897 Queensland*). With this history in mind, racism has thrived, and like many Indigenous Australians, the experience of racial discrimination is unfortunately common (Markwick et al., 2019; Paradies & Cunningham, 2009). With such a complex and traumatic history for its residents, contrastingly, many Indigenous people from Cherbourg are positive and proud of being from Cherbourg. At the same time, grappling with its history and ensuring truth-telling is at the forefront of moving forward has been articulated by many Cherbourg Elders and people over the years. The need to have some balance in materials about Cherbourg was the impetus for this project.

Some people from Cherbourg have published stories about their experiences growing up in Cherbourg and living under the Act. For example, Aunty Ruth Hegarty published her story "Is That You, Ruthie" as a non-fiction novel in 1999. Aunty Ruth's novel is a deeply intimate narration of her experiences being forced away from her mother into Cherbourg's dormitory system. Rita Huggins and Jackie Huggins AM published the memoir "Auntie Rita" in 1994, sharing their story of struggle, activism, hope, and resilience after being forcibly removed to Cherbourg at the age of 14 years. Aunty Lesley Williams and her daughter Tammy Williams published their memoir "Not Just Black and White" in 2015, which details many aspects of their stories and connections to Cherbourg, in particular, Aunty Leslie's fight for justice around the issue of Aboriginal people and stolen wages in Queensland. While there is a growing number of people writing and sharing their stories about Cherbourg, there was recognition of the need to grow these stories and ensure there were many voices and stories available to the community and schools who want to learn from local people. There was also a recognised need to have stories available in diverse genres, such as videos and audio recordings, such as podcasts. There was a sense of urgency from the Wakka Wakka Elders group with whom we codesigned the project to create contemporary resources that privilege local knowledge, stories, and perspectives that provide some much-needed balance to the history and cultures of Cherbourg.

Ethics and Cultural Protocols

The team on this project was guided by the AIATSIS Code of Ethics for Aboriginal and Torres Strait Islander Research 2020 guidelines (AIATSIS, 2020). These guidelines were developed by diverse Indigenous leaders and groups. As such, we respect and embed the ethical principles of Indigenous self-determination, Indigenous leadership, impact and value, sustainability, and accountability. Indigenous leadership and self-determination principles are evident in how the team is comprised, including Wakka Wakka traditional owner Fred Cobbo as a Chief Investigator on the project; the codesign with the Wakka Wakka Advisory group; key research partner, the Cherbourg Aboriginal Shire Council (members are elected by the community), and the employment of local researchers. Impact and value were included in how the research was designed to include research outputs (digital and written stories, podcasts, and books) that the storytellers own. Sustainability and accountability were also a key consideration in decisions made about where the stories are located and who governs them long term. Through the process of codesign, it was determined that the Cherbourg Aboriginal Shire Council website was the best location to house the stories, as elected members of the Council can work with CI Fred Cobbo to govern the stories in the future. For sustainability, the team also collaborated with Cherbourg Radio. There are plans for Cherbourg Radio to continue the podcast project to preserve and share local stories and knowledge.

The ethics process and cultural protocols of this community are distinct and, as such, we applied the below to ensure we were respecting local knowledge and practices:

a Talking to the elected body of the community/shire, in our context, the Cherbourg Aboriginal Shire Council.
b The traditional owners are the Wakka Wakka people. On 12 April 2022, Wakka Wakka people were formally recognised by the Federal Courts of Australia as Native Title Holders of the area where we did this project.

Recognising and working with traditional owners is part of working ethically with Indigenous peoples and communities.

c Both groups of Elders (Wakka Wakka Elders and Historical Elders) were involved in the codesign of the project. Historical Elders are Respectful Elders along with families who have been brought to Wakka Wakka country from their homeland under government policies. Understanding this complexity is critical in following protocol.

d Giving feedback to partners on the project at all stages.

e Giving copyrights to the storytellers and ownership back to the people and community.

Engaging the Community in the Project

We often have colleagues ask how we had such high levels of community engagement in the project (especially from non-Indigenous colleagues). We propose that some surprises are steeped in deficit presuppositions that Indigenous communities are difficult to engage with. We started with the assumption that Indigenous people care about developing local knowledge-based resources for all students to learn in their local schools. It was the correct assumption, and our data, which will be shared in this chapter, reflects our assumption. The success of engaging the community was also in the team and having a local Chief Investigator (Fred Cobbo), who was also at the commencement of the project working in the local high school and an elected Council member with the Cherbourg Aboriginal Shire Council. Fred's connection and influence in the community undoubtedly played a significant role in effectively engaging a wide range of communities. For educators and policymakers who want to engage meaningfully with Indigenous people and communities, find out who the influential people in the community are and provide leadership opportunities for them in the process.

When designing the project, the research partners and team identified a need to provide multiple ways to inspire the community on the topic of storytelling. The funding application included funding for eminent Indigenous authors, Professor Anita Heiss and Uncle Boori Monty Pryor, to facilitate workshops across the schools and community. The workshops were very well attended, with children as young as five years old and Elders attending the workshops. Over 250 Indigenous people participated in the storytelling workshops. Under Fred's leadership, we were invited by Cherbourg Radio to promote when the workshops were happening, as well as other methods such as word of mouth, school communications, and social media.

The Research Process and Key Findings

This chapter focuses on privileging local knowledge and perspectives when applying SBA in Indigenous education contexts. We will focus on sharing data from the project that speaks to this topic. The research used collaborative yarning methodology (Shay, 2021), where yarning is used to work through research topics and questions. Participants had two choices about how the data was recorded: audio recorded and transcribed or storyboarded, whereby the researcher and participants together would create a textual recording of the yarning responses and undertake an in-situ cross-check and analysis of the data (Shay, 2021). Further analysis was undertaken by the team using qualitative thematic analysis (Braun & Clarke, 2006).

Twenty-eight adults participated in collaborative yarning about codesigning local curriculum resources. Seventy-nine per cent, or twenty-two participants, were Indigenous people who contributed to the research data. The Indigenous participant cohort were Aboriginal and/or Torres Strait Islander people who live in Cherbourg or Murgon. They were either community members or worked at the primary or secondary school. The non-Indigenous cohort were school leaders at the primary or secondary school or key staff involved in the project.

Compellingly, 100% of participants felt it was of great importance that curriculum resources are informed by local knowledges. One community member explained, "it's very important to have us find ourselves again and to make us, you know, proud of our heritage and ancestors because... they teach us who we are". Another community member shared, "It's very important to create local curriculum resources developed by local people. This empowers us community people [to have] an equal say in curriculum". A further community member felt it was important for reconciliation, "local curriculum resources developed by local people...this shows the true spirit of reconciliation and valued partnership between two parties". One school principal also made the point that local curriculum resources are vital because "they don't age".

One hundred per cent of all participants agreed that having local Indigenous knowledge and perspectives included in the curriculum was of benefit to Indigenous and non-indigenous students. Forty-two per cent of participants felt having local knowledge present within the curriculum has a direct relationship with identity affirming of Indigenous students. One Elder described this connection, "[including local knowledge] help[s] them understand and also give them the strength to look at that the old people–the ancestors–achieved or what they want through so they can also look at building their own strength and confidence of 'if they can do it, I can'". Another Elders shares, "it's just a pride...being able to say 'well I'm worth something'... it's about making our children feel proud. Not just of themselves, but of their people, of their ancestors".

The theme to emerge under benefit to non-Indigenous students was centred on understanding cultural difference and building relationships. One non-Indigenous educator observed, "it also provides a realisation around the past mistreatment of Indigenous peoples and hopefully builds respect for the culture". One Aboriginal community member felt strongly about the benefit to non-Indigenous students, "the big benefits I see for non-Indigenous students is they will be blessed to learn and value their own rich Australian history. Learning the local language, cultures and stories from a local perspective".

Research Outputs and Impact

For some Indigenous people and communities, the research outcome is sometimes more important than the research itself. It is well documented that Indigenous peoples and communities have been the subject and object of research, which resulted in little outcomes or change for their communities (Tuhiwai Smith, 2021). The research partners in this project wanted tangible outcomes, specifically contemporary resources to support Wakka Wakka language revitalisation.

After the storytelling/author workshops, Fred worked closely with different Elders and community members to develop a list of people interested in contributing a story and how they would like to contribute it. We initially only had funding for videos and written stories. However, after many yarns with the community, the idea for podcasts emerged so that people who chose not to be filmed could still share their stories orally.

Short Films

We finished with 13 stories in short video form. The stories and storytellers are diverse in topics and offer an intergenerational perspective. Some examples include "Keeping Language Alive" by Uncle Eric Law, "Education and History" by Aunty Patty Bond, "Growing up in Cherbourg–History and Strength", and "Healing and Community" by Aunty Sylvie Bond. Each story is rich in content, context, culture, and humanity.

The videos were filmed by an Indigenous filming company across communities and in various locations. Once the films were completed, they were reviewed by the storytellers and the team worked with the Cherbourg Aboriginal Shire Council and Cherbourg Radio to develop a link on the Council webpage. Posters were created that showed the storytellers and included a QR code to access the website. The posters were gifted to all of the research partners as well as key places around the community where community members would see the posters and be able to access the stories. In addition to the video stories, there is a full report about the project freely available for all of the partners and community to access. This was very important for transparency and to ensure anything related to the project was available in a format that was easy to access (Figure 7.1).

Bilingual Books

In partnership with the Culture Studies and Wakka Wakka Language Teachers and the primary school and high school, bilingual books were developed by students at each school. The primary school wrote a book, "For Our

Figure 7.1 Binung Ma Na Du poster (this will take a whole page).

Elders" – a series of stories from different children about their Nans, Pops, and Elders. Their stories are in Standard Australian English, Aboriginal English, and Wakka Wakka language. The secondary school book, "Out in the Bush" was by two students and is in Standard Australian English and Wakka Wakka language. The aim of the books was to use local stories and storytelling to support Wakka Wakka language teaching.

Community Forums

Fundamental to valuing local wisdom and knowledge is providing forums for all community members to attend and contribute meaningfully. For this project, the team decided on a community forum in Cherbourg, as well as a community forum at the University of Queensland, which provided opportunities for community members to connect with the university and showcase the project in that forum. Both events were very well attended. We had colleagues ask why attendance was so strong and we propose that it was because of how we designed the project and how central local Indigenous leadership was to how the project was delivered.

Conclusion

Learning from local wisdom and expertise requires a significant investment in relationships. It also begins with a strengths approach in that engagement must start with the premise that despite communities and individuals in communities struggling with various issues (and sometimes serious issues), this does not define the community and people in it. There are always strengths to draw from and different possibilities and outcomes available.

We shared a case study from the communities of Cherbourg and Murgon on a project that, at its essence, was about using an SBA to enhance the visibility and presence of local Indigenous knowledge and perspectives in the curriculum of the primary and secondary schools in the communities. We demonstrated how important the process is when working in partnership or codesign with Indigenous peoples and communities. The success of this project hinged on the expertise and leadership of people from the community where we were working. Indigenous knowledges and perspectives come from Indigenous people; ensuring these knowledges are deeply localised and contextual is critical in applying SBA in Indigenous education.

References

Australian Institute of Aboriginal and Torres Strait Islander Studies (AIATSIS) (2020). *Code of ethics for Aboriginal and Torres Strait Islander research*. https://aiatsis.gov.au/sites/default/files/2020-10/aiatsis-code-ethics.pdf

Barr, J., & Saltmarsh, S. (2014). "It all comes down to leadership": The role of the school principal in fostering parent-school engagement. *Educational Management, Administration & Leadership*, 42(4), 491–505. https://doi.org/10.1177/1741143213502189

Bishop, M., Vass, G., & Thompson, K. (2021). Decolonising schooling practices through relationality and reciprocity: Embedding local Aboriginal perspectives in the classroom. *Pedagogy, Culture & Society, 29*(2), 193–211.

Bodkin-Andrews, G., & Carlson, B. (2016). The legacy of racism and Indigenous Australian identity within education. *Race Ethnicity and Education, 19*(4), 784–807.

Bourdieu, P., & Passeron, J.-C. (1990). *Reproduction in education, society and culture* (2nd ed.). Sage.

Braun, V., & Clarke, V. (2006). Using thematic analysis in psychology. *Qualitative Research in Psychology, 3*(2), 77–101.

Burgess, C. M., & Evans, J. R. (2017). Culturally responsive relationships focused pedagogies: The key to quality teaching and creating quality learning environments. In J. Keengwe *(Ed.), Handbook of research on promoting cross-cultural competence and social justice in teacher education* (pp. 1–31). IGI Global.

Cherbourg Aboriginal Shire Council (2025). *Our history about Cherbourg*. Retrieved from https://cherbourg.qld.gov.au/council/our-history/

Commonwealth of Australia (2013). *Sustainable school and community partnerships: A research study*. National Curriculum Services.

Dockery, A. M. (2013). *Cultural dimensions of Indigenous participation in vocational education and training: New perspectives*. NCVER. https://eric.ed.gov/?id=ED541752

Dockett, S., Mason, T., & Perry, B. (2006). Successful transition to school for Australian Aboriginal children. *Childhood Education, 82*(3), 139–144. https://doi.org/10.1080/00094056.2006.10521365

Fricker, A., Moodie, N., & Burgess, C. (2023). Why can't we be smart? Exploring school community partnerships through decolonising race theory. *Australian Educational Researcher, 50*(1), 55–71. https://doi.org/10.1007/s13384-022-00590-9

Gillan, K., Mellor, S., & Krakouer, J. (2017). The case for urgency: Advocating for Indigenous voice in education. Australian Education review no. *62. Australian Council for Educational Research*

Godinho, S. C., Woolley, M., Webb, J., & Winkel, K. D. (2015). Sharing place, learning together: Perspectives and reflections on an educational partnership formation with a remote Indigenous community school. *Australian Journal of Indigenous Education, 44*(1), 11–25. https://doi.org/10.1017/jie.2015.1

Gower, G., Ferguson, C., & Forrest, S. (2021). Building effective school–community partnerships in Aboriginal remote school settings. *Australian Journal of Indigenous Education, 50*(2), 359–367. https://doi.org/10.1017/jie.2020.11

Guenther, J., & Osborne, S. (2017). *Red Dirt education leaders' perceptions about what is important for Aboriginal and Torres Strait Islander education*. AIATSIS National Indigenous Research Conference. https://eprints.batchelor.edu.au/id/eprint/597/

Hayes, D., Johnston, K., Morris, K., Power, K., & Roberts, D. (2009). Difficult dialogue: Conversations with Aboriginal parents and caregivers. *Australian Journal of Indigenous Education, 38*(1), 55–64. https://doi.org/10.1375/S1326011100000594

Langton, M. (1994). *Valuing cultures: Recognizing Indigenous cultures as a valued part of Australian heritage*. Commonwealth of Australia.

Lea, T., Wegner, A., McRae-Williams, E., Chenhall, R., & Holmes, C. (2011). Problematising school space for Indigenous education: Teachers' and parents' perspectives. *Ethnography and Education, 6*(3), 265–280. https://doi.org/10.1080/17457823.2011.610579

Lonsdale, M., & Anderson, M. (2012). *Preparing 21st century learners: The case for school–community collaborations*. ACER. https://research.acer.edu.au/policy_analysis_misc/16/

Lowe, K. (2011). A critique of school and Aboriginal community partnerships. In N. Purdie, G. Milgate, & H. Bell (Eds.), *Two way teaching and learning* (pp. 13–34). ACER Press.

Lowe, K. (2017). Walanbaa Warramildanha: The impact of authentic aboriginal community and school engagement on teachers' professional knowledge, *Australian Education Researcher, 44*, 35–54, https://doi.org/10.1007/s13384-017-0229-8

Lowe, K., Harrison, N., Tennent, C., Guenther, J., Vass, G., & Moodie, N. (2019). Factors affecting the development of school and Indigenous community engagement: A systematic review. *Australian Educational Researcher, 46*(2), 253–271. https://doi.org/10.1007/s13384-019-00314-6

Markwick, A., Ansari, Z., Clinch, D., & McNeil, J. (2019). Experiences of racism among Aboriginal and Torres Strait Islander adults living in the Australian state of Victoria: A cross-sectional population-based study. *BMC Public Health, 19*, 1–14.

Martin, K. (2008). *Please knock before you enter: Aboriginal regulation of outsiders and the implications for researchers*. Post Pressed.

McKnight, A. (2016). Meeting country and self to initiate an embodiment of knowledge: Embedding a process for aboriginal perspectives. *The Australian Journal of Indigenous Education, 45*(1), 11–22.

Murray, G., & Campton, S. (2024). Reducing racism in education: Embedding Indigenous perspectives in curriculum. *The Australian Educational Researcher, 51*(5), 1771–1790.

Paradies, Y., & Cunningham, J. (2009). Experiences of racism among urban Indigenous Australians: Findings from the DRUID study. *Ethnic and Racial Studies, 32*(3), 548–573.

Queensland Government. (2015). *Cherbourg*. Retrieved from https://www.qld.gov.au/firstnations/cultural-awareness-heritage-arts/community-histories/community-histories-c-d/community-histories-cherbourg

Riley, L., & Genner, M. (2011). Bemel-Gardoo: Embedding cultural content in the science and technology syllabus. In N. Purdie, G. Milgate, & H. Bell (Eds.), *Two way teaching and learning* (pp. 35–48). ACER Press.

Shay, M. (2021). Extending the yarning yarn: Collaborative yarning methodology for ethical Indigenist education research. *The Australian Journal of Indigenous Education, 50*(1), 62–70.

Shay, M., & Lampert, J. (2024). Community according to whom? An analysis of how Indigenous 'community' is defined in Australia's through growth to achievement 2018 report on equity in education. In *Critical studies and the international field of Indigenous education research* (pp. 47–63). Routledge.

Tuhiwai Smith, L. (2021). *Decolonizing methodologies: Research and Indigenous peoples* (3rd ed.). Bloomsbury Publishing Plc. https://doi.org/10.5040/9781350225282

Woodrow, C., Somerville, M., Naidoo, L., & Power, K. (2016). *Researching parent engagement: A qualitative field study*. Australian Research Alliance for Children and Youth.

8 Fostering Cultural Identity through Education

Indigenous Strength Perspectives from Singapore and New Zealand

Suraiya Abdul Hameed and Toni Torepe

Introduction

> With 60,000 years of genius and imagination in our hearts and minds, we can be one of the groups of people that transform the future of life on Earth, for the good of us all.
>
> We can design the solutions that lift islands up in the face of rising seas, we can work on creative agricultural solutions that are in sync with our natural habitat, we can re-engineer schooling, we can invent new jobs and technologies, and we can unite around kindness.
>
> We are not the problem, we are the solution...
>
> *Imagination Declaration, 2019 (Shay et al., 2019)*

This excerpt from the *Imagination Declaration* conveys important messages from 65 Indigenous and non-Indigenous students from years 6 to 12 who have come together for a Youth Forum to address the deficit narratives that have infiltrated educational discourse in Australia. It highlights how education systems, like Australia's, are grappling with the need to provide inclusive, equitable, and culturally responsive learning environments. Despite their invaluable contributions, Indigenous students often face barriers to accessing quality education, leading to persistent achievement gaps and diminished opportunities (Naepi, 2019; Shay, 2022). This inequity not only perpetuates cycles of disadvantage but also deprives educational institutions of diverse perspectives that could drive innovation and progress.

This is a common phenomenon in a globalised setting with a more diversified demographic, where embracing diverse identities, knowledge systems, and ways of being is important in shaping educational policies, pedagogies, and practices. There is a need to establish learning environments that are respectful and responsive to the diversity of students' backgrounds and identities. Strengths-based perspectives have emerged as a counter-act in dispelling the powerful actions of deficit discourses (Askew et al., 2020; Fogarty et al., 2018; Shay et al., 2024). With a strength-based perspective, there is the promotion of set values and practices that centre around Indigenous self-determination and assist in reframing the expectations and opportunities

DOI: 10.4324/9781003372783-8

within institutional interventions, policies, and programmes (Bond, 2019; Kana'iaupuni, 2005). According to Hameed et al. (2021), "achieving Indigenous educational excellence in Australian schools will require a focus on achievement through learning growth for all students, complemented by policies which support an adaptive, innovative, and continuously improving education system" (p. 1).

A recent Organisation for Economic Cooperation and Development (OECD) international study in Australia, Canada, and New Zealand investigated strength-based practices and showed great success for Indigenous students (OECD, 2017). These studies showcased the many promising practices underpinned by the discourses of success and excellence, which benefited both Indigenous and non-Indigenous young peoples by providing a safer and more inclusive learning environment. From a strength-based perspective, there is a recognition of the importance of promoting culturally responsive education, fostering positive identity formation, and fostering collaborations between Indigenous communities and educational institutions (Castagno & Brayboy, 2008; Hackett et al., 2021). One area of critical importance is the integration of Indigenous perspectives and knowledge into educational frameworks. Western, Eurocentric epistemologies have dominated the educational landscape for too long, marginalising and devaluing the rich traditions and understandings of Indigenous peoples worldwide (Michie & Linkson, 1999; Silvestru, 2023). This exclusion not only perpetuates the erasure of Indigenous cultures but also deprives education of alternative ways of knowing that could enrich and expand our collective understanding (Bang & Medin, 2010). Scholars have emphasised the need to critically examine the role of education in a globalised world, addressing issues of equity, social justice, and the recognition of diverse knowledge and identities (Lingard et al., 2015; Rizvi & Lingard, 2010; Shay et al., 2024).

Singapore and New Zealand provide compelling examples of educational approaches that centre on strengths-based perspectives rather than deficit narratives, each shaped by their unique cultural contexts and aspirations. In our analysis, we chose Singapore and New Zealand as a focus because of who we are and our positionality as educational leaders and scholars within the two contexts.

As an Indigenous Malay educator and former school leader in Singapore, my cultural heritage and professional experiences have shaped my deep commitment to equity-focused educational research. Growing up in a multicultural context while navigating my own Malay Indigenous identity has given me unique insights into the importance of honouring diverse cultural knowledge systems in education. I am passionate about challenging deficit narratives and instead emphasising the rich cultural capital, wisdom, and strengths that diverse communities bring to educational spaces. This perspective, combined with Singapore's demonstrated success in building an education system that celebrates multiculturalism while pursuing excellence, offers powerful lessons for creating more culturally responsive and equitable educational frameworks.

As a Māori academic, I have Indigenous tribal affiliations across the Ngāi Tahu region in the South Island of Aotearoa New Zealand. While I live in Christchurch, I identify Arowhenua as my whānau (family) home. Growing up in a small South Canterbury town, I was privileged to be raised in a multigenerational household with my grandparents, who were instrumental in shaping my identity, worldview, and confidence as a bicultural and bilingual woman. I feel fortunate to have navigated an education system that did not always recognise my ways of knowing and being, an experience I know is not shared by all Māori. This understanding has inspired my career in education, particularly in teacher education and research that aims to make positive contributions to Māori advancement.

A closer examination of Singapore's model showcases the country's emphasis on culturally inclusive classrooms that celebrate diversity while promoting national unity, primarily through its innovative language policy. The synergy between Singapore's bilingual policy, mandatory Mother Tongue instruction, and comprehensive National Education (NE) programme creates a powerful framework for nurturing cultural awareness and national consciousness (Gearin et al., 2017). This approach enables students to develop strong personal cultural identities while fostering a shared national ethos that prepares them for life in a multicultural society. New Zealand, in contrast, has pioneered culturally responsive pedagogies that deliberately incorporate Indigenous Māori knowledge systems, beliefs, and practices into English medium education. New Zealand's colonial history is founded on Te Tiriti o Waitangi, a treaty signed by representatives of the British Crown and Māori rangatira (chiefs) in 1840. In subsequent years, Māori have sought redress and reconciliation of Crown actions that have not upheld the promises exchanged in the treaty which have systematically undermined Māori sovereignty through land confiscations, warfare, and policies of assimilation resulting in economic, social, and cultural impacts. This impact is also seen in the education sector and much has been done to develop teaching pedagogies that are culturally responsive to Māori. The concept of "ako," which positions teaching and learning as a reciprocal process, exemplifies how Indigenous perspectives can enrich educational practices for all students. Both nations demonstrate how educational systems can leverage linguistic and cultural diversity as assets rather than obstacles. Their success in implementing policies and teaching methods that affirm cultural identity while promoting social cohesion offers valuable insights for other diverse societies seeking to create more equitable and inclusive educational environments (Bishop et al., 2009).

This chapter examines the implementation of strength-based approaches in education through the lens of Singapore and New Zealand's distinctive experiences. It focuses on two fundamental domains: first, how language serves as a vehicle for cultural identity and national unity, and second, how cultural connectedness is nurtured through responsive pedagogical approaches. Through detailed country-specific narratives, the chapter illuminates how each nation has developed unique strategies that reflect their specific historical, cultural, and demographic contexts. The comparative analysis reveals both shared principles and distinct approaches in how these nations have successfully implemented strength-based educational frameworks. Singapore's strategy demonstrates how cultural and linguistic diversity can be transformed into assets for national cohesion, while New Zealand's approach shows how Indigenous knowledge systems can enrich mainstream education. Together, these narratives offer valuable insights into how education systems can effectively embrace cultural diversity while fostering inclusive learning environments. By examining these contrasting yet complementary approaches, the chapter identifies both context-specific solutions and universal strengths-based principles that can inform the development of culturally responsive education in diverse societies.

Language as a Vehicle for Cultural Identity and National Ethos

In this section, we explore how languages shape cultural and national identity. Languages are deeply intertwined with culture, transcending mere communication to serve as powerful tools that connect cultural and national identities. They are woven into the history, customs, and values of communities, representing cultural heritage and fostering a sense of belonging and identity within diverse groups (Edensor, 2020). Languages reflect cultural knowledge and traditional values, and belief systems passed down through generations. They serve as mediums through which stories, myths, and legends are shared, preserving historical narratives that contribute to a group's identity. Names, places, and events holding cultural or national significance gain meaning through language, reinforcing the emotional and symbolic connections that bind community members together (Velayutham, 2007).

In many contexts, the language(s) spoken by individuals or communities become badges of cultural or national pride, signifying roots, heritage, and belonging. For example, in Singapore, while English is the primary language of communication, the Malay language – Indigenous to the region before colonisation – remains the lingua franca of the Malay Indigenous peoples. It is still used in the national anthem and military commands, underscoring its cultural significance. Similarly, in New Zealand, the Māori language holds a special place in the nation's identity. Te reo Māori, an official language of New Zealand, is integral to Māori culture and has experienced a revival in recent decades. Its incorporation into public life, education, and media reflects a growing recognition of its importance in preserving and celebrating New Zealand's Indigenous heritage.

Language can also be a source of contention and struggle, particularly when minority or Indigenous languages are threatened by dominant languages or where language policies marginalise certain cultural or national identities

(May, 2013). The Australian context provides a compelling example of these challenges. Indigenous Australian languages have faced significant threats since colonisation, with many languages becoming extinct or endangered. However, recent efforts to revitalise and preserve these languages highlight their crucial role in maintaining Indigenous cultural identities. Recognising Indigenous languages in education and public spaces is increasingly seen as vital to reconciliation and cultural preservation efforts in Australia (Gaudry & Lorenz, 2018; Marmion et al., 2014).

These challenges highlight the importance of language preservation efforts in maintaining cultural diversity and identity. As globalisation continues to shape our world, preserving linguistic diversity becomes ever more critical. Languages serve as repositories of unique worldviews, traditional knowledge, and cultural practices that might otherwise be lost. Efforts to document, teach, and revitalise endangered languages are not merely academic exercises but vital endeavours in maintaining the rich tapestry of human culture. Thus, language serves as a powerful marker of cultural and national identities, a repository of collective knowledge, a vehicle for cultural expression, and a symbol of group solidarity and pride. Its importance in defining and asserting these identities cannot be overstated. Language is deeply intertwined with the shared histories, values, and experiences that shape communities' cultural and national fabric worldwide. Understanding and preserving linguistic diversity is crucial for maintaining the rich tapestry of human culture and identity (Velayutham, 2007).

The relationship between language, culture, and identity is complex and multifaceted. It extends beyond mere communication to encompass the very essence of how communities perceive themselves and their place in the world. In an increasingly interconnected global society, the role of language in preserving and promoting cultural and national identities becomes even more significant. It serves as a bridge between generations, carrying forward traditions and values while adapting to new realities. As we move forward, it is essential to recognise the profound impact of language on cultural and national identities. Policies and practices that support linguistic diversity promote language preservation and encourage multilingualism, which can contribute to a more inclusive and culturally rich global society. By valuing and protecting diverse languages, we preserve invaluable cultural heritage and foster understanding and respect among different communities, contributing to a more harmonious and diverse world. This intrinsically aligns with strength-based approaches as it recognises language as a powerful cultural asset and source of community wealth, rather than viewing linguistic diversity as a barrier to be overcome.

Building upon this understanding of the intricate relationship between language, culture, and identity, Singapore and New Zealand offer compelling narratives that illuminate how these concepts manifest in real-world educational contexts. In Singapore, the bilingual policy mandates proficiency in English and a mother tongue language (typically Mandarin, Malay, or

Tamil), reflecting the nation's multicultural makeup and its aim to balance global competitiveness with cultural preservation. This approach is complemented by the NE programme, which permeates the curriculum and school life, fostering a shared national identity while respecting diverse cultural heritages. New Zealand, on the other hand, places significant emphasis on the revitalisation of te reo Māori, the Indigenous language, through initiatives like Māori-medium education and the integration of Māori culture and values across the education system. This is exemplified in the Te Whāriki early childhood curriculum and the Ka Hikitia strategy, which aim to affirm Māori cultural identity and improve educational outcomes for Māori students. Both nations have developed culturally responsive pedagogical approaches that go beyond language policies. Singapore's emphasis on values education and community involvement programmes, and New Zealand's incorporation of Māori concepts like ako (reciprocal learning) and tuakana-teina relationships (peer tutoring), demonstrate how cultural responsiveness is woven into the fabric of their educational systems. These approaches not only honour the cultural diversity within each country but also prepare students to navigate an increasingly interconnected world, showcasing how language and culturally responsive practices can be leveraged to create inclusive, effective, and forward-looking educational environments. In the following section, we will unveil the narratives from Singapore and New Zealand to better understand their educational approach towards strength-based perspectives.

Singapore Story

Singapore, a small island nation with a population of approximately 5.97 million, is renowned for its cultural diversity and unique approach to fostering national identity through education. The country's demographic composition reflects its multicultural heritage, with a mix of Chinese, Malay, Indian, and other ethnic groups making up its citizenry of 3.61 million, alongside 0.53 million permanent residents and 1.57 million non-residents (Department Statistics Singapore, 2024).

Central to Singapore's education policy is its emphasis on bilingualism, recognising the importance of both English as a global language and mother tongue languages (Mandarin, Malay, or Tamil) in preserving cultural roots. This bilingual policy, implemented since the 1960s, aims to equip students with linguistic skills that enhance their global competitiveness while maintaining strong ties to their cultural heritage. National identity formation is another crucial aspect of Singapore's education system. The Ministry of Education has integrated NE into the curriculum, focusing on cultivating a shared Singaporean identity that transcends ethnic and religious boundaries. This initiative includes teaching students about Singapore's unique history, its challenges as a young nation, and the importance of social cohesion in a diverse society.

Despite its small size, Singapore has leveraged its human capital through a carefully crafted education system that balances academic excellence with character development. The nation's success in international assessments like Program for International Student Assessment (PISA) and Trends in International Mathematics and Science Study (TIMSS) reflects not only its strong emphasis on STEM subjects but also its adaptability in incorporating 21st-century skills such as critical thinking and creativity into its curriculum (Hameed, 2020). Through these educational strategies, Singapore strives to nurture a cohesive yet diverse society, preparing its citizens to thrive in an increasingly globalised world while maintaining a strong sense of national identity and cultural awareness.

In exploring Singapore's innovative approach to nurturing cultural connectedness through culturally responsive pedagogical strategies, we will examine several key strengths of the nation's educational landscape. This exploration will highlight how Singapore leverages its cultural diversity as an asset, fostering a unique national identity while celebrating individual cultural heritages. Our discussion will unfold in three main sections.

We will begin by examining Singapore's pioneering approach to bilingualism, the cornerstone of its strength-based educational initiative. This section will illuminate how the policy adeptly balances cultural preservation with national unity, equipping students with linguistic versatility that enhances both personal cultural connections and national cohesion. Next, we will examine the ways into which Singapore embeds cultural connectedness in its curricula, particularly through the NE and Citizenship programmes. This discussion will showcase the government's strategic efforts in crafting a strong, inclusive national identity that harmoniously incorporates diverse cultural backgrounds, highlighting how these initiatives celebrate Singapore's multicultural fabric while fostering a unified national ethos. The ambitious objectives of these initiatives in fostering culturally aware, globally competitive citizens will be outlined, underscoring how Singapore prepares its youth to thrive in both local and international contexts. Finally, there will be an exploration of Singapore's innovative initiatives in promoting rich intercultural relationships through both curricular and co-curricular programmes. This section will analyse the multi-faceted, creative approaches taken by educational institutions to nurture understanding, respect, and collaboration among students from different ethnic and cultural backgrounds, transforming diversity into a source of strength and innovation.

By examining these three interconnected aspects, we aim to provide a comprehensive understanding of Singapore's culturally responsive pedagogical approach, showcasing how it successfully nurtures cultural connectedness while fostering a shared national identity, and offering valuable insights for multicultural education in other diverse societies.

The Bilingual Policy

Starting with Singapore's bilingual policy, this stands as a cornerstone in the nation's effort to forge a unique national identity while celebrating its multicultural heritage. Rather than viewing linguistic diversity as a challenge, Singapore has ingeniously leveraged it as a strength, using bilingualism as a bridge between cultural preservation and national unity (Gearin et al., 2017). The implementation of bilingualism in Singapore goes beyond mere language acquisition; it serves as a powerful tool for cultivating a shared national ethos. By encouraging proficiency in both English and a mother tongue language (typically Mandarin, Malay, or Tamil), Singapore has created a linguistic framework that simultaneously connects its citizens to their cultural roots and to each other.

Prime Minister Lee Kuan Yew's (1972) inaugural speech on language exemplifies the importance placed upon bilingualism as part of its key educational policies. According to Lee, the importance placed upon bilingualism is more than just the acquisition of different languages. They are, instead, languages to be learned for different purposes.

> As he put it,…when I speak of bilingualism, I do not mean just the facility of speaking two languages. It is more basic than that, first, we understand ourselves: what we are, where we came from, what life is, or should be about, and what we want to do. Then the facility of the English language gives us access to the science and technology of the West.
>
> (Lee Kuan Yew, 1972, p. 8)

Singapore's aim to retain its "Asian core" by means of bilingualism was an intentional move towards establishing a cohesive identity. This approach also recognises the inherent value of each community's linguistic and cultural heritage. Instead of promoting assimilation into a single dominant culture, Singapore's bilingual policy celebrates diversity as a national asset. It allows each ethnic group to maintain and deepen its cultural connections while participating fully in a shared national narrative. The success of Singapore's bilingual policy lies in its dual capacity to preserve cultural heritage through mother tongue languages while fostering national unity through English as a common language. Rather than viewing this as a trade-off between cultural identity and national cohesion, Singapore positions bilingualism as an asset that strengthens both dimensions. This approach empowers citizens to be cultural bridges, capable of expressing their heritage while contributing to a shared Singaporean identity. The policy exemplifies how national strength can emerge from embracing and harmonising cultural diversity rather than pursuing uniformity, creating an inclusive national ethos deeply rooted in Singapore's rich cultural tapestry.

Beyond Language Acquisition-Building Intercultural Relationships

Building upon Singapore's bilingual policy, the nation's approach to fostering intercultural relationships further exemplifies its commitment to cultivating a cohesive yet diverse society. This strategy, rooted in Singapore's official recognition of its 4Ms – Multiracial, Multicultural, Multilingual, and Multi-Religious nature – demonstrates how the country has transformed potential challenges of diversity into pillars of national strength.

The emphasis on character building and citizenship education serves as a natural extension of the bilingual policy, creating a comprehensive framework for nurturing culturally aware and globally competent citizens. While bilingualism provides the linguistic tools for intercultural communication, these educational initiatives focus on developing the attitudes, values, and skills necessary for meaningful cross-cultural engagement.

The former Prime Minister Goh Chok Tong's (1999) metaphor of four overlapping circles eloquently captures the essence of Singapore's approach to intercultural relationships. This model acknowledges the unique cultural spaces of each community while emphasising the importance of a shared national space. The "overlapping area" he describes aligns closely with the common ground created by the bilingual policy – a space where Singaporeans of all backgrounds can interact, collaborate, and contribute to the national narrative. Singapore's notion of multiculturalism reinforces the idea of "equal representation and fair allocation of resources" without marginalisation of minority groups (Ooi & Shaw, 2004, p. 54). Importantly, this approach does not seek to erase cultural differences but rather to create a harmonious coexistence of distinct cultural identities within a unified national framework. It builds upon the linguistic duality fostered by the bilingual policy, extending it to a broader cultural context. Just as Singaporeans are encouraged to be proficient in both English and their mother tongue, they are also encouraged to be comfortable in both their specific cultural milieu and the broader Singaporean society.

This strategy of maintaining "two playing fields" – one shared and one culturally specific – complements the bilingual policy's dual focus on global competitiveness and cultural preservation. It allows for the cultivation of deep cultural roots while simultaneously nurturing a sense of national belonging and intercultural understanding. Moreover, Singapore's emphasis on "equal representation and fair allocation of resources" in its multicultural approach reinforces the inclusive ethos established by the bilingual policy. Both strategies recognise diversity as an asset rather than a liability, and both are designed to ensure that no community feels marginalised or left behind in the nation's progress. In practice, this approach to building intercultural relationships manifests in various educational and social initiatives. These might include cultural exchange programmes in schools, community events that celebrate diverse traditions, and national campaigns that promote racial and religious harmony. Such initiatives, underpinned by the linguistic versatility fostered through bilingualism, create multiple avenues for Singaporeans to engage meaningfully across cultural lines.

By intertwining language policy with broader strategies for intercultural relationship-building, Singapore has created a comprehensive approach to national cohesion. This model not only respects and preserves cultural diversity but actively leverages it as a source of national strength and global competitiveness. In doing so, Singapore offers a unique paradigm for managing diversity in an increasingly interconnected world – one that balances cultural preservation with national unity, and local identity with global engagement.

Nurturing Cultural Connectedness through Culturally Responsive Pedagogical Approaches

Building upon Singapore's robust bilingual policy and its emphasis on fostering intercultural relationships, the nation's approach to embedding cultural connectedness in curricula, particularly through the NE and Citizenship programmes, further exemplifies its commitment to culturally responsive pedagogy. These initiatives serve as a natural extension of the linguistic and cultural foundations laid by the bilingual policy, creating a comprehensive framework for nurturing culturally aware and nationally conscious citizens.

Just as the bilingual policy recognises the importance of both English and Mother tongue languages in shaping identity, the NE and Citizenship programmes acknowledge the crucial role of education in cultivating a strong sense of national belonging while respecting cultural diversity. This approach aligns closely with Prime Minister Goh Chok Tong's metaphor of overlapping circles, where the NE curriculum represents a significant part of the "shared space" where all Singaporeans, regardless of their cultural background, come together to form a cohesive national identity (Goh, 1999).

Introduced in 1997, the NE initiative marked a significant step in Singapore's efforts to strengthen national cohesion through education. This programme complements the linguistic duality fostered by the bilingual policy by extending it to a broader cultural and civic context. While bilingualism provides the tools for intercultural communication, NE and Citizenship education focus on developing the knowledge, values, and attitudes necessary for meaningful engagement with Singapore's multicultural society.

The NE curriculum is designed with the understanding that cultural connectedness must be cultivated through both cognitive and affective learning. As stated in the original assumptions of the NE program, "To be effective, National Education must appeal to both heart and mind" (Edun N09-01-057,1997). This holistic approach ensures that students not only learn about their nation's history and challenges but also internalise a deep sense of belonging and commitment to their multicultural society, mirroring the dual focus of the bilingual policy on global competitiveness and cultural preservation.

The NE and Citizenship program's emphasis on experiential learning and active participation reflects a culturally responsive approach that builds upon the intercultural competence fostered by bilingualism. By engaging students in real-world experiences and encouraging them to reflect on their cultural identities within the context of the larger national identity, the curriculum helps students develop a nuanced understanding of cultural connectedness that goes beyond linguistic proficiency. Moreover, the integration of values education into the broader curriculum, focusing on respect, responsibility, integrity, care, and harmony, further reinforces the importance of cultural connectedness. These values are presented not as abstract concepts but as essential tools for navigating and contributing to a cohesive multicultural society, complementing the practical linguistic skills developed through the bilingual policy. The current curriculum aims to balance a focus on languages, mathematics and science, and humanity and the arts (Singapore Ministry of Education, 2015). Through these focal points, students receive explicit instruction in "respect, responsibility, integrity, care, and harmony; [...which] are important for safeguarding [a] cohesive and harmonious multiracial and multicultural society" (Singapore Ministry of Education, 2015 n.p).

Singapore's approach also demonstrates adaptability in the face of changing demographics, much like its evolving language policies. With an increasing proportion of the population born outside the country, the NE and Citizenship programmes have had to evolve to address the challenge of fostering a shared national identity among an increasingly diverse student body, while still maintaining the emphasis on cultural roots that the mother tongue component of the bilingual policy provides. Between 2005 and 2009, the number of permanent residents grew an average of 8.4% per year; and the proportion of the population born outside of the country increased from 18.1% in 2000 to 22.8% in 2010 (Yeoh & Lin, 2012). The majority of immigrants were born in Malaysia (386,000); China, Hong Kong, and Macau (175,200); South Asia (123,500); and Indonesia (54,400) (Gearin et al., 2017; Yeoh & Lin, 2012). This has resulted in a greater need for Singapore to constantly attend to, and potentially redefine, national goals and ideologies.

Singapore's approach to embedding cultural connectedness in curricula through the NE and Citizenship programmes offers a comprehensive extension of its bilingual and intercultural relationship-building strategies. By integrating cultural awareness and national identity formation into all aspects of education, Singapore has created a model that nurtures culturally connected citizens who are not only bilingual but also equipped with the knowledge, values, and skills to thrive in both their local multicultural context and the global community. This holistic approach to education reflects Singapore's commitment to leveraging its cultural diversity as a source of national strength and global competitiveness.

New Zealand Story

Māori are the Indigenous people of Aotearoa New Zealand representing 19.6% of the New Zealand population in 2023 (Stats NZ) and are recognised as a people rich in custom, culture, and language. Prior to colonisation, Māori developed a structural and economic system based on iwi, hapū, and whanau. They also reinforced a distinct culture and language premised on people's relationship to the land and the natural environment (Torepe, 2024). Following waves of European arrival in the early 19th century and a period of increasing interactions and conflict between Māori and the settlers, the British government sought to formalise a relationship to manage the increasing conflicts. In 1840, a treaty was drafted by the then British Governor of New Zealand, Captain William Hobson, and translated into te reo Māori by missionary Henry Williams and his son.

A foundational document in New Zealand, Te Tiriti o Waitangi was first signed at Waitangi on 6 February 1840 between Māori rangatira (chiefs) and the British Crown. Te Tiriti sought to establish a legal framework for British settlers and to recognise Māori authority of their lands and properties. Both an English text and a te reo Māori text were drafted and signed over a period of months with an overwhelming number of over 500 signatories signing the text written in te reo Māori compared to 39 signatories on the English document (Manatū Māori – Ministry of Culture and Heritage, n.d.). In the years following, Te Tiriti was often ignored or overlooked by the British authorities when drafting legislation, developing policy, and engaging with Māori communities. Through the Government's actions since the signing of Te Tiriti, Māori have been dispossessed of millions of hectares of land (Thom, 2022) and dislocated from their culture and language which have had significant impact on the status of Māori today. Assimilation policies and language suppression have had an impact on the health of the Māori language.

From the 1970s onwards, there has been a resurgence in Māori culture and language with protests and resistance movements responding to both historical and contemporary grievances and ongoing legislative decisions marginalising Māori, their culture, language, and rights under Te Tiriti. In recent decades, te reo Māori has experienced a significant revitalisation effort by the Crown, Iwi, and community. These efforts have been aimed at reversing the language decline that has occurred and to preserve New Zealand's only Indigenous language for future generations. In 2018 the New Zealand Government set a target of 1 million speakers of basic te reo Māori by 2024, and 150,000 speakers proficient to use as a primary language (Neilson, 2018). There have been several key strategies and initiatives that have contributed to the increasing health of the Māori language. The government has enacted legislation that has established Te Taura Whiri i te Reo Māori (Māori Language Commission), which is tasked with the promotion of te reo Māori and supporting language learning initiatives and the *Māori Language Act 2016* that recognises te reo Māori as an official language and ensures its protection and promotion. In addition, the Government has developed Māori language strategies and supported Māori Media and Broadcasting to provide te reo Māori content catering to all levels of language proficiency.

Iwi have also been prominent in their language revitalisation efforts. Many Iwi now have targeted policy and initiatives to support the teaching and learning of te reo Māori, often providing funding, resources, and opportunities for tribal members to develop their proficiency. "Kotahi Mano Kāika, Kotahi

Mano Wawata: One thousand homes, One thousand aspirations", is one example of an Iwi developed language strategy by Te Rūnanga o Ngāi Tahu. Prioritising intergenerational transmission, the 25-year strategy aims to have at least 1000 households speaking te reo Māori by 2025 (Te Rūnanga o Ngāi Tahu). Māori community-led movements and initiatives such as kōhanga reo (Māori language preschools) have also supported the resurgence of the Māori language and have been the catalyst for Māori immersion education.

Language as a Pathway to Cultural Identity

Te reo Māori holds immense importance not only as an Indigenous language but also as one of two official languages of Aotearoa New Zealand. Declared an official language in 1987 under the Māori Language Act, te reo Māori holds prominence as enacted through legislation. Greetings and simple words and phrases are very much embedded in the wider community and place names, geographic features, and government organisations are often reflected by dual bilingual signage.

In addition to national identity, te reo Māori is more than a means of communication. It provides insight into the preservation of heritage and Indigenous knowledge and provides an understanding into mātauranga Māori (traditional knowledge) about the natural world and traditional practices. It also provides a sense of belonging and pride and serves as a pathway to understanding a people and their worldview. The importance of language is also inextricably linked to culture and identity. It is the primary medium through which cultural traditions, genealogy, and cultural practices are transmitted from one generation to the next. Through the medium of waiata (song), pūrākau (ancient stories), and whakataukī (proverb) and the display of haka (cultural performance) we gain an insight into the value systems and knowledge of Māori culture and heritage. This significance of this relationship is best encapsulated in the Māori whakataukī (proverb), "Ko te reo te mauri o te mana Māori" translating as "The Māori language is the life force of Māori existence" (Te Ara, - The Encyclopedia of New Zealand).

Nurturing Cultural Connectedness through Culturally Responsive Pedagogical Approaches

Classroom Strategies for Language and Identity Affirmation

Māori achievement or underachievement in education has been, and continues to be, an issue in Aotearoa, New Zealand (Hargraves, 2022). It has been identified as one of the most inequitable among the 38 OECD countries (UNICEF, 2018). Smith (1999) explains that these disparities result from the curriculum's failure to recognise Māori worldviews, while Bishop et al. (2003) attribute them to teaching styles that are not suited to Māori students. However, in recent years, there has been a shift in thinking and practice where attention has been made to incorporate Māori pedagogy into classroom teaching to support Māori student engagement and achievement. Four examples have been recognised as addressing Māori underachievement and enhancing Māori learner experiences and success.

TUAKANA-TEINA

The tuakana-teina pedagogical approach is a philosophy rooted in traditional Māori society and according to Winitana (2012), is underpinned by both whakapapa (genealogy) and mana (social prestige). Still evident in today's cultural practices, tuakana and teina recognises the roles and responsibilities of siblings in for example, whaikōrero (speech making) and karanga (ceremonial call). Tuakana, as defined by Te Aka Māori Dictionary, is the "elder brother (of a male), elder sister (of a female), cousin (of the same gender) from a more senior branch of the family)" while a teina recognises "younger brother (of a male), younger sister (of a female), cousin (of the same gender) of a junior line, junior relative" (Te Aka, n.d.). While this model has been used in different contexts (Industry training) it is frequently seen throughout the education sector through the lens of peer mentoring. As understood by the definition above this approach in an education context recognises an older or more experienced individual (tuakana) supporting a less experienced or younger student (teina). The benefits of such an approach are numerous. An example of success was at Fruitvale school in West Auckland. Two years into a tuakana-teina program, the school noted an increase in student engagement and oral language skills. From a holistic viewpoint, a culture of wellbeing was identified with the tuakana tending to the needs of younger students as well as developing leadership skills (Education Gazette, 2022).

AKO

Ako is a traditional Māori principle increasingly used in the Aotearoa New Zealand education system. According to Glynne et al. (2010), it is a "responsive and reciprocal process, through which both teaching and learning roles are shared" (p. 118) and where the roles are flexible and adaptable. The foundation of this principle, ako (Glynne & Bishop, 1995; Glynne et al., 2010; Metge, 1983; Pere, 1982) is illustrated in two Māori words, kaiako (teacher) and akonga (learner), which reflects the interchangeability of roles and but importantly allows from both parties to learn from one another. Positioning the learner as both a learner and a teacher fosters reciprocal learning and challenges traditional hierarchical structures and addresses the power imbalance often seen in New Zealand learning spaces.

Glynne et al. (2010) recognise that the Māori principles of ako and whanaungatanga effectively support knowledge transmission in ways that closely align with culturally relevant pedagogy, as outlined by Ladson-Billings (1995, 2009), and transformative education for culturally diverse learners, as described by Hale et al. (2007). The alignment of these international studies with the pedagogical approach of ako clearly acknowledges the value of Indigenous knowledges and ways of thinking.

CULTURALLY RESPONSIVE PEDAGOGY

Kaupapa Māori theory and practice asserts the cultural aspirations and practices of Māori (Bishop & Glynne, 2000). When used in an education context, Bishop (1996) argues that it addresses the structural inequalities of power and control, as well as inequalities in initiation and representation. The use of kaupapa Māori theory and practice enhances accountability and legitimisation. Many studies have explored kaupapa Māori in education (see Bishop, 1996; Smith, 1997; Smith, 1999), including research conducted in Māori medium primary schooling. Graham Smith (1992, p. 1997) identified six key principles underpinning a power-sharing model: tino rangatiratanga (autonomy/self-determination), taonga tuku iho (cultural aspirations), ako (reciprocal learning), kia piki ake i nga raruraru o te kainga (mediation of socio-economic and home difficulties), whanau (extended family), and kaupapa (collective vision, philosophy). These fundamental principles form a model that posits relational interactions as central to successful learning experiences. The model acknowledges all individuals involved in learning and teaching interactions, fostering meaningful cultural engagement and recognising diverse cultural knowledges while challenging monocultural patterns of thinking and behaviours (Bishop & Glynne, 2000). Berryman et al. (2018) recognise the importance of relationships by reframing the idea of culturally responsive pedagogy and renaming it as cultural relationships for responsive pedagogy. Here, the authors position cultural relationships as fundamental to successful student learning and draw on six Māori principles that they consider effective in contributing to this successful pedagogy (wānanga, ako, mahi ngātahi) and effective relationships (whanaungatanga, whakapapa, kaupapa). Fundamental to this pedagogical approach is that students acquire skills and knowledge for the future, but they do so being strong and confident in their cultural identity.

MĀORI MEDIUM AND MĀORI IMMERSION EDUCATION

A result of an upsurge in discontent with the education system, Māori communities have led a renaissance of Māori language and culture in recent decades. One of the outcomes of this has been the emergence of Māori medium and immersion education throughout Aotearoa. Māori medium education recognises education programmes where te reo Māori is the language of instruction for at least 51% of the curriculum delivery (Education Counts, 2024) whereas most Māori immersion programmes such as kohanga reo, kura kaupapa Māori and whare kura use te reo Māori fully as the language of classroom instruction. With over 460 Kohanga Reo throughout Aotearoa,

Kohanga Reo (early childhood) has been recognised as providing more than an Early childhood education service (Waitangi Tribunal, 2012) and is a model that has been adopted in other Pacific Island communities, with one example being Pūnana Leo, established in Hawaii to revitalise the Indigenous Hawaiian language. Kura kaupapa Māori (years 1–8) and whare kura (years 9–13) are Māori language immersion schools in the compulsory sector where the philosophy and practices within these schools are underpinned by Māori cultural values and world views. As an alternative to English medium schooling in the compulsory sector, these schools provide a learning experience that privileges Māori ways of being, doing, and knowing.

The success of Māori immersion education contributing to an increase of te reo Māori speakers in our community is evident. 2023 Census data has shown that there are now over 200,000 speakers of te reo Māori, an increase of 15% since the last census in 2018 (Stats NZ). In addition to the language revitalisation in our communities, research has shown that achievement rates for students at kura Māori schools are superior to their peers in English medium schools. Gerritsen (2024) highlights that students from kura are more likely to achieve merit and excellence endorsements in the National Certificate of Education Achievement (NCEA) than those at comparable English medium schools. This is also evident in university entrance rates, which were higher for students in Māori medium education (41%) compared to 24% for comparable students in English medium schools, and 18% for Māori students in these schools.

Fostering Cultural Connectedness and Community Engagement

Research consistently demonstrates that cultural connectedness and authentic community engagement are fundamental to effective teaching and learning in New Zealand's educational context (e.g., Bishop & Glynne, 1999; Lucido et al., 2024). The New Zealand Curriculum explicitly recognises that students learn best when teachers create caring, inclusive environments and foster positive relationships. This aligns with the principles outlined in Tātaiako, which emphasises the essential nature of genuine connections between teachers, students, and whānau. There has also been a recognition of the importance of whānau, iwi, and the wider community in effective teaching and learning (See Bishop & Berryman, 2009; Bishop & Glynne, 1999; Ministry of Education, 2011, 2018).

The evidence for culturally responsive teaching is particularly compelling for Māori learners. Glynne et al. (1999) research reveals that Māori students often struggle to express their authentic selves in English-medium education when their cultural knowledge and worldviews are marginalised. However, studies show that, when Māori learners' cultural identity is affirmed and valued within the educational setting, they experience greater academic success. This finding aligns with New Zealand's shift towards strengths-based approaches in education, moving away from deficit thinking to recognise and build upon the cultural capital that students bring to their learning. Research by Bennett and Flett (2001), Webber (2011), and others demonstrates a clear correlation between strong cultural identity and educational achievement, suggesting that cultural connectedness is not merely beneficial but essential for student success.

Professional Development for Educators

With an increasing emphasis on teachers integrating culturally responsive practice and approaches, and ongoing professional growth, educators are encouraged to commit to professional learning development to deepen understanding and competence on bicultural practices. A notable programme is Te Kōtahitanga, a transformative, research-based professional development initiative developed by Professor Russell Bishop and Professor Mere Berryman that focuses on improving cultural responsiveness to Māori students. The research found that improving interactions and relationships between teachers and Māori learners has a more significant impact on their achievement than specific academic interventions in literacy or numeracy. In addition to individual ongoing professional learning, teachers in Aotearoa New Zealand are also supported by Kāhui Ako or Communities of Learning. These communities of learning cluster education providers from early learning centres to compulsory sector schools to collaborate, share and support expertise and professional learning goals.

Conclusion

The exploration of Singapore's and New Zealand's educational approaches reveals a profound transformation in understanding cultural diversity as a fundamental strength rather than a deficit. By positioning cultural and linguistic heritage as dynamic assets, these nations have developed sophisticated educational frameworks that transcend traditional paradigms of assimilation. Their strategies demonstrate that national identity can be constructed through a nuanced recognition of cultural differences, where diversity becomes a source of collective resilience and innovation. Singapore's bilingual policy and New Zealand's Indigenous knowledge integration represent more than linguistic preservation; they are powerful mechanisms of social cohesion, offering a model of how education can simultaneously honour individual cultural identities and forge a shared national narrative.

These approaches challenge conventional educational narratives by repositioning cultural knowledge as intellectual capital. Through comprehensive policy frameworks, both countries have embedded cultural competencies into teacher training, curriculum design, and institutional practices, recognising that true educational equity requires more than surface-level representation. Their models illustrate how strength-based perspectives can transform educational systems from sites of potential marginalisation to spaces of empowerment, where students' cultural backgrounds are not just acknowledged but actively celebrated and leveraged as learning resources.

The significance of these approaches extends beyond national boundaries, offering critical insights for multicultural societies globally like Australia. By demonstrating that cultural diversity can be a strategic advantage in an interconnected world, Singapore and New Zealand provide a compelling alternative to deficit-oriented models of education. Countries with a diversified population can further examine their current practices and reflect upon the potential of educational systems to be transformative spaces that not only recognise but actively cultivate the rich cultural wealth present within diverse communities. As global demographics continue to shift, these models offer a provocative blueprint for reimagining education as a dynamic, inclusive process that honours complexity, builds mutual understanding, and prepares students to navigate an increasingly interconnected global landscape.

References

Askew, D., Brady, K., Mukandi, B., Singh, D., Sinha, S., Brough, M., & Bond, C. J. (2020). Closing the gap between rhetoric and practice in strengths-based approaches to Indigenous public health: A qualitative study. *Australian and New Zealand Journal of Public Health, 44*(2), 102–105. https://doi.org/10.1111/1753-6405.12953

Bang, M., & Medin, D. (2010). Cultural processes in science education: Supporting the navigation of multiple epistemologies. *Science Education, 94*(6), 1008–1026.

Bennett, S., & Flett, R. (2001). Te hua o te ao Māori [The fruit of The Māori world]. *He Pukenga Kōrero—A Journal of Māori Studies, 6*(2), 29–34.

Berryman, M., Lawrence, D., & Lamont, R. (2018). Cultural relationships for responsive pedagogy: A bicultural mana ōrite perspective. *Set: Research Information for Teachers, 1*, 3–10. https://doi.org/10.18296/set.0096

Bishop, R. (1996). *Collaborative research stories: Whakawhanaungatanga*. The Dunmore Press.

Bishop, R., & Berryman, M. (2009). The Te Kotahitanga effective teaching profile, *Set: Research Information for Teachers, 2*, 27–34, https://doi.org/10.18296/set.0461

Bishop, R., Berryman, M., Cavanagh, T., & Teddy, L. (2009). Te Kotahitanga: Addressing educational disparities facing Māori students in New Zealand. *Teaching and Teacher Education, 25*(5), 734–742.

Bishop, R., Berryman, M., Tiakiwai, S., & Richardson, C. (2003). *Te Kōtahitanga: The experiences of Year 9 and 10 Māori students in mainstream classrooms*. Report to the Ministry of Education. Ministry of Education.

Bishop, R., & Glynn, T. (1999). Kaupapa Maori: Maori educational initiatives. In R. Bishop, & T. Glynn (Eds.), *Culture counts: Changing power relations in education* (1st ed., pp. 61–99). Dunmore Press Limited.

Bishop, R., & Glynn, T. (2000). Kaupapa Māori messages for the mainstream. *Set: Research Information for Teachers, 1*, 4–7.

Bond, C. (2019). The Inala Manifesto: A call to arms for Indigenous health researchers. In *Lowitja Indigenous Health and Wellbeing Conference*, 2019.

Castagno, A. E., & Brayboy, B. M. J. (2008). Culturally responsive schooling for Indigenous youth: A review of the literature. *Review of Educational Research, 78*(4), 941–993.

Department Statistics Singapore (2024). *Population and population structure 2024.* Retrieved from https://www.singstat.gov.sg/find-data/search-by-theme/population/population-and-population-structure/latest-data

Edensor, T. (2020). *National identity, popular culture and everyday life.* Routledge.

Edun N09-0l-057 (1997). *Press release no: 017/97 [Concerning the launch of national education].* Singapore Ministry of Education. Retrieved from: https://www.moe.gov.sg/media/press/1997/pr01797.htm

Fogarty, W., Lovell, M., Lagenberg, J., & Heron, M. J. (2018). *Deficit discourse and strengths-based approaches: Changing the narrative of Aboriginal and Torres Strait Islander health and wellbeing.* The Lowitja Institute.

Gaudry, A., & Lorenz, D. (2018). Indigenization as inclusion, reconciliation, and decolonization: Navigating the different visions for indigenizing the Canadian Academy. *AlterNative: An International Journal of Indigenous Peoples, 14*(3), 218–227.

Gearin, B., Hameed, S., Christensen, M., & Thier, M. (2017). Educating for nationalism in an age of educating for economic growth. In Y. Zhao and B. Gearin (Eds.), *Imagining the future of global education* (pp. 160–175). Routledge.

Gerritsen, J. (2024, Oct 16). *Kaupapa Māori studentsmore likely to get NCEA merit and excellence endorsements.* Radio New Zealand. https://www.rnz.co.nz/news/te-manu-korihi/530891/kaupapa-maori-students-more-likely-to-get-ncea-merit-and-excellence-endorsements

Glynne, T., & Bishop, R. (1995). Cultural issues in educational research: A New Zealand perspective. *He Pukenga Korero, 1*(1), 37–43.

Glynne, T., Cowie, B., Otrel-Cass, K., & Macfarlane, A. (2010). Culturally responsive pedagogy: Connecting New Zealand teachers of science with their Māori students. *The Australian Journal of Indigenous Education, 39*, 118–127.

Goh Chok, T. (1999). The Singapore tribe: Speech by Prime Minister Goh Chok Tong on "Singapore 21 debate" *in parliament,* 5 May Retrieved from http://www.moe.gov.sg/media/speeches/1999/sp120599a.htm

Hale, A., Snow-Gerono, J., & Morales, F. (2007). Transformative education for culturally diverse learners through narrative and ethnography. *Teacher and Teacher Education, 24*(6), 1413–1425. https://doi.org/10.1016/j.tate.2007.11.013

Hameed, S. (2020). Global citizenship education practices in Singapore and Australia: The fusion of the global eye with the national eye. *International Journal of Comparative Education and Development, 22*(3), 169–184.

Hameed, S., Shay, M., & Miller, J. (2021). 'Deadly leadership'in the pursuit of Indigenous education excellence. In *Future alternatives for educational leadership* (pp. 93–110). Routledge.

Hargraves, V. (2022). Seven principles to effectively support Māori students as Māori. *The Education Hub.* https://theeducationhub.org.nz/seven-principles-to-effectively-support-maori-students-as-maori/#:~:text=M%C4%81ori%20underachievement%20is%20of%20critical,to%20enrol%20in%20tertiary%20education.

Kana'iaupuni, S. M. (2005). Ka'akālai Kū Kanaka: A call for strengths-based approaches from a Native Hawaiian perspective. *Educational Researcher, 34*(5), 32–38. https://doi.org/10.3102/0013189X034005032

Ladson-Billings, G. (1995). Toward a theory of culturally relevant pedagogy. *American Educational Research Journal, 32*(3), 465–491.

Ladson-Billings, G. (2009). *The dreamkeepers: Successful teachers of African American children* (2nd ed.). Jossey-Bass.

Lee, K. Y. (1972). Bilingualism is more than just learning two languages. Speech given at the Singapore Teachers' Union dinner, 11 November. Document number 1ky19721105. Retrieved from http://stars.nhb.gov.sg/public/

Lingard, B., Martino, W., Rezai-Rashti, G., & Sellar, S. (2015). *Globalizing educational accountabilities*. Routledge.

Lucido, F., Jimenez, D., & Tang, S. (2024). Affirming culture and cultural identity in the bilingual/ESL classrooms. *Front, 9*, 1338671. https://doi.org/10.3389/feduc.2024.1338671

Manatū Taonga – Ministry of Culture and Heritage (n.d.). *Signing the treaty*. Retrieved January 10, 2025 from https://nzhistory.govt.nz/politics/treaty/making-the-treaty/signing-the-treaty

Marmion, D., Obata, K., & Troy, J. (2014). *Community, identity, wellbeing: The report of the Second National Indigenous Languages Survey*. Australian Institute of Aboriginal and Torres Strait Islander Studies.

May, S. (2013). *Language and minority rights: Ethnicity, nationalism and the politics of language*. Routledge.

Metge, J. (1983). *Learning and teaching He tikanga Māori*. New Zealand Department of Education.

Michie, M. G., & Linkson, M. (1999). Interfacing western science and Indigenous knowledge: A northern territory perspective.

Ministry of Education – Te Tāhuhu o te Mātauranga (2011). *Tātaiako: Cultural competencies for teachers of Māori learners*. https://teachingcouncil.nz/assets/Files/Code-and-Standards/Tataiako-cultural-competencies-for-teachers-of-Maori-learners.pdf

Ministry of Education – Te Tāhuhu o te Mātauranga (2017). *Te whāriki: He whāriki mātauranga mō ngā mokopuna o Aotearoa: Early childhood curriculum*. https://www.education.govt.nz/assets/Documents/Early-Childhood/Te-Whariki-Early-Childhood-Curriculum-ENG-Web.pdf

Ministry of Education–Te Tāhuhu o Te Mātauranga (2018). *Tapasā: Cultural competencies framework for teachers of Pacific learners*. https://teachingcouncil.nz/assets/Files/Tapasa/Tapasa-Cultural-Competencies-Framework-for-Teachers-of-Pacific-Learners-2019.pdf

Naepi, S. (2019). Pacific research methodologies. In *Oxford research encyclopedia of education*. Retrieved from https://oxfordre.com/education/view/10.1093/acrefore/9780190264093.001.0001/acrefore-9780190264093-e-566

Ooi, G. L., & Shaw, B. J. (2004). *Beyond the port city: Development and identity in 21st century Singapore*. Pearson Prentice Hall.

Organisation for Economic Cooperation and Development [OECD] (2017). *Promising practices in supporting success for Indigenous students*. OECD Publishing.

Pere, R. (1982). *Ako: Concepts and learning in the Māori tradition: Working Paper No 17*. Department of Sociology, University of Waikato.

Rizvi, F., & Lingard, B. (2010). *Globalizing education policy*. Routledge.

Shay, M. (2022). The ripple effect: Epistemic and professional justice in Indigenous education. *Asia-Pacific Journal of Teacher Education, 50*(2), 144–149.

Shay, M., Sarra, G., Proud, D., Blow, I. J., & Cobbo, F. (2024). "Strive with pride": The voices of Indigenous young people on identity, wellbeing, and schooling in Australia. *International Journal of Qualitative Studies in Education, 37*(2), 327–341.

Shay, M., Woods, A., & Sarra, G. (2019, August 13). The imagination declaration: Young Indigenous Australians want to be heard–but will we listen? *The Conversation*. https://theconversation.com/the-imagination-declaration-young-indigenous-australians-want-to-be-heard-but-will-we-listen-121569

Silvestru, A. (2023). *Weaving relations: Exploring the epistemological interaction between Indigenous & traditional ecological knowledge and Eurowestern paradigms in education for sustainable development-an umbrella review* [Unpublished Maasters dissertation]. University of Gothenburg.

Singapore Ministry of Education (2015). *"Bringing out the best in every child" corporate brochure.* Retrieved from https://www.moe.gov.sg/docs/default-source/document/about/files/moe-corporate-brochure.pdf

Smith, G. H. (1992). Tane-nui-a-rangi's legacy ...propping up the sky: Kaupapa Māori as resistance and intervention. Paper presented at the Aotearoa/New Zealand Association for Research in Education/Australia Association for Research in Education joint conference, Dakin University, Australia, 20–25 November.

Smith, L. (1999). *Decolonizing methodologies: Research and Indigenous people.* Zed Books/University of Otago Press.

Te Ara – The Encyclopedia of New Zealand, Ministry for Culture and HeritageTe Ara The Encyclopedia of New Zealand (n.d.) *Te Tiriti o Waitangi – the Treaty of Waitangi.* https://teara.govt.nz/en/te-tiriti-o-waitangi-the-treaty-of-waitangi

Thom, R. R. M. (2022). Land loss, confiscation, arability and colonisation: The experience of iwi in Aotearoa New Zealand. *AlterNative: An International Journal of Indigenous Peoples, 18*(4), 556–565. https://doi.org/10.1177/11771801221122810

Torepe, T. (2024). *Cultural Taxation: Cultural Myth or Workplace Reality?* [Unpublished doctoral thesis]. University of Queensland.

UNICEF. (2018). *An unfair start: Inequality in children's education in rich countries.* https://www.unicef-irc.org/publications/pdf/an-unfair-start-inequality-children-education_37049-RC15-EN-WEB.pdf

Velayutham, S. (2007). *Responding to globalization: Nation, culture, and identity in Singapore.* Institute of Southeast Asian Studies.

Waitangi Tribunal (2012). *The Report on the Kōhanga Reo Claim (Report No. Wai 2336).* https://forms.justice.govt.nz/search/Documents/WT/wt_DOC_68775144/Matua%20Rautia%20W.pdf

Webber, M. (2011). Look to the past, stand tall in the present: The integral nature of positive racial-ethnic identity for the academic success of Māori students. In W. Vialle (Ed.), *Giftedness from an Indigenous perspective,* 100–110. University of Wollongong.

Winitana, M. (2012). Remembering the deeds of Māui: What messages are in the tuakana –teina pedagogy for tertiary educators? *MAI Journal, 1*(1), 29–37.

Yeoh, B., & Lin, W. (2012). *Rapid growth in Singapore's immigrant population brings policy challenges.* Migration Policy Institute. Retrieved from: http://www.migrationpolicy.org/article/rapid-growth-singapores-immgrant-population-brings-policy-challenges

9   Thriving through Strengths

A New Generation of Indigenous Education Researchers

Ren Perkins

Who I Am

My name is Ren Perkins and I am a Quandamooka man with connections to the Wakka Wakka Nation. My Grandmother was the eldest of 10 children to Jessie and Alec Landers. She was born in the Cherbourg Aboriginal Reserve in Queensland. My Grandmother was moved to the Myora Mission on Minjerribah (North Stradbroke Island). My Grandfather was the youngest child of Paddy and Gladys Perkins. He was born in Eidsvold, Queensland in Wakka Wakka Country. My Grandfather served Australia in World War 2, despite he and his people not being recognised as citizens in his own country. I was born in Brisbane and raised in Quandamooka Country and I have a strong spiritual connection to Minjerribah. I have recently completed my PhD journey at the University of Queensland. My research topic was *Learning from the lived experiences of Indigenous teachers who have remained in the profession*. I have worked in Indigenous education for over 20 years. I am a lecturer at Griffith University and continue my research to support our communities. My personal history and professional experience have shaped my perspective on the strengths-based approach (SBA) in Indigenous education, which forms the core of this chapter.

Introduction

Indigenous research, particularly Indigenous researchers, are an invaluable asset for academic institutions in Australia and globally. While Indigenous education has historically been dominated by narratives of deficit and disadvantage (Hogarth, 2017; Stacey, 2024; Vass, 2012), a new generation of Indigenous researchers is emerging to reframe this conversation. This chapter examines the growing presence of Indigenous researchers in academia and their transformative impact on Indigenous education. By leveraging unique cultural knowledge, lived experiences, and community strengths, these scholars are shaping a more empowering future for Indigenous education. Additionally, I will share my personal journey of employing a strengths-based approach (SBA) in my PhD research with Indigenous teachers.

DOI: 10.4324/9781003372783-9

The chapter unfolds by first discussing the limitations of deficit-based research in Indigenous education. I will then explore the key principles of SBA and their application in various educational research contexts and examine why I chose to apply a strengths-based lens to my research topic. Finally, I will look at the potential impact of this new wave of Indigenous scholarship and its strengths in educational systems and our Indigenous communities. Drawing on Indigenous peoples' lived experiences and cultural knowledge, this chapter showcases the innovative and culturally grounded research methodologies employed by this emerging generation of scholars.

Background

Australia's history of colonialism and the ongoing exclusion of Indigenous perspectives have created an educational system that disadvantages Indigenous students. This cycle of marginalisation perpetuates educational challenges for Indigenous Australians (Bodkin-Andrews & Carlson, 2016). The existing literature on Indigenous education often dwells on difficulties, reinforcing a deficit model that portrays Indigenous students as lacking (Moodie et al., 2018). Herbert (2012) argues that the very structure of Indigenous education reinforces negative assumptions about Indigenous abilities.

Deficit thinking severely limits Indigenous education, particularly affecting the educational achievements of Aboriginal and Torres Strait Islander students. Sarra et al. (2018) suggest that persistent deficit stereotypes about Indigenous peoples can permeate classroom environments, impacting both teacher and student expectations of academic achievement and behaviour. This deficit language has been used to identify perceived deficiencies in Indigenous people, including gaps in education, health, and employment outcomes (Hogarth, 2017). While past research on Indigenous education has focused on systemic barriers and negative experiences (Lowe et al., 2019; Vass, 2012), raising important awareness, a critical shift is now underway.

Rigney (1997) and Smith (2021) argue that research on Indigenous peoples and communities should be conducted by Indigenous researchers for the benefit of local families and communities. Historically, universities have been enclaves of Western knowledge (Connell, 2016; Nakata, 2010), resulting in a scarcity of Indigenous researchers to counter colonial narratives. However, as more Indigenous people enter higher education, there has been a steady increase in Indigenous graduate research students in Australia (Moodie et al., 2018). The cultural knowledge and lived experiences of these emerging Indigenous researchers are key strengths in countering the long-standing deficit narrative in Indigenous education. This shift towards Indigenous-led research aligns with the SBA that forms the core of this chapter, offering a new paradigm for understanding and advancing Indigenous education.

Countering through Strengths: Key Principles of Strengths-Based Approaches in Education

In his 2005 work, McCashen defines SBA as a transformative philosophy prioritising people's unique strength, inherent dignity, and right to self-determination. As outlined by Saint-Jacques et al. (2009 p. 454), the SBA is founded on six key principles:

1 every individual, family, group, and community possesses strengths, with a focus on these strengths rather than on pathology;
2 the community is viewed as a rich source of resources;
3 interventions are guided by client self-determination;
4 collaboration is central, with the practitioner-client relationship being primary and essential;
5 outreach is employed as a preferred mode of intervention; and
6 all people have the inherent capacity to learn, grow, and change.

The core principles of SBA in education focus on building upon a student's strengths and abilities to foster their overall development (Lopez & Louis, 2009). SBA in education acknowledge that all students possess inherent strengths and talents regardless of their backgrounds or academic level. SBA to Indigenous education in Australia focus on leveraging Indigenous communities' inherent strengths, cultural knowledge, and existing capabilities to enhance educational outcomes (Sarra et al., 2018).

SBA empower Indigenous students by recognising and valuing their cultural identities and knowledge systems (Davis, 2024). This recognition fosters a sense of pride and self-worth, encouraging students to take ownership of their learning. By acknowledging the richness of Indigenous cultures, languages, and traditions, these approaches support the broader goal of self-determination, enabling communities to assert control over their educational pathways and outcomes. This empowerment supports the work of Indigenous academics in Australia and the contribution they are making to higher education.

According to Yip and Chakma (2024), integrating Indigenous perspectives and knowledge into education makes it more culturally relevant and inclusive. SBA integrate Indigenous ways of knowing and learning, making the curriculum more engaging and meaningful for Indigenous students. This relevance helps to bridge the gap between home and school environments, reducing feelings of alienation and increasing student engagement and attendance (Sarra, 2011). For example, incorporating traditional ecological knowledge into the science curricula not only enriches the content but also validates and respects Indigenous students' cultural backgrounds (Australian Curriculum, Assessment and Reporting Authority [ACARA], 2024).

SBA promote stronger connections between schools and Indigenous communities. According to Lowe's (2017) research in four remote Australian communities, building genuine and authentic relationships between teachers and the community requires teachers to go beyond simply acknowledging the presence of Aboriginal and Torres Strait Islander cultures. By involving community members, elders, and families in the educational process, schools can create a supportive and collaborative environment. This partnership ensures that educational practices are culturally appropriate and responsive to the needs of the community. Additionally, community involvement can provide valuable insights and resources, enriching the educational experience for both students and teachers (Lowe, 2017; Sarra, 2011).

Strengths-Based Approaches to Indigenous Education

Why Adopt Strengths-Based Approached to Indigenous Education

Research conducted by Shay et al. (2021) highlights the importance of relationships in schools developing meaningful partnerships with their local communities. A SBA builds bridges between Indigenous communities and educational institutions. By fostering collaboration and reciprocity (Shay et al., 2021), this approach works on dismantling the damaging legacy of colonisation. When educators actively seek input from Indigenous communities, a more inclusive learning environment is created. This collaboration allows for the local community to be able to contribute to the school with enthusiasm for their children's success, openly share their cultural knowledge, provide a strong advisory voice in decision-making, and form a partnership in the learning outcomes of all students (Milgate, 2016).

Benefits of Strengths-Based Approaches

1 Fostering Cultural Identity: One of the most significant benefits is the promotion of a strong sense of cultural identity (Sarra, 2011; Shay & Miller, 2021; Shay et al., 2021). By recognising the vibrant and diverse nature of Indigenous cultures, including their deep connections to language, storytelling, and land (Australian Institute of Aboriginal and Torres Strait Islander Studies [AIATSIS], 2020b; Grieves, 2009; Martin & Mirraboopa, 2003), SBA affirm students' heritage and foster self-esteem crucial for academic success.
2 Active Participation: SBA empower students to become active participants in their education. Students are encouraged to contribute their unique perspectives and strengths, fostering a sense of ownership and confidence in their abilities (Sarra, 2011).
3 Resilience Building: By acknowledging inherent strengths, these approaches foster resilience (Saleebey, 2013), a crucial quality for Indigenous students facing historical and ongoing challenges (Dudgeon et al., 2017). A positive cultural identity supports mental health and overall wellbeing, independent of academic success (Kickett-Tucker, 2009; Zubrick et al., 2005).

What Is the Evidence for Strengths-Based Approaches to Indigenous Education and Research?

The shift from deficit-based and problems-focused to strength-based approaches is evident in the research (Caiels et al., 2021; Peters, 2010; Saint-Jacques et al., 2009; Sarra, 2011; Scerra, 2012; Shay et al., 2021). Saleebey (2013) suggests that society is preoccupied with focussing on problems. There is a greater emphasis on discussing problems compared to highlighting strengths. This is true for research. Research is often framed around solving problems. For example, the University of Sydney (n.d.) claims that "Our researchers are tackling the world's greatest problems, from creating a more sustainable world to developing new treatments for chronic diseases" (para. 1). Another example is from the Commonwealth Scientific and Industrial Research Organisation (CSIRO) website which states "Our research focuses on the biggest challenges facing the nation" (n.d., para. 1).

As research on Indigenous peoples is increasingly conducted by Indigenous researchers, the focus is shifting from this deficit discourse mode of thinking that is overly focused on problems to a SBA that highlights the knowledges that our Mob bring. SBA to Indigenous research challenge these traditional views by valuing Indigenous knowledge and capacities that Indigenous researchers bring with them. The following section explores my PhD journey and why I incorporated a SBA to my research.

My Research Story: Why I Chose a Strengths-Based Approach for My PhD Research Project.

The Deficit Paradigm in Indigenous Education Literature

When I started my PhD journey, I read much literature around Indigenous teachers and Indigenous education more generally. What I discovered was that there was a tendency for most of the literature to be framed around a deficit paradigm. This was particularly true for education policy which focussed on Indigenous education and Aboriginal and Torres Strait Islander students. A majority of the policy literature was centred on addressing the "gaps" or "learning needs" or "challenges" that were experienced by Aboriginal and Torres Strait Islander young people. The focus was on Aboriginal and Torres Strait Islander students as being deficient and a problem that needed fixing. As an Aboriginal person who had gone to school and learnt through the lens of a westernised curriculum, these assumptions made me doubt my strengths, knowledges, skills, and abilities. This process of self-doubt which was a result of the deficit language is discussed in great depth by Aboriginal scholar, Chris Sarra. Sarra (2011) speaks about the impact that a deficit framework can have on Aboriginal people.

This issue of self-doubt continued into my undergraduate degree at the University of New England (UNE) in Armidale, New South Wales. By this time, universities around Australia had identified that they needed to provide additional support to their Aboriginal and Torres Strait Islander students (Pechenkina et al., 2011) and Aboriginal student support centres were being implemented throughout Australian universities. Dedicated Indigenous centres are now commonplace at Australian universities, a significant shift since the first support unit founded in 1973 (Pechenkina & Anderson, 2011; Trudgett, 2009). While internally acknowledging how great this was, I could not find the strength or courage to respond to letters to attend the Oorala centre. According to the University of New England (2024):

> For over 35 years, the Oorala Aboriginal Centre has offered services, programs and facilities of a nationally recognised standard to Aboriginal and/or Torres Strait Islander students who have chosen to study at UNE. The name "Oorala" was chosen by Indigenous students enrolled at UNE when the Centre first opened in 1986. It was chosen based on a local Aboriginal word meaning "a camp" or "a place where people come together".
>
> (para. 1)

Navigating Identity and Imposter Syndrome

On reflection, the reason I didn't accept the offer of support from Oorala was because I was suffering from imposter syndrome. The term imposter syndrome was first used by Clance and Imes (1978) to describe the experience of women who felt like academic impostors despite possessing the necessary credentials, believing their success to be a result of deception rather than merit. This feeling of inadequacy and being able to "cover-up" would stay with me during much of my working life. I felt inadequate because while my father was Indigenous, my mother was of Irish heritage and I therefore, was not "black" enough in appearance to satisfy some people, including our own Mob. This justification of our identity based on other people's perceptions has been covered in the literature and in the media (Grant, 2015; Heiss, 2012; Sarra, 2011). Unfortunately, the notion of imposter syndrome would rear its ugly head again during my PhD journey, which will be highlighted further in this chapter. Another reason for avoiding the support of Oorala was to evade questions about my Aboriginal identity. Growing up, there was so much "shame" associated with identifying as Aboriginal. Shame is an emotion experienced by many Indigenous peoples in Australia. "It has been suggested that shame develops when one is unprepared and feels they are exposed, looked at, from all around" (Louth, 2017, p. 188). The history of Aboriginal and Torres Strait Islander peoples post-colonisation is chequered with racial discrimination, oppression, and marginalisation, which still occurs today. The long-term negative impact of this on Indigenous peoples can be seen in all areas, including health and education (Smallwood et al., 2021). From these ongoing negative perceptions of identity and culture, it is clear where the concept of shame has come from. However, by the end of my undergraduate degree, I had developed strong relationships with people who accepted and celebrated my identity, which was reaffirmed after my negative experiences at school (Perkins, 2020).

Throughout most of my professional life, I have experienced different levels of imposter syndrome. I always felt like I had to prove myself to my non-Indigenous colleagues that I belonged and that I did not just get my job because I was "Blak". Additionally, in the back of my head was the insidious thinking that someone would discover that I was a fraud and not good enough to do the job I was being paid to do. This would be counter-productive because of the stress it caused me and the anxiety that would continue to build up. So, rather than focus on my strengths, I was clearly aware of my deficiencies. What this situation created was a vicious cycle of shame, stress, and anxiety, which chipped away at my confidence and, indeed, my self-esteem and mental health. The things that always kept me grounded were the strength of my family and my sense of belonging.

Confronting Racism and Finding Strength

The Turning Point: Recognising Indigenous Strengths

Another experience I encountered in my professional career was dealing with racism in the workplace. The experience of racism of Aboriginal and Torres Strait Islander peoples has been well documented within the literature (Marwick et al., 2019; Mellor, 2003; Paradies et al., 2015; Priest et al., 2019). Indigenous Australians are still experiencing discrimination today. In 2023, data from the Diversity Council of Australia showed "that exclusion of Indigenous Australians in the workplace has gotten worse, with 59% of Aboriginal and/or Torre Strait Islander workers experiencing discrimination and/or harassment in the workplace in 2023" (Diversity Council of Australia, 2023, para. 2). Dealing with racism is an everyday occurrence for Mob, and it takes its toll on you, physically and mentally. Again, I could draw on my family's strengths and the growing sense of being at ease with my cultural identity, which gave me the ability to navigate these often-hostile environments from a position of strength and resilience.

Along my professional and life journey, I have met many remarkable, strong, and deadly Aboriginal and Torres Strait Islander people, including my family. I was privileged to conduct some research for the Stronger Smarter Institute and met Professor Chris Sarra. The work of the Institute and the scholarship of Professor Sarra was inspirational to me. His book, *Strong and Smart – Towards a Pedagogy for Emancipation: education for First Peoples* (Sarra, 2011), demonstrates how Indigenous people have agency and can take control of their own emancipation. The book was a call for Indigenous Australians to radically transform and not simply reproduce the identity that mainstream W\white Australia has sought to foster for us. At this point in my life and learning journey, it made me reflect on the incredible strengths and knowledge we have as Aboriginal and Torres Strait Islander people. Recognising our strengths was the moment I was aware of how important it was for Mob to celebrate our culture, identity, and connections.

Choosing a Strengths-Based Approach

From my lived experiences, I could reflect on how far I had come professionally, emotionally, and spiritually. The following quote from my PhD methodology chapter explains why I chose to use a SBA in my thesis:

> I had an epiphany while sitting in the waiting room of my local Aboriginal Health Service, Yulu-Burri-Ba recently. There was a television that was playing messages from the Aboriginal Health Television (2021) service, on loop. After waiting for 15 minutes after my Covid-19 vaccination, I was about to leave when I noticed the message on the television. It displayed the words:
>
> • Culture is strength;
> • Family is strength;
> • Community is strength.

This epiphany convinced me that Indigenous teachers' stories needed to be told through a strengths-based lens, not a deficit-focused one (Perkins, 2024, pp. 109–110).

My journey from self-doubt to recognising the inherent strengths of Indigenous cultures and communities led me to adopt a SBA in my research. This approach not only aligns with my personal growth but also contributes to a broader shift in Indigenous education research, moving away from deficit narratives towards recognising and building upon Indigenous strengths and knowledge systems.

Indigenous Researchers: Bringing Our Strengths to the Academy

History of Indigenous Academics in Australia

Australia's higher education sector boasts a rich but relatively brief history. The first higher education institution, the University of Sydney, was established in 1850 (University of Sydney, n.d.). By 1914, Australia was home to six universities: the University of Sydney, University of Melbourne, University of Adelaide, University of Tasmania, University of Queensland, and University of Western Australia, all under the control of their respective state governments (Breem, 2002). Today, nearly a century after the founding of the initial "sandstone" universities, there are now 39 universities across the country (Universities Australia, 2024).

Historically, universities have been dominated by a white, wealthy, and predominantly male demographic (Gunawardena & McIsaac, 1994), failing to reflect the diversity of the broader Australian population. For instance, the first female student graduated from the University of Melbourne in 1883, more than three decades after the inception of higher education in Australia (Australian Bureau of Statistics [ABS], 1994; University of Melbourne, n.d.). The situation has been even more challenging for Aboriginal and Torres Strait Islander peoples (Anderson, 2008). Despite significant progress in recent years, these communities remain notably under-represented in Australian universities (Behrendt et al., 2012). Key achievements in Aboriginal and Torres Strait Islander higher education, such as the first Indigenous student earning a degree or the first Indigenous doctor graduating, occurred almost a century later than similar milestones in other countries with comparable colonial histories, including the United States, Canada, and New Zealand (Anderson, 2008).

Indigenous Pioneers

The first Indigenous students did not graduate from an Australian university until 1966, when Charles Perkins completed his studies at the University of Sydney (University of Sydney, 2005) and Margaret Valadian graduated from the University of Queensland (Australian Museum, 2020). Although participation rates among under-represented groups in higher education have increased, access rates for Indigenous peoples remain significantly below the levels needed to achieve equitable representation based on their population share in Australia. Indigenous student enrolments increased by 121.6% between 2008 and 2019, climbing from 9,490 to 21,033 students (Universities Australia, 2021). During this period, the proportion of Indigenous students among all domestic enrolments rose from 1.3% to 2.0%. However, despite these gains, Indigenous enrolments in 2019 still fell short of the population parity of 3.1% (Australian Bureau of Statistics [ABS], 2024).

Increasing Participation

As a result of the increased participation of Mob at university, there has been an increase in the number of Indigenous academics working within Australian universities. Researchers produce knowledge and ideas that translate into innovation, drive productivity, and improve the wellbeing of all Australians. According to Behrendt et al. (2012), Aboriginal and Torres Strait Islander perspectives must be included in this process by increasing the number of Aboriginal and Torres Strait Islander people completing higher degrees by research. Universities Australia (2021) has called for universities to ensure adequate support for Indigenous research and researchers within publicly funded research.

Commitments

This increased participation will allow Australian universities to enhance their uniqueness and deepen their understanding by valuing and integrating Indigenous knowledge and value systems, better reflecting the country's history and diversity while creating more inclusive learning environments (Universities Australia, 2021). Embracing both Western and Indigenous perspectives is vital for universities and advancing contemporary research and higher education. According to the *Indigenous Strategy 2022–25* (Universities Australia, 2021), Indigenous people should lead the development, implementation, monitoring, and evaluation of efforts to integrate Indigenous knowledge and values into university structures and research to achieve this. This includes embedding these perspectives within curricula and establishing formal strategies to ensure students leave with a solid foundation of Indigenous knowledge and values. It is also crucial that the intellectual property rights of Indigenous knowledge are properly acknowledged and compensated in this process. Indigenous academics have been and continue to contribute to this critical space. These are the strengths that Indigenous academics bring to higher education, which benefit the sector and all students.

The history of Indigenous academics in Australia reflects a journey from exclusion to increasing inclusion and recognition. While challenges remain, the growing presence of Indigenous academics brings unique strengths to higher education, benefiting the sector and all students. As universities continue to embrace Indigenous perspectives, they pave the way for a more inclusive and diverse academic landscape that better reflects Australia's rich cultural heritage.

Contributions

Contributions of Indigenous Academics: Transforming Australian Higher Education

Indigenous academics in Australia have been pivotal in reshaping the landscape of higher education, bringing unique perspectives and knowledge that challenge traditional paradigms and enrich academic discourse. Their work spans multiple disciplines and has far-reaching impacts on research, policy, and community outcomes. Following will be a brief insight into some of their contributions and the impact they have had for Indigenous academics coming through.

Promoting Indigenous Knowledges and Methodologies

One of the most significant contributions of Indigenous academics is their promotion of Indigenous knowledges and methodologies. Scholars such as Professor Lester Irabinna-Rigney, Professor Aileen Moreton-Robinson, and Professor Martin Nakata have been at the forefront of this movement. Their work offers alternative ways of understanding the world that are deeply connected to cultural heritage and land. For example, Professor Nakata's concept of the "cultural interface" has been instrumental in understanding the complexities of Indigenous and non-Indigenous knowledge systems interacting in educational contexts (Nakata, 2010). This framework has been widely adopted in curriculum development across Australian universities.

Indigenous scholars have led efforts to embed this knowledge into curricula, research, and institutional policies. As a result, many universities now offer Indigenous studies programmes that educate all students about Australia's rich cultural history, social justice, and contemporary issues facing Indigenous communities (Nakata et al., 2014). Indigenous academics have also been instrumental in developing culturally appropriate educational resources and advocating for the inclusion of Indigenous knowledge in mainstream curricula (Shay & Oliver, 2021).

Advancing Critical Research

Another contribution Indigenous academics have made is advancements in research that addresses critical issues affecting Indigenous peoples, such as health disparities, education, social policy, and environmental sustainability (Behrendt et al., 2012; Bennett, 2019; Briggs, 2022; Griffiths et al., 2016; Kennedy, 2021). In fields such as health, Indigenous academics have advocated for culturally appropriate healthcare models that address the unique needs of Indigenous communities. In law and politics, they have influenced discussions on land rights, sovereignty, and self-determination, contributing to significant legal reforms and policy changes (Dodson, 2012; Foley, 2006; Gainsford, 2021). Their research often adopts a community-focused approach, prioritising Indigenous communities' voices, needs, and aspirations (Rigney, 1999). This work not only contributes to academic knowledge but also directly impacts policy development and community outcomes, improving the lives of Indigenous Australians.

Mentorship and Role Modelling

Indigenous academics serve as mentors and role models for Indigenous students, providing crucial support, guidance, and inspiration for the next generation of scholars (Povey et al., 2023). This SBA highlights the positive impact of Indigenous presence and success in academia. It challenges stereotypes and paves the way for greater representation and participation of Indigenous peoples in higher education. In addition, Indigenous academics advocate for protecting Indigenous intellectual property rights and ensure that Indigenous knowledges are respected and appropriately credited within academic and research contexts. Their contributions reshape the academic landscape, making it more inclusive, diverse, and reflective of Australia's rich Indigenous heritage. The contributions of

Indigenous academics align closely with SBA in Indigenous education. By centring Indigenous knowledges, prioritising community needs, and providing strong role models, these scholars demonstrate the power and potential of Indigenous-led education and research. Their work not only advances academic knowledge but also directly improves the lives of Indigenous Australians, paving the way for a more equitable and inclusive higher education system.

The Current Landscape of Indigenous Academia in Australia

The landscape of Indigenous academia in Australia has been significantly shaped by the collaborative efforts of various organisations across the higher education sector. These institutions play crucial roles in supporting Indigenous academics, funding research, and promoting ethical practices. Their combined efforts have created an environment that increasingly recognises and values the contributions of Indigenous scholars.

Government Support: The Australian Research Council (ARC)

The Australian Research Council (ARC) stands at the forefront of funding research and innovation in Australia. As a government agency, the ARC promotes high-quality research that advances knowledge and addresses national and global challenges (Australian Research Council [ARC], 2022). Through competitive funding schemes, it supports researchers, projects, and research centres in universities and other eligible organisations. In 2024, the ARC announced the commencement of the inaugural ARC Indigenous Forum, which is made up of a cross-section of eminent Indigenous members with significant experience in research, as well as engagement with end-users of research. The ARC Indigenous Forum is significant in terms of the Australian research funding and supporting Indigenous knowledge and researchers. According to the ARC (2024):

> The establishment of the ARC Indigenous Forum is such a positive and important moment for Australia's research sector. The Forum will work closely with the ARC Board, bringing a unique and strategic focus to initiatives that will strengthen Indigenous leadership in the research sector, build opportunities for Indigenous-led and focused research, and support career pathways for emerging Indigenous researchers.
>
> (para. 2)

Also of importance to Indigenous academics is the ARC's Discovery Indigenous scheme. This programme provides grant funding to Aboriginal and/or Torres Strait Islander researchers with multiple objectives. It supports both basic and applied research, fosters national and international collaboration, aligns research with government priorities, and aims to retain established Indigenous researchers in higher education institutions. By offering this targeted support, the ARC plays a vital role in nurturing Indigenous academic talent and research capabilities (ARC, 2024).

Collaborative Networks: NATSIHEC

The National Aboriginal and Torres Strait Islander Higher Education Consortium (NATSIHEC) focuses on fostering collaboration and mutual support among Indigenous academics. This incorporated organisation provides mentoring for Indigenous scholars at various career stages and organises conferences that create culturally safe and supportive environments for knowledge sharing. NATSIHEC's (2024) goal to "increase the availability of higher education for our communities and to develop and grow research and scholarship for and by Aboriginal and Torres Strait Islander peoples" underscores its commitment to expanding Indigenous participation in academia (p. 1).

Ethical Research: AIATSIS

Another key organisation which supports the role of Indigenous academics in Australia is the Australian Institute of Aboriginal and Torres Strait Islander Studies (AIATSIS). AIATSIS has developed a comprehensive Code of Ethics to guide ethical research involving Aboriginal and Torres Strait Islander peoples (Australian Institute of Aboriginal and Torres Strait Islander Studies [AIATSIS], 2020a). This code is designed to ensure that research is conducted with respect, integrity, and in accordance with Indigenous values and rights. Compliance with the AIATSIS Code of Ethics is essential for conducting ethical and responsible research with Aboriginal and Torres Strait Islander communities. A SBA has been used in developing the AIATSIS Code of Ethics. The code ensures that Indigenous peoples' knowledge is central to conducting research with Indigenous peoples and their communities. One of the key principles of the code is that Indigenous people should be involved in the leadership and governance of research projects (AIATSIS, 2020a). This includes decision-making, oversight, and representation of Indigenous interests.

Sector-Wide Commitment: Universities Australia

Universities Australia is the peak body for the university sector that advocate for the vast social, economic, and cultural value of higher education and research to Australia and the world (Universities Australia, 2024). In 2017, Universities Australia launched a whole-of-sector strategy, with the aim of supporting Indigenous people's advancement in higher education in Australia. To emphasise their commitment to supporting Indigenous academics and others in higher education, Universities Australia launched their current Indigenous strategy in 2021. Regarding Indigenous academics, the strategy states:

> In particular, universities should commit to further developing pathways through higher degrees by research (HDRs) and into academic work. Universities commit to fostering Aboriginal and Torres Strait Islander academic staff and supporting them to become leading researchers and teachers in their academic disciplines.
>
> (Universities Australia, 2021, pp. 31–32)

The current landscape of Indigenous academia in Australia is characterised by a collaborative network of support spanning government agencies, Indigenous-led organisations, research institutions, and university bodies. While challenges remain, the combined efforts of these organisations have contributed significantly to the growth and recognition of Indigenous scholarship.

As an Aboriginal academic, I find inspiration in the commitment Australian universities have made to supporting and recognising Aboriginal and Torres Strait Islander peoples and our knowledges. The capacity building of Indigenous academics and recognising our strengths within the sector are particularly encouraging. While achieving parity in academic staffing remains a goal, the progress made and the increasing recognition of Indigenous contributions by individual universities are heartening developments in Australian higher education.

Conclusion

As we move forward, it is crucial that both Indigenous and non-Indigenous readers engage actively with SBA in academia. For Indigenous scholars and students, I encourage you to embrace and showcase your unique cultural knowledge and perspectives in your work. Your voices and experiences are invaluable in reshaping the academic landscape.

For non-Indigenous readers, I urge you to actively seek out and incorporate Indigenous knowledge systems in your research and teaching practices. This could involve collaborating with Indigenous scholars, integrating Indigenous methodologies into your work, or advocating for more inclusive policies in your institutions.

All readers can contribute by:

- Challenging deficit-based narratives about Indigenous peoples in academic discourse and beyond.
- Supporting and mentoring Indigenous students and early career researchers.
- Promoting the inclusion of Indigenous perspectives in curriculum development across all disciplines.
- Advocating for increased funding and resources for Indigenous-led research projects.

- Engaging respectfully with Indigenous communities in research partnerships.
- By embracing these actions, we can collectively work towards a more equitable, diverse, and enriching academic environment that values and amplifies Indigenous strengths.

As an Indigenous academic who has just completed their PhD, I am grateful for the opportunities open before me. On reflection, the choice of using a SBA for my research study allowed me to draw on the strengths that all Aboriginal and Torres Strait Islander peoples have in their culture, identity, connection to Country, and strong relationships with our families. These values underpin Indigenous ways of knowing, doing, and being and the knowledge we bring into the spaces we work in. The incredible strengths, resilience, and knowledge of the Indigenous teachers I met throughout my PhD research study further highlighted the importance of using a SBA to my research.

Given the recent commitment from Universities Australia (2021) of Aboriginal and Torres Strait Islander peoples in their *Indigenous Strategy 2022–25*, I sense there is a powerful momentum for our Mob in Australian universities. This chapter highlighted the strengths that Indigenous peoples bring into their research. It is heartening to see this being valued by the university sector. The real beneficiaries from this new wave of strong, deadly Indigenous academics will be our communities and young people who will now have their cultures, identity, and knowledges represented in the research that is supporting them and creating a future where they can see themselves represented in policies and programmes throughout all aspects of Australian society.

As we stand at this pivotal moment in the evolution of Indigenous academia, we must recognise that SBA are not just methodologies or theories – they are pathways to empowerment, self-determination, and cultural resurgence. By centring Indigenous knowledge, values, and perspectives, we are not only enriching the academic landscape but also contributing to the healing and flourishing of our communities. The transformative potential of these approaches extends far beyond the walls of universities; it has the power to reshape societal narratives, inform policy decisions, and inspire future generations. As Indigenous and non-Indigenous scholars alike embrace these approaches, we are collectively writing a new chapter in the story of Australian academia – one where Indigenous strengths are celebrated, Indigenous voices are amplified, and Indigenous wisdom is recognised as fundamental to addressing the complex challenges of our time. In this journey, every step taken towards recognising and building upon Indigenous strengths is a step towards a more just, inclusive, and enlightened future for all.

References

Anderson, I. (2008, 13 May). *The knowledge economy and Aboriginal health development* [Dean's lecture], Melbourne.

Australian Bureau of Statistics (2024). *Estimates of Aboriginal and Torres Strait Islander Australians.* https://www.abs.gov.au/statistics/people/aboriginal-and-torres-strait-islander-peoples/estimates-aboriginal-and-torres-strait-islander-australians/30-june-2021

Australian Curriculum, Assessment and Reporting Authority (2024). *Aboriginal and Torres Strait Islander Histories and Cultures.* https://v9.australiancurriculum. edu.au/teacher-resources/understand-this-cross-curriculum-priority/aboriginal-and-torres-strait-islander-histories-and-cultures#accordion-38e6895a00-item-800b79132c

Australian Institute of Aboriginal and Torres Strait Islander Studies (2020a). *AIATSIS code of ethics for Aboriginal and Torres Strait Islander research.* https://aiatsis.gov. au/sites/default/files/2020-10/aiatsis-code-ethics.pdf

Australian Institute of Aboriginal and Torres Strait Islander Studies (2020b). *Indigenous Australians: Aboriginal and Torres Strait Islander people.* https:// aiatsis.gov.au/explore/indigenous-australians-aboriginal-and-torres-strait-islander-people

Australian Museum (2020). *Indigenous Australia Timeline: 1901 to 1969.* http://aus-tralianmuseum.net.au/Indigenous-Australia-Timeline-1901-to-1969

Australian Research Council. (2022). *About the ARC.* https://www.arc.gov.au/ about-arc

Australian Research Council (2024). *Forum to bring collaboration and knowledge exchange.* https://www.arc.gov.au/about-arc

Behrendt, L. Y., Larkin, S., Griew, R., & Kelly, P. (2012). *Review of higher education access and outcomes for Aboriginal and Torres Strait Islander People: Final report.* Department of Industry, Innovation, Science, Research and Tertiary Education. https://apo.org.au/node/31135

Bennett, B. (2019). The importance of Aboriginal history for practitioners. In B. Ben-nett, & S. Green (Eds.) *Our voices – Aboriginal social work* (pp. 10–22). Red Globe Press.

Bodkin-Andrews, G., & Carlson, B. (2016). The legacy of racism and Indigenous Australian identity within education. *Race Ethnicity and Education, 19*(4), 784–807. https://doi.org/10.1080/13613324.2014.969224

Breem, J. (2002). *Higher education in Australia: Structure, policy & debate.* http:// www.csse.monash.edu.au/~jwb/aused/aused.html

Briggs, C. (2022). Australian government social policy – where are Aboriginal and Torres Strait Islander people positioned in policy-making? *social work & policy studies: social justice, Practice and Theory, 5*(1), Special focus on Women and Children.

Caiels, J., Milne, A., & Beadle-Brown, J. (2021). Strengths-based approaches in so-cial work and social care: Reviewing the evidence. *Journal of Long Term Care,* 401–422. https://doi.org/10.31389/jltc.102

Clance, P. R., & Imes, S. A. (1978). The imposter phenomenon in high achieving women: Dynamics and therapeutic intervention. *Psychotherapy: Theory, Research and Practice, 15*(3), 241–247.

Commonwealth Scientific and Industrial Research Organisation (n.d.). *Research.* https://www.csiro.au/en/research

Connell, R. (2016). Southern Theory and world universities. *Higher Education Re-search & Development, 36*(1), 4–15. https://doi.org/10.1080/07294360.2017. 1252311

Davis, J. (2024). *Strength basing, empowering and regenerating Indigenous knowl-edge education: Riteway flows.* Routledge.

Diversity Council of Australia (2023). *First Nations facing increased discrimination & cultural load.* https://www.dca.org.au/news/media-releases/first-nations-facing-increased-discrimination

Dodson, M. (2012). Constitutional recognition of Indigenous Australians. *Papers on Parliament, 57,* 11–22.

Dudgeon, P., Calma, T., & Holland, C. (2017). The context and causes of the suicide of people in Australia. *The Journal of Indigenous Wellbeing, 2*(2), 5–15.

Foley, G. (2006). Land rights and Aboriginal voices. *Australian Journal of Human Rights, Special Issue: Marginality and Exclusion, 12*(1), 83–107.

Gainsford, A. (2021). *Embedding Indigenous Knowledges in the Design of the Higher Education Curriculum: An International Study in Law Education* [Unpublished doctoral thesis]. Charles Sturt University.

Grant, S. (2015, December 14). The politics of identity: We are trapped in the imaginations of white Australians. *The Guardian.* https://www.theguardian.com/commentisfree/2015/dec/14/the-politics-of-identity-we-are-trapped-in-the-imaginations-of-white-australians

Grieves, V. (2009). *Aboriginal spirituality: Aboriginal philosophy, the basis of Aboriginal social and emotional wellbeing. Discussion paper no. 9.* Cooperative Research Centre for Aboriginal Health.

Griffiths, K., Coleman, C., Lee, V., & Madden, R. (2016). How colonisation determines social justice and Indigenous health—a review of the literature. *Journal of Population Research, 33,* 9–30.

Gunawardena, C. N., & McIsaac, M. S. (1994). Distance education. In D.H. Jonassen (Ed.), *Handbook of research on educational communications and technology* (2nd ed., pp. 355–395). Mahwah, NJ: Lawrence Earlbaum Associates.

Heiss, A. (2012). *Am I Black enough for you?* Random House Books Australia.

Herbert, J. (2012). "Ceaselessly circling the centre": Historical contextualisation of Indigenous education within Australia. *History of Education Review, 41*(2), 91–103. https://doi.org/10.1108/08198691311269484

Hogarth, M. (2017). Speaking back to the deficit discourses: A theoretical and methodological approach. *The Australian Educational Researcher, 44,* 21–34.

Kennedy, B. (2021). *Engaging Stakeholder Participation to Improve Animal Management in a Remote Australian Aboriginal Community* [Unpublished doctoral thesis]. University of New England.

Kickett-Tucker, C. S. (2009). Moorn (Black)? Djardak (White)? How come I don't fit in Mum? Exploring the racial identity of Australian Aboriginal children and youth. *Health Sociology Review, 18*(1), 119–136. https://doi.org/10.5172/hesr.18.1.119

Lopez, S. J., & Louis, M. C. (2009). The principles of strengths-based education. *Journal of College and Character, 10*(4). https://doi.org/10.2202/1940-1639.1041

Louth, S. (2017). Indigenous Australians: Shame and respect. In E. Vanderheiden, & C. Mayer (Eds.), *The value of shame* (pp. 187–200). Springer. https://doi.org/10.1007/978-3-319-53100-7_8

Lowe, K. (2017). Walanbaa warramildanha: The impact of authentic Aboriginal community and school engagement of teachers' professional knowledge. *Australian Educational Researcher, 44,* 35–54.

Lowe, K., Tennent, C., Guenther, J., Harrison, N., Burgess, C., Moodie, N., & Vass, G. (2019). "Aboriginal Voices": An overview of the methodology applied in the systematic review of recent research across ten key areas of Australian Indigenous education. *The Australian Educational Researcher, 46,* 213–229. https://doi.org/10.1007/s13384-019-00307-5

Martin, K., & Mirraboopa, B. (2003). Ways of knowing, being and doing: A theoretical framework and methods for Indigenous and Indigenist re-search. *Journal of Australian Studies, 27*(76), 203–214. https://doi:10.1080/14443050309387838

McCashen, W. (2005). *The strengths approach: A strengths-based resource for sharing power and creating change.* St Luke's Innovative Resources.

Mellor, D. (2003). Contemporary racism in Australia: The experiences of Aborigines. *Personality and Social Psychology Bulletin, 29*(4), 474–486. https://doi.org/10.1177/0146167202250914

Milgate, G. (2016). Building empowering partnerships between schools and communities. In N. Harrison, & J. Sellwood (Eds.), *Learning and teaching in Aboriginal and Torres Strait Islander education* (pp. 193–206). Oxford University Press.

Moodie, N., Ewen, S., McLeod, J., & Platania-Phung, C. (2018). Indigenous graduate research students in Australia: A critical review of the research. *Higher Education Research & Development*, 37(4), 805–820. https://doi.org/10.1080/07294360. 2018.1440536

Nakata, M. (2010). Australian Indigenous studies: A question of discipline. *The Australian Journal of Anthropology*, 17(3), 265–275.

Nakata, M., Nakata, V., Keech, S., & Bolt, R. (2014). Rethinking majors in Australian Indigenous studies. *The Australian Journal of Indigenous Education*, 43(1), 8–20.

National Aboriginal and Torres Strait Islander Higher Education Consortium (2024). *About*. https://natsihec.edu.au/about/

Paradies, Y., Ben, J., Denson, N., Elias, A., Priest, N., Pieterse, A., Gupta, A., Kelaher, M., & Gee, G. (2015). Racism as a determinant of health: A systematic review and meta-analysis. *PloS One*. https://doi.org/10.1371/journal.pone.0138511

Pechenkina, E., & Anderson, I. (2011). *Background paper on Indigenous Australian higher education: Trends, initiatives and policy implications*. Department of Education, Employment and Workplace Relations.

Pechenkina, E., Kowal, E., & Paradies, Y. (2011). Indigenous Australian students' participation rates in higher education: Exploring the role of universities, *The Australian Journal of Indigenous Education*, 40, 59–68, https://doi.org/10.1375/ajie.40.59

Perkins, R. (2020). Where ya from? In K. Kilner (Ed.), *Growing up Indigenous in Australia*. AustLit. https://www.austlit.edu.au/austlit/page/18774590

Perkins, R. (2024). *Learning from the lived experiences of Indigenous teachers who have remained in the profession* [Unpublished doctoral thesis]. University of Queensland.

Peters, S. (2010). *Literature review: Transition from early childhood to school. Report to the New Zealand Ministry of Education*. http://www.educationcounts. govt.nz/publications/ece/literature-review-transition-from-early-childhood-education-to-school/executive-summary

Povey, R., Trudgett, M., Page, S., Locke, M. L., & Harry, M. (2023). Raising an Indigenous academic community: A strength-based approach to Indigenous early career mentoring in higher education. *The Australian Educational Researcher*, 50(4), 1165–1180.

Priest, N., Chong, S., Truong, M., Sharif, M., Dunn, K., Paradies, Y., Nelson, J., Alam, O., Ward, A., & Kavanagh, A. (2019). *Findings from the 2017 speak out against racism (SOAR) student and staff surveys*. Western Sydney University.

Rigney, L. (1999). Internationalization of an Indigenous anticolonial cultural critique of research methodologies: A guide to Indigenist research methodology and its principles. *Wicazo Sa Review*, 14(2), 109–121. https://doi.org/10.2307/1409555

Rigney, L. I. (1997). Internationalism of an Aboriginal or Torres Strait Islander anticolonial cultural critique of research methodologies: A guide to Indigenist research methodology and its principles. *Research and Development in Higher Education: Advancing International Perspectives*, 20, 629–36.

Saint-Jacques, M.-C., Turcotte, D., & Pouliot, E. (2009). Adopting a strengths perspective in social work practice with families in difficulty: From theory to practice. *Families in Society*, 90(4), 454–461. https://doi.org/10.1606/1044-3894.3926

Saleebey, D. (Ed.). (2013). *The strengths perspective in social work practice* (2nd ed.). Pearson.

Sarra, C. (2011). *Strong and smart - towards a pedagogy for emancipation: Education for first peoples*. Routledge.

Sarra, C., Spillman, D., Jackson, C., Davis, J., & Bray, J. (2018). High-expectations relationships: A foundation for enacting high expectations in all Australian schools. *The Australian Journal of Indigenous Education*, 49(1), 32–45. https://doi. org/10.1017/jie.2018.10.

Scerra, N. (2012). Strengths-based practices: An overview of the evidence. *developing practice: The child. Youth and Family Work Journal, 31*(Autumn), 43–52.

Shay, M., & Miller, J.. (2021). Excellence in Indigenous education. In K-A. Allen, A. Reupert, & L. Oades (Eds.), *Building better schools with evidence-based policy: Adaptable policy for teachers and school leaders* (pp. 46–54). Routledge. https://doi.org/10.4324/9781003025955-7

Shay, M., Miller, J., & Hameed, S. (2021, October 4). Excellence is the future of Indigenous education. *Teacher Magazine.* https://www.teachermagazine.com/au_en/articles/excellence-is-the-future-of-indigenous-education

Shay, M., & Oliver, R. (2021). *Indigenous education in Australia.* Taylor & Francis Group. https://doi.org/10.4324/9780429263453

Smallwood, R., Woods, C., Power, T., & Usher, K. (2021). Understanding the impact of historical trauma due to colonization on the health and well-being of Indigenous young peoples: A systematic scoping review. *Journal of Transcultural Nursing, 32*(1), 59–68. https://doi.org/10.1177/1043659620935955

Smith, L. T. (2021). *Decolonizing methodologies: Research and Indigenous peoples* (3rd ed.). Zed Books. https://doi.org/10.5040/9781350225282

Stacey, M. (2024). Deficit discourses and teachers' work: The case of an early career teacher in a remote Indigenous school. In G. Vass & M. Hogarth (Eds.), *Critical studies and the international field of Indigenous education research* (pp. 64–79). Routledge.

The University of Sydney (n.d). *Research.* https://www.sydney.edu.au/research.html

Trudgett, M. (2009). Build it and they will come: Building the capacity of Indigenous units in universities to provide better support for Indigenous Australian postgraduate students. *The Australian Journal of Indigenous Education, 38,* 9–18.

Universities Australia (2021). *Universities Australia's Indigenous strategy: 2022-2025.* https://universitiesaustralia.edu.au/policy-submissions/diversity-equity/universities-australias-indigenous-strategy-2022-2025/

Universities Australia (2024). *Who we are.* https://universitiesaustralia.edu.au/about/who-we-are/

University of Melbourne (n.d.). *Women at the University of Melbourne.* https://library.unimelb.edu.au/asc/collections/archives/resources/research-guides/women-in-the-archives/women-at-the-university-of-melbourne#:~:text=In%20December%201883%2C%20Julia%20Margaret,including%20in%20campaigns%20for%20suffrage.

University of New England (2024). *The Oorala Aboriginal Centre.* https://www.une.edu.au/info-for/indigenous-matters/oorala/about-oorala

Vass, G. (2012). "So, what is wrong with Indigenous education?" Perspective, position and power beyond a deficit discourse. *The Australian Journal of Indigenous Education, 41*(2), 85–96.

Yip, S. Y., & Chakma, U. (2024). The teaching of Indigenous knowledge and perspectives in initial teacher education: A scoping review of empirical studies. *Journal of Further and Higher Education, 48*(3), 287–300. https://doi.org/10.1080/0309877X.2024.2327029

Zubrick, S., Silburn, S., Lawrence, D., Mitrou, F. G., Dalby, R. B., Blair, E. M., & Griffin, J. et al. (2005). *The Western Australian Aboriginal Child Health Survey: The social and emotional wellbeing of Aboriginal Children and young people.* Curtin University of Technology and Telethon Institute for Child Health Research.

10 A Theoretical Lens for Strengths-Based Knowledge Production in Indigenous Education

Marnee Shay and Grace Sarra

Introduction

This is a chapter we have spent much time conceptualising, thinking about, and yarning about. Like other concepts discussed in the book, such as "codesign" and "Indigenous community", the term theory is somewhat contested and has different meanings when used by different people in different contexts (Thomas, 1997). On the note of conceptual clarity, when we use the term "knowledge production" in this chapter, we refer to the practice of research. We also use the term to include knowledge produced through policy and practice. We recognise that, as researchers, the knowledge we produce is within the realms of the academy and subject to processes such as human research ethics approval within university settings. However, knowledge is also produced every day in educational and policy settings. Both can be harmful to Indigenous people or help to advance our current circumstances.

We are two Indigenous women scholars with decades of experience applying strengths-based approaches (SBA) in Indigenous education in our teaching and leadership practice and research. We have reached a point where, in the absence of other theoretical models to use SBA in knowledge production in the field of Indigenous education, there is an urgency to publish our ideas for testing, debate, and reflection. We understand there is considerable substantiation required for any social researcher to call anything a theory, so it is critical that we draw on sociological and Indigenous scholarship to be clear about our intent in proposing a theoretical SBA to knowledge production in Indigenous education.

Abend (2008) analyses how sociological research defines and uses theory. Though we define ourselves as Indigenous researchers who work within Indigenous knowledge paradigms and with Indigenous theories and methodologies, we also consider ourselves sociological researchers in education rather than purist educational researchers by the very definition of our scholarship as Indigenous researchers. In this chapter, we look to sociological theoretical scholarship to clarify our propositions. We recognise the polysemy of language with sociological theory and that there are nuances in how each field considers the role of theory in research (Abend, 2008). We also acknowledge consistency across the literature, namely, that there is a general consensus for

DOI: 10.4324/9781003372783-10

a precondition of empiricism to underpin one's theoretical claims (Sutton & Staw, 1995). However, some authors propose that theory has broader objectives, and that theory development is about challenging and extending existing knowledge to "push back the boundaries of our knowledge by providing compelling and logical justification for altered views" (Whetten, 1989, p. 491).

While theory can include theorising the social world, "a theory is a *Weltanschaunng*, that is, an overall perspective from which one sees and interprets the world" (Abend, 2008, p. 179). Abend further outlines that theory can be about how we examine and represent topics. It is this position that we situate our chapter and the theoretical model we put forward for researchers who are seeking a strengths-based theoretical lens for undertaking educational research, particularly on any topics involving Indigenous peoples or interests.

The Problem with Research Problems

Research is inherently a problem-based undertaking; the most impactful research aims to solve some of our most persistent and complex problems. But what if the problems are so unsolvable because of how we approach the research? There is an increasing need to justify rigorous research-based inquiry and rationalise why research is another way of addressing a problem. Research can solve real-world problems and critique and deconstruct many elements of a problem. But has research been so concerned with critical interrogation of problems that it has overlooked extant and potential strengths and solutions?

Frequent views of social science research are "overwhelmingly explanation-oriented, where the central question is 'why'" (Chakraborty, 2019, p. 6). Common answers to "why" research a topic include (intellectual) curiosity, whether it is a significant or a persistent issue or simply because it is a hot topic. It is uncommon to find research that seeks existing solutions or strengths.

Problem identification or research purpose is significant when thinking about SBA in Indigenous education research. Silverman (2001) cautions researchers about how particular problems are constructed via the media and political agendas. We know the impact of the media in identifying and (re)presenting issues in schooling and education more broadly. We also know the Australian media's long history of negative and racist stereotyping and misreporting on matters relating to Indigenous people, cultures, and topics (McCallum et al., 2022). It is common for media reporting and political commentary on education issues to impact how problems in schooling and education policy are identified (Hattam et al., 2009). Sometimes, the body of research can reproduce dominant understandings of particular issues. Therefore, research plays an important role in countering these representations.

Consider the potential of SBA in balancing how we understand pervasive issues, such as the current teacher shortages. Media and other coverage generally present a dire situation about teacher recruitment and retention (Shine, 2015). Indigenous teachers have been recognised as under-represented in Australian classrooms (Australian Institute for Teaching and School Leadership, 2024). The body of research has looked at the issue of Indigenous teacher experiences and it has swiftly identified a range of issues in how Indigenous teachers navigate their careers and why they leave the profession (Santoro & Reid, 2006). Quandamooka researcher Ren Perkins (and the author of Chapter 9) recently completed a PhD study examining why Indigenous teachers remain in the profession. He looked for Indigenous teachers who have navigated the challenges and stayed in the profession despite these challenges. Ren's research demonstrates how overlooked SBA has been in research on this topic of Indigenous teacher shortages and increasing the number of Indigenous teachers in Australian schools. By looking at the problem through a SBA lens, this study provided a new understanding of factors that enable mob to stay in the profession.

Foregrounding the Theoretical Lens

Like many other concepts discussed in this book, there is contestation in the literature about whether SBA are a practice approach, theory, or methodology. As Chapter 2 outlines, increasing scholarly theories underpinned by SBA have been developed to focus on a particular cohort or issue. For example, appreciative inquiry (AI) developed in organisational development, with its distinct purpose of identifying strengths, is focused on inquiry and change (Ludema et al., 2006). Funds of Knowledge (FoK) theorised how students from minorities bring strengths from their homes and communities and how this impacts classroom learning and outcomes (Hogg, 2011). The salutogenic theory aims to move away from biological understandings of health to understanding health and wellbeing as a spectrum encompassing the many dimensions of health and wellbeing (Brolin et al., 2018; Eriksson, 2022).

SBA are recognised as emerging from the social work field, particularly as practitioners sought less pathological approaches to supporting their clients, especially those experiencing disenfranchisement, oppression, and disadvantage (Caiels et al., 2024). From being described as a philosophy to a practice approach, there has been so much development across fields and scholarly paradigms that it is increasingly recognised for its ability to shape how knowledge and discourse are produced in the academy. The Department of Health and Social Care (2019) recognises the multitude of definitions of SBA, acknowledging consistent reference to practice approaches and recognising its status as a social work practice theory.

Chapter 2 explained that strengths-based theories have developed across disciplines, including organisational development, health sciences, education, and community development. The educationally focused theories, FoK and Funds of Identity (FoI), emphasise a focus on family and community knowledge and cultural identities in understanding school engagement and outcomes, particularly of culturally minoritised cohorts. These theories are highly relevant to Indigenous education. However, as educational researchers who primarily research Indigenous education in schools and communities with high Indigenous populations, we found we had to piece together theories to accompany Indigenous theories to contextualise our research, which, across projects, always had a different focus and, therefore a need for different theoretical cross-stitching.

We know that the Indigenous health field was quick to adopt SBA. As an increasing critique of deficit epistemologies that dominated the field, researchers invested in conceptualising a reframing for researchers looking for strengths-based theories to shift the focus of their studies to incorporate SBA. We looked to the health literature for Indigenous scholarship and theoretical conceptualising of strengths-based research in Indigenous health. While SBA are recognised as critical (Bullen et al., 2023), Lines and Jardine (2025) outline limited examples of applying SBA as a research approach with Indigenous people. Bryant et al. (2021) analysed how SBA in Indigenous health research were presented in the literature. Bryant et al. (2021) found three predominant ways these were reflected: resilience, social-ecological, and sociocultural approaches. They further outlined some consensus in the literature that the most effective SBA draw from Indigenous ways of being, knowing, and doing. We concur with this proposition as we attempt to advance SBA to a theoretic lens for undertaking Indigenous education research.

Strengths-Based Approaches – A Theoretical Lens for Indigenous Education Research

We have illustrated a compelling argument for the need for a theoretical lens for Indigenous education research across the chapters in this book. While deficit discourses are shaped by many elements (such as historical, political, racial, and social), educational institutions in Australia must consider their roles in the perpetual cycle of low expectations and deficit ideologies. We cannot ignore that the persistent deficit discourses in Indigenous education are somewhat shaped by knowledge production or research. In this chapter, we intend to provide any researcher with a strengths-based theoretical lens to undertake Indigenous educational research. We hope this may contribute to generating new knowledge about persistent problems, as the data shows that Indigenous education is not advancing as it should.

What Is Indigenous Education Research?

Clearly, defining what we mean by "Indigenous education research" is important. Indigenous education research could be the established field where many published studies investigate topics in and around Indigenous education. These may include but are not limited to:

- Close the Gap
- Indigenous literacy
- Indigenous numeracy
- Embedding Indigenous knowledge and perspectives

- Indigenous STEM (science, technology, education, mathematics)
- Indigenous pedagogies
- Technology and Indigenous education
- Relationships between Indigenous communities and schools
- Indigenous language curriculum and teaching
- Indigenous identity affirming in schools
- Indigenous career development
- Indigenous wellbeing in schools
- Indigenous teachers and leaders
- Indigenous boarding schools
- Indigenous cultural programmes
- Remote schooling
- Indigenous school attendance and engagement
- Reconciliation in schools
- Whole of school change approaches
- Indigenous community/support teachers/aides
- Indigenous arts
- Indigenous games
- Teacher preparedness and Indigenous education
- Indigenous educational sovereignty
- Indigenous rights in education
- Indigenous access to tertiary education
- Indigenous post-schooling pathways.

This is not an exhaustive list, but it provides some tangible examples of the array of published topics under the umbrella of Indigenous education. The Australian Institute of Aboriginal and Torres Strait Islander Studies (AIATSIS, 2020) Code of Ethics for Aboriginal and Torres Strait Islander Research are the key guideline for ethical Indigenous research in Australia. These guidelines were developed with input and leadership from various stakeholders, including Indigenous Pro-Vice Chancellors, groups from AIATSIS, and public submissions. The AIATSIS (2020) *Guidelines* state that Indigenous research should be defined as research that:

concerned or impacts Aboriginal and Torres Strait Islander peoples in any of the following ways:

- The research is about Aboriginal and Torres Strait Islander peoples, society, culture and/or knowledge, Aboriginal and Torres Strait Islander policies or experience
- The target population is Aboriginal and Torres Strait Islander individuals, groups, communities or societies
- The target population is not explicitly Aboriginal and Torres Strait Islander individuals or communities but the research population includes a significant number of Aboriginal and Torres Strait Islander people

- Aboriginal and/or Torres Strait Islander people have been incidentally recruited and researchers wish to do separate analysis of Indigenous-specific data
- There are Aboriginal and Torres Strait Islander individuals or communities contributing to the research
- There is new or pre-existing data related to Aboriginal and Torres Strait Islander people being used in the research
- The research concerns Aboriginal and Torres Strait Islander peoples' land or waters.

(AIATSIS, 2020, p. 6)

It is critical to take a moment to unpack the definition of Indigenous research outlined by AIATSIS. Being two experienced Indigenous academics, we have observed many instances whereby researchers have insisted their study is not Indigenous research. Worse, they have deliberately framed their work as focused on a broader topic involving Indigenous people to avoid engaging with the principles for ethical Indigenous research. We will provide a couple of educational research examples. The first example is a non-Indigenous researcher invited by a non-Indigenous principal of a remote Indigenous school and provided significant funding to undertake research within the school. This researcher has extensive experience working in Indigenous research with Indigenous colleagues. When they develop the research design, all questions are framed as generic questions about the science curriculum. Questions such as "How do students engage with science?" frame their study, knowing that one hundred per cent of the students they are researching are Indigenous, with the school being located in an Indigenous community. Their research would meet the definition of Indigenous research across the numerous points outlined above.

A further example is a researcher examining the issue of young people in child protection care and their schooling experiences. The researcher insists that the study concerns children in care and how they engage with school. Their research questions are generic: "Why do children in care experience poorer educational outcomes?". This is another way of avoiding recognition that this will inherently be defined as Indigenous research because it is well acknowledged that Indigenous children and young people are over-represented in this cohort in Australia. The latest data shows that Aboriginal children are 11 times more likely to be placed in out-of-home care than non-Aboriginal children (Lima et al., 2024). An expert on children and young people interacting with child protection systems would know this statistic. Therefore, the researcher appears to avoid engaging with Indigenous research ethics, guidelines, literature, and theories.

We want to be clear that using a strengths-based theoretical lens to undertake Indigenous education research means being transparent about the research topic, context, and participants. Any other approach (such as the two examples provided) suggests complicity with the harmful and damaging research practices that render/ed Indigenous peoples objects of research. As Tuhiwai Smith (2012) explains:

> it galls us that Western researchers and intellectuals can assume to know all that is possible to know of us, on the basis of their brief encounters with some of us. It appals us that the West can desire, extract and claim ownership of our ways of knowing, our imagery, the things we create and produce and then simultaneously reject the people who created and developed those ideas and seek to deny them further opportunities to be creators of their own culture and own nations.
>
> (p. 1)

We encourage our non-Indigenous colleagues to continue the work needed to change educational systems and transform Indigenous education. We propose that this can be achieved by fully embracing these concepts and considering theories concerning Indigenous peoples' emancipation, such as SBA. Undertaking strengths-based Indigenous education research requires some personal qualities from any researcher. These include honesty, respect, transparency, commitment, integrity and relationality. These values and qualities are present throughout most literature and guidelines. Still, it is important to recognise that our theoretical lens encompasses and recognises values as equally important as other core tenets of the theory.

We introduce our Strengths-Based Theory for Indigenous Education Research in Figure 10.1. The values mentioned above are in the centre of the figure. Without those inherent values, many of which align with Indigenous ways of being, knowing, and doing, the rest of the core tenets outlined are unlikely to be present. We propose six core tenets for a theoretical lens in Indigenous education research:

1 Strong Indigenous voices
2 Indigenous leadership
3 Indigenous agency
4 Strengths-based knowledge
5 Community strengths
6 Reimagining Futures.

Redefining Research Problems with the Core Tenets

The foundational aspect of the Strengths-Based Theory for Indigenous Education Research is how research problems are approached. While we have critiqued how problem-based research is, using a strengths-based lens can still allow for research to be based on problems. It is how the inquiry is approached from there. For example, one State government policymaker approached us some years ago and said they were looking for research on

Figure 10.1 Strengths-Based Theory for Indigenous Education Research.

improving school attendance of Indigenous students in their region. They said they had all the attendance data, showing a picture of lower attendance (than non-Indigenous students) across schools. We suggested that using the same data to investigate the same issue, they could look at patterns of individual students where their attendance may have dropped but then improved. We explained that, once those students were identified, further qualitative data could be collected from their Indigenous school-based workers, their families, and teachers to understand the circumstances that shifted the increase. Using a strengths-based lens may tell you something new about why students are not attending.

A further example would be a research project investigating the persistent problem of Indigenous students' lower year 12 completion rates. Applying strengths-based theory in this situation, the research would focus on understanding the stories and perspectives of Indigenous students who have finished year 12. What were the compelling factors that enabled completion? Shifting the focus of the inquiry may generate new knowledge about the issue instead of focusing on why Indigenous students are not completing year 12.

We also want to be clear that SBA can be used to research wicked and complex problems such as racism. In one of our research projects, we had an explicit research question about how Indigenous young people experienced racism in school settings. We applied a strengths-based lens by including strengths-based questions such as "Tell us about what support you have around you if you have experienced racism" and "Can you share an example of a positive relationship with a non-Indigenous person?". By including these questions, we had additional information from those young people about the strengths they draw from when experiencing racism. We also understood how they conceive of positive relationships with non-Indigenous people. Again, these inclusions generated new knowledge and understanding of a well-traversed topic.

Strong Indigenous Voices

We recognise eminent Narungga education researcher Professor Lester Irabinna Rigney for his ground-breaking Indigenist scholarship, which rigorously advocates for Indigenous voices as central in knowledge production (Rigney, 1999, 2001, 2017). Prof Rigney's work has been so influential in our scholarship across many projects now that we use his theory in most of our work. The substratum of our work has been ensuring we are committed to the centring of diverse Indigenous voices across our research – not just the Indigenous voices that already have a platform, but also the wisdom and knowledge holders in our communities who have so much to contribute but may miss out for a myriad of reasons.

We are also deeply influenced by the scholarship of Distinguished Professor and Quandamooka scholar Aileen Moreton-Robinson and her development of Indigenous women's standpoint theory, as Indigenous women and in asserting our standpoints in developing this work. Moreton-Robinson's work further provides the theoretical underpinnings for why strong Indigenous voices must be present in a strengths-based theory for Indigenous education. As Moreton-Robinson articulates, "we are involved in a constant battle to authorise Indigenous knowledges and methodologies as legitimate and valued components of research" (Moreton-Robinson, 2013, p. 331). Moreton-Robinson's (2013) scholarship analyses why feminist theory inadequately theorises our standpoints and epistemes and subsequently developed an Indigenous women's standpoint theory. Indigenous women's standpoint theory is "constituted and constitutive of the interconnectedness of our ontology (our way of being); our epistemology (our way of knowing) and our axiology (our way of doing)" (Moreton-Robinson, 2013, p. 340).

These theoretical positions inform strong Indigenous voices, and applying this in research means recognising and embracing the gendered and other identities that shape one's positionality as an Indigenous person. Understanding that there are many dimensions of a person's identity, particularly for Indigenous people, is critical. The homogenising and exoticising of Indigenous identities by

Western cultures are well acknowledged (Bodkins-Andrews & Carlson, 2016). We draw from key Indigenous theorists such as Rigney and Moreton-Robinson to apply strong Indigenous voices as a strength-based approach in research. We also concur with Saleebey's (2013) sentiment that "we have fabulous powers and potentials. Some are muted, unrealized, and immanent. Others glimmer brilliantly about us. All around are people and policies, circumstances and conventions, contingencies and conceptions that may nurture and emancipate these powers or that may crush or degrade them" (p. 8). Strong Indigenous voices in strengths-based theory for Indigenous research requires demonstratable markers in the research design to seek out diverse Indigenous voices proactively. It also requires researchers to centre and represent diverse Indigenous voices with integrity in the analysis and reporting of the research.

Indigenous Leadership

In the colonial context of Australia and recognising that while we are the First People of these lands, with a history of some 65,000 years (Clarkson et al., 2017), in 2025, we are a minority with very limited access to systemic power. We are under-represented in school leadership roles, senior educational policy roles, and the political structures that make educational decisions. Furthermore, we are still under-represented in the research workforce and in academia (Universities Australia, 2021). Because of this context, Indigenous leadership is a core tenet of our strengths-based theory for Indigenous research.

Our current context does not define our power and strengths. A critical tenet of this theory is ensuring there are ways of incorporating Indigenous leadership in the research design, the research team, and the analysis and dissemination of data. In practice, Indigenous leadership means having mechanisms for key decision-making throughout the research. This may not mean that an Aboriginal or Torres Strait Islander person is the lead person on the research project. If an Indigenous person cannot lead, it means that there are ways for Indigenous people (whether they are other team members, partners, or participants) to be enabled to make decisions about the process or project and that they are listened to and respected as leaders in the process.

Indigenous Agency

Like many concepts in this book, the concept of agency has been a source of contestation and debate across many disciplines, such as philosophy, psychology, education, political science, gender studies, culture studies, and more. Campbell (2009) outlines the dualities of how the term agency is engendered; in one way, it can be about an individual's power; in another, it can be about individuals acting as agents. Bhattacharyya (1995) defines agency within the context of community development as the ability to define oneself and not be defined by others, further suggesting that "agency is the antithesis of dependency" (p. 61).

Many people in the world are structurally oppressed, and while they may not be able to change the institutions and governments responsible for their oppression, they still possess enormous agency. Applying our theory in research means starting from this position and thus developing a research design that embraces this premise and enables Indigenous agency across the many dimensions of research design. Indigenous agency is a presupposition; reciprocity is innately related and required as part of this tenet. Reciprocity means ensuring a balance in benefits between researchers or governments and Indigenous people and communities. Enacting reciprocity means tangible reciprocal practices should be present when applying this theory. It is our premise in developing this theory that Aboriginal and Torres Strait Islander people are agentic in the multiplicities of the term's meaning (there are many more theories and ideas about human agency).

Strengths-Based Knowledge

A core tenet of our theory is a deliberate inclusion of the development of strengths-based knowledge in undertaking research. This may include developing research questions that seek strengths-based perspectives from a larger problem-based inquiry. It may also shift the research premise that enables the macro view of the problem to include inquiry that allows for strengths-based knowledge to emerge. Theories such as AI, as outlined in chapter two, demonstrate how research can be shaped from a strengths-based lens within organisational development research. For example, if a researcher were to examine how health workers can increase safe practices in their clinical work by using AI, the researcher would first look at the current safety practices and centre these as the beginning point of the research.

In applying strength-based knowledge in our theory within the context of Indigenous education, intently seeking strength-based perspectives is a critical way of producing new knowledge. We have many examples of how we have done this in our research over the years. One example is a project that explored codesign to develop local curriculum resources to support Aboriginal language revitalisation. We purposefully included strengths-based research questions that informed our data on how schools and communities can work together to develop and include local Indigenous knowledges and perspectives. We also ensured that the digital stories that were an output from the project (and an artefact that provided direct benefit to the community and schools) were based on the strengths of the storytellers and the community.

Community Strengths

In chapter seven, we elaborate extensively on community strengths and how invaluable local expertise and wisdom are. Aboriginal and Torres Strait Islander communities across the nation are incredibly diverse, each with its own strengths, languages, politics, histories, cultures, practices, and dynamics. As

Thomas et al. (2016) explain, the strength of Indigenous resilience and cultures is the collective nature of all Indigenous communities. To apply a SBA in Indigenous education research, the strengths and perspectives on the Indigenous community are vital in encompassing Indigenous worldviews and ontological dispositions.

Indigenous communities across Australia know what is best for them. They are the only consistent, yet they are so often overlooked when governments intervene to address complex issues within the community. The Community Strengths tenet of Strengths-Based Theory for Indigenous Education Research requires researchers to develop explicit mechanisms within the research design to ensure that community strengths are incorporated into the research design and, where possible and relevant, the research questions. Applying community strengths also means developing dissemination and communication pathways that are fit for purpose and useful to the communities involved in the research. As communities are the experts, these communication strategies would need to be developed with local community partners, adhering to local cultural protocols (for more on cultural protocols, see Chapter 7).

Reimagining Futures

A key feature of AI is ensuring distinct processes that allow for reimagining the current situation or status quo (Willoughby & Tosey, 2007). In developing our Strengths-Based Theory for Indigenous Education Research, we looked to further scholarship incorporating Indigenous worldviews. As Indigenous education researchers, we know there can be a narrow lens of emphasising the past and present when discussing Indigenous education. The emphasis on the past and present is inherently a deficit way of conceiving our work in Indigenous education. It is underpinned by colonial discourses that continue to overlook Indigenous strengths and aspirations for better futures.

Indigenous futurity can be seen as a form of resistance to the ongoing imaginings of Indigenous people in the past (Teuton, 2018). The reimagining futures tenet of our Strengths-Based Theory for Indigenous Education Research should allow for Indigenous perspectives on reimagined futures or alternative futures and solutions. The inclusion of reimagining futures will contribute to the development of Indigenous-informed, future-orientated data that is currently very limited in the corpus of literature.

Conclusion

This chapter outlined six key tenets of a Strengths-Based Theory for Indigenous Education Research: Strong Indigenous voices, Indigenous leadership, Indigenous agency, Strengths-based knowledge, Community strengths, and Reimagining Futures. These are underpinned by six core values: honesty, respect, transparency, commitment, integrity, and relationality. Like many

Indigenous knowledge systems, these are highly interrelated, and one of these tenets or values is no more important than the other.

In chapter 2, we unpacked the significance of epistemology, particularly its role in producing and (re)producing knowledge about Indigenous people and education. In developing a Strengths-Based Theory for Indigenous Education, we aim to give researchers, policymakers, and school leaders conceptual tools that may contribute to developing new knowledge in a field that urgently needs new ideas, actions, and aspirations. We encourage colleagues working across the spectrum of Indigenous education to share their experiences of applying our theory for further exploration, debate, and testing.

References

Abend, G. (2008). The meaning of "theory". *Sociological Theory, 26*(2), 173–199.

AIATSIS (2020) AIATSIS *Code of ethics for Aboriginal and Torres Strait Islander research*. Available from: https://aiatsis.gov.au/research/ethical-research#:~:text=The%20 AIATSIS%20Code%20of%20Ethics,or%20communities%20involved%20in%20the

Australian Institute for Teaching and School Leadership (2024). *In focus: Aboriginal and Torres Strait Islander teachers*. Australian Institute for Teaching and School Leadership. https://www.aitsl.edu.au/research/australian-teacher-workforce-data/ in-focus/aboriginal-and-torres-strait-islander-teacher

Bhattacharyya, J. (1995). Solidarity and agency: Rethinking community development. *Human Organization, 54*(1), 60–69. https://doi.org/10.17730/ humo.54.1.m459ln688536005w

Brolin, M., Quennerstedt, M., Maivorsdotter, N., & Casey, A. (2018). A salutogenic strengths-based approach in practice - An illustration from a school in Sweden. *Curriculum Studies in Health and Physical Education, 9*(3), 237–252. https://doi. org/10.1080/25742981.2018.1493935

Bryant, J., Bolt, R., Botfield, J. R., Martin, K., Doyle, M., Murphy, D., Graham, S., Newman, C. E., Bell, S., Treloar, C., Browne, A. J., & Aggleton, P. (2021). Beyond deficit: 'Strengths-based approaches' in Indigenous health research. *Sociology of Health & Illness, 43*(6), 1405–1421. https://doi. org/10.1111/1467-9566.13311

Bullen, J., Hill-Wall, T., Anderson, K., Brown, A., Bracknell, C., Newnham, E. A., Garvey, G., & Waters, L. (2023). From deficit to strength-based Aboriginal health research—Moving toward flourishing. *International Journal of Environmental Research and Public Health, 20*(7), 5395. https://doi.org/10.3390/ ijerph20075395

Caiels, J., Silarova, B., Milne, A. J., & Beadle-Brown, J. (2024). Strengths-based approaches - Perspectives from practitioners. *The British Journal of Social Work, 54*(1), 168–188. https://doi.org/10.1093/bjsw/bcad186

Campbell, C. (2009). Distinguing the power of agency from agentic power: A note on Weber and the "black box" of personal agency. *Sociological Theory, 27*(4), 407–418.

Chakraborty, A. (2019). An approach toward methodological appraisal of social research. *Occasional Paper*. Institute of Development Studies Kolkata. Retrieved from https://idsk.edu.in/wp-content/uploads/2019/01/OP-63.pdf

Clarkson, C., Jacobs, Z., Marwick, B., Fullagar, R., Wallis, L., Smith, M., Roberts, R. G., Hayes, E., Lowe, K., Carah, X., Florin, S. A., McNeil, J., Cox, D., Arnold, L. J., Jua, Q., Huntley, J., Brand, H. E. A., Manne, T., Fairbairn, A., Schulmeister, J., & Pardoe, C. (2017). Human occupation of northern Australia by 65,000 years ago. *Nature, 547*, 306–310. https://doi.org/10.1038/nature22968

Department of Health and Social Care (2019). *Strengths-based approach: Practice framework and practice handbook.* Retrieved from https://assets.publishing. service.gov.uk/media/5c62ae87ed915d04446a5739/stengths-based-approach-practice-framework-and-handbook.pdf

Eriksson, M. (2022) Key concepts in the salutgenic model. In *Handbook of Salutogensis* (2nd ed., pp. 59–60). Springer.

Hattam, R., Prosser, B., & Brady, K. (2009). Revolution or backlash? The mediatisation of education policy in Australia. *Critical Studies in Education, 50*(2), 159–172.

Hogg, L. (2011). Funds of knowledge: An investigation of coherence within the literature. *Teaching and Teacher Education, 27*(3), 666–677. https://doi.org/10.1016/j.tate.2010.11.005

Lima, F., O'Donnell, M., Gibberd, A. J., Falster, K., Banks, E., Jones, J., Williams, R., Eades, F., Harrap, B., Chenhall, R., Octoman, O., & Eades, S. (2024). Aboriginal children placed in out-of-home care: Pathways through the child protection system. *Australian Social Work, 77*(4), 471–485. https://doi.org/10.1080/0312407X.2024.2326505

Lines, L. A., & Jardine, C. G. (2025). Identifying and applying a strength-based research approach in Indigenous health. *International Journal of Qualitative Methods, 24*, 16094069241310273.

Ludema, J. D., Cooperrider, D. L., & Barrett, F. J. (2006). Appreciative inquiry: The power of the unconditional positive question. *Handbook of action research: The concise paperback edition* (pp. 155–165). SAGE.

McCallum, K., Ryan, T., & Caffery, J. (2022). Deficit metrics in Australian Indigenous education: Through a media studies lens. *Discourse: Studies in the Cultural Politics of Education, 43*(2), 266–281.

Moreton-Robinson, A. (2013). Towards an Australian Indigenous women's standpoint theory: A methodological tool. *Australian Feminist Studies, 28*(78), 331–347. https://doi.org/10.1080/08164649.2013.876664

Rigney, L. I. (1999). Internationalization of an Indigenous anticolonial cultural critique of research methodologies: A guide to Indigenist research methodology and its principles. *Wicazo sa Review, 14*(2), 109–121.

Rigney, L. I. (2001). A first perspective of Indigenous Australian participation in science: Framing Indigenous research towards Indigenous Australian intellectual sovereignty.

Rigney, L. I. (2017). Indigenist research and Aboriginal Australia. In *Indigenous peoples' wisdom and power: Affirming our knowledge through narratives* (pp. 32–48). Routledge.

Saleebey, D. (2013). *The strengths perspective in social work practice* (6th ed.). Pearson.

Santoro, N., & Reid, J. A. (2006). "All things to all people": Indigenous teachers in the Australian teaching profession. *European Journal of Teacher Education, 29*(3), 287–303.

Shine, K. (2015). Reporting the 'exodus': News coverage of teacher shortage in Australian newspapers. *Issues in Educational Research, 25*(4), 501–516.

Silverman, D. (2001). *Interpreting qualitative data: Methods for analysing talk, text and interaction* (2nd ed.). Sage.

Smith Tuhiwai, L. (2012). *Decolonizing methodologies: Research and Indigenous peoples* (2nd ed.). Zed Books; Otago University Press.

Sutton, R. I., & Staw, B. M. (1995). What theory is not. *Administrative Science Quarterly, 40*(3), 371–384. https://doi.org/10.2307/2393788

Teuton, S., (2018). *Native American literature: A very short introduction* (online ed, ch. 7). Oxford University Press.

Thomas, D., Mitchell, T., & Arseneau, C. (2016). Re-evaluating resilience: From individual vulnerabilities to the strength of cultures and collectivities among Indigenous communities. *Resilience, 4*(2), 116–129. https://doi.org/10.1080/21693293.2015.1094174

Thomas, G. (1997). What's the use of theory? *Harvard Educational Review, 67*(1), 75–104. https://doi.org/10.17763/haer.67.1.1x807532771w5u48

Universities Australia (2021). *Indigenous strategy annual report.* Retrieved from https://universitiesaustralia.edu.au/wp-content/uploads/2021/06/Indigenous-Strategy-Annual-Report_Mar21_FINAL.pdf

Whetten, D. A. (1989). What constitutes a theoretical contribution? *The Academy of Management Review, 14*(4), 490–495. https://doi.org/10.2307/258554

Willoughby, G., & Tosey, P. (2007). Imagine "Meadfield": Appreciative inquiry as a process for leading school improvement. *Educational Management Administration & Leadership, 35*(4), 499–520. https://doi.org/10.1177/1741143207081059

Index

For Product Safety Concerns and Information please contact our EU
representative GPSR@taylorandfrancis.com
Taylor & Francis Verlag GmbH, Kaufingerstraße 24, 80331 München, Germany

www.ingramcontent.com/pod-product-compliance
Lightning Source LLC
Chambersburg PA
CBHW052009270326
41929CB00015B/2851

9 781032 445618